C000171609

IN PURSUIT OF THE QUALITY OF LIFE

IN PURSUIT OF THE QUALITY OF LIFE

Edited by

AVNER OFFER

OXFORD UNIVERSITY PRESS

1996

Oxford University Press, Walton Street, Oxford OX2 6DP
Oxford New York
Athens Auckland Bangkok Bogota Bombay
Buenos Aires Calcutta Cape Town Dar es Salaam
Delhi Florence Hong Kong Istanbul Karachi
Kuala Lumpur Madras Madrid Melbourne
Mexico City Nairobi Paris Singapore
Taipei Tokyo Toronto
and associated companies in
Berlin Ibadan

Oxford is a trade mark of Oxford University Press

Published in the United States by
Oxford University Press Inc., New York

British Library Cataloguing in Publication Data
Data available

Library of Congress Cataloging in Publication Data
In pursuit of the quality of life / edited by Avner Offer.
Includes bibliographical references.
1. Quality of life. 2. Quality of Life—Great Britain.
I. Offer, Avner.
HN25.I49 1996 306—dc20 96–31301
ISBN 0–19–828002–5

1 3 5 7 9 10 8 6 4 2

Typeset by Graphicraft Typesetters Ltd., Hong Kong
Printed in Great Britain by
Biddles Ltd, Guildford and King's Lynn

PREFACE

This book originated in an interdisciplinary seminar on 'the quality of life' which took place at Oxford University during 1993 and 1994, under the auspices of Nuffield College. Together, these essays may be taken as a survey, intended for non-specialists, of current empirical work on 'the quality of life'. I am grateful to the authors for their papers and for their patience, and to the many keen participants, who made those Tuesday evenings so memorable. Ray Fitzpatrick, Jay Gershuny, and David Halpern helped to convene the seminars and chaired many of the sessions. Nuffield College does not, as a corporate body, bear any responsibility for the book. Annie Chan, Leonie Forman, and Martin Spät assisted ably in the editorial work.

A.O.

Oxford, 15 February 1996

CONTENTS

CONTRIBUTORS

Michael Argyle was Reader in Social Psychology at the University of Oxford, and is a Fellow of Wolfson College.

Christopher Bliss is Nuffield Professor of International Economics at the University of Oxford, and a Fellow of Nuffield College.

Janet Finch is Vice-Chancellor of the University of Keele.

Ray Fitzpatrick is Professor of Medical Sociology at the University of Oxford and a Fellow of Nuffield College.

Duncan Gallie is Professor and Official Fellow in Sociology at Nuffield College, Oxford.

Jonathan Gershuny is Professor of Sociology and Director of the ESRC Centre for Micro-social Change at the University of Essex.

Brendan Halpin is Senior Research Fellow at the ESRC Centre for Micro-social Change at the University of Essex.

Heather Joshi is Professor of Social Statistics and Director of the Social Statistics Research Unit at the City University.

Robert E. Lane is Sterling Professor of Political Science (Emeritus) at Yale University.

Avner Offer is Reader in Recent Social and Economic History at the University of Oxford, and a Fellow of Nuffield College.

Frances Stewart is Professor and Director of Queen Elizabeth House, a research centre in Development at the University of Oxford.

1

Introduction

AVNER OFFER

Aristotle says that just talking about virtue does not make a man virtuous. To be virtuous, one has to *act*, to *make a choice*.[1] More famously in the same vein, Marx said that it was no longer good enough to talk about the world, what was necessary was to change it. What is the pursuit of the quality of life? Since the 1940s (when the performance of the economy began to be measured systematically) it has focused on the pursuit of economic growth, striving to increase the flow of traded goods and services. Command of such goods, expressed for convenience in money, provided a clear measure of welfare, both individual and social. If that were the end of the story, there would be no call for this book. We are more than twice as affluent as in the 1940s by the measure of real income per head, and better off in a great many ways, but there is no end in sight to our discontents.

The study of well-being and the quality of life often begins with a top-down approach, spelling out constraints, preconditions, measures, and objectives at a level of philosophical generality.[2] A good deal of attention is devoted to rules that will generate the good life, rather than on its actual content.[3] This collection approaches the problem from the other direction: it builds from the bottom up, starting with concrete experience, and approaching generality only in its last chapter. Each of these essays comes out of a particular research programme. Each is a report from the field. Like the seminar in which it began, the purpose is practical: to bring problems into clear view, and to acquaint workers in different fields with each other's findings. This introduction is similarly practical, providing a short outline of the contributions, and of the common issues that they raise.

Despite its ancient pedigree and impressive scope, philosophical analysis of the quality of life is but one approach among many. Problems

[1] Aristotle (1976: 98, 117).

[2] e.g. Griffin (1986); the majority of articles in Nussbaum and Sen (1992); Dasgupta (1993: chs. 1–3).

[3] e.g. Harsanyi (1994).

cannot wait, and reality requires that they be engaged even if not fully comprehended. The pursuit of quality of life is open-ended, and finality is not within reach. Most of the essays combine (in different measures) a survey of empirical work, conceptual investigation, and the authors' own personal contribution to the field. They are rich in implications, but all stop short of detailed policy proposals. Here are brief summaries of the essays. Similar insights and conclusions resonate through all of them, and I proceed, after these short outlines, to draw these common threads together.

SUMMARY OUTLINE

Michael Argyle writes as a social psychologist about the experience of subjective well-being (SWB). This can be measured with some validity, and consists of satisfaction, positive affect, and the absence of distress. It has a small positive relation with wealth, and satisfaction is greater for the elderly. Social relationships like marriage and friendship are a major source of SWB. Work is another cause, via intrinsic and social job satisfaction, and unemployment a cause of distress. Leisure of various kinds is beneficial—leisure groups and serious leisure in particular. There are happy people, and the main personality variables here are extroversion, social skills like assertiveness and co-operation, and certain cognitive styles, for example, a small goal-achievement gap, and attributing good events but not bad ones to the self. SWB has some effect on length of life, mental health, sociability, and altruism. Happy workers do work a little harder, but the direction of causation is not known. Satisfied workers are absent less and have lower labour turnover. Happiness can be enhanced by social skills training, cognitive therapy, increasing pleasant activities, or twice-daily positive mood induction.

Pervasive destitution world-wide remains a standing reproach to the wealthy and to their satisfactions. Indeed, achieving a juster distribution depends to some extent on understanding the driving force of acquisitiveness. It is reasonable to assume that the benefits of material improvement would be felt most strongly by the poor. In conditions of destitution, priorities are clearer and therefore choice, which is what market economies cherish, is less relevant. *Frances Stewart* is a development economist and her essay defines and contrasts three recent approaches to identifying development objectives and strategies. The *basic needs* approach had its origin in the 1970s, and focuses on the objective of meeting the basic needs of all people; the *capabilities* approach, developed by Amartya Sen, sees the enhancement of human capabilities as the central objective; the *human development* approach, advocated by the United Nations Development Programme, puts human development at the centre, building on the two previous approaches and attempting to measure progress through the Human Development Index. The essay follows the evolution of these approaches in the context of the history of development thought; looks for similarities and differences; and considers how the adoption of these perspectives alters assessment of country performance, compared with the more conventional focus on economic variables. Finally, there is a brief analysis of types of success and failure, at a country level, in achieving 'human development'.

As we grow wealthy, we run down irreplaceable natural resources, and often the quality of our immediate environment as well. This is held to be a prime contradiction between economic welfare and the quality of life by many writers, and by the 'green' movement in particular, one of the most important reforming social and political movements in the affluent world. *Christopher Bliss* does not agree: he applies standard micro-economic analysis, but in doing so, provides a wide-ranging impression of dissenting, 'green' points of view. His paper starts out with a historical survey of estimates of the capacity of the earth's natural endowment to sustain economic growth. It sets out possible objectives for environmental policy, and the considerations and concepts which affect the choice among them. The final part considers the policies and tools that are available for implementing personal and policy choice, entering a case for respecting revealed preferences, especially the 'domesticated nature' paradigm of suburbia. His essay indicates both the extent to which quality of life concerns have entered and modified professional economics discourse, and the flexibility of this analytical framework in accommodating new concerns. Like most of the essays it is moderately optimistic in its faith that the application of reason is capable of increasing the quality of life.

For women, abundance has presented a dilemma. The potential of motherhood offers women a different set of choices to those facing men. Since the Second World War, women in Britain have had to choose or to compromise between two broad clusters of goods: on the one hand, family, household, and children; on the other, vocational opportunity, paid work, and personal autonomy. Most women attempt to combine both in some measure, with varying levels of success. *Heather Joshi* has opened up the study of the costs and rewards of the different life trajectories newly available to women, based on large longitudinal samples. It is common knowledge that paid work and child-rearing have increasingly been combined. She finds that once returning to the labour market became an established norm, the period outside it has tended to shorten. The standard British broken employment pattern is internationally, and historically unique. Before the 1970s, women of different classes had increasingly divergent life-courses; since the 1970s, their choices have converged. By the 1990s women were polarized between continuous careers among the most advantaged women and exclusion from the labour market of the least advantaged. Among a mass of ordinary women entering childbearing in their twenties, sharp distinctions emerge between teenage mothers, seldom employed, and 'elderly primagravidea', coming to motherhood after 30, utilizing maternity leave and maintaining full-time employment records. The middle ground is characterized by mothers working part-time, and mainly dependent for day-care on the school system. Such women are typically only minor contributors of earnings to the family budget.

The economic benefits of increased female employment are largely felt in the secondary earnings of two-earner families. For a minority, recently, it has also involved gains in more equally matched dual-full-time-earner couples. There are also positive impacts on women's self-esteem, and perhaps improved health, workplace companionship, economic autonomy, and social status, gains that are moderate for most but considerable for a minority. The impact on the distribution of income of these trends is complex, and depends on the solidarity and permanence of conjugal partnership.

Rising employment may have a negative effect on *unpaid* output, e.g. quality of housework and child care. There is little evidence on related variables such as trends in leisure, productivity of home time or the effect of mother's employment on the 'quality' of children. New opportunities on the labour market may also have affected the number and timing of births, though there is no unanimity about the effect. While opportunities for women may have improved over the long run, a continued inequality maintains the traditional division of domestic labour. Concurrently, women's work outside the home may exacerbate the trend of marital instability: one woman's independence gained is another's security lost.

As Argyle shows, satisfaction with family is a central component of overall life satisfaction. It provides the pleasures of personal interaction and enhances the sense of security. Families constitute a web of obligations and entitlements, and *Janet Finch's* essay explores the ways in which such commitments are established. How supportive is the family? Survey research indicates that most people acknowledge substantial obligations for intergenerational care in case of disability and dependency within the family. In practice, such obligations are discharged when the need arises, in a high proportion of cases. Who carries the burden? That depends on accumulated experiences of mutual exposure and exchange, and also on the vagaries of residential location, job, and life-cycle position of siblings and other relatives. The strength of obligations appears to depend (to some extent) on reciprocity. Within the family, obligation is the more intense when it has been earned.

By far the most intense programme of quality of life research is in the field of illness. The medical ethos of prolonging life regardless of cost has increasingly run against economic resource limitations, and modern therapies often prolong lives of unalleviated suffering. *Ray Fitzpatrick's* contribution describes the increasing preoccupation of socio-medical research with these dilemmas. A rapid expansion of studies using quality of life concepts and measures has occurred in medicine and health care over the last twenty years. Applications of the concept vary. They may be used as outcome measures in clinical trials or as population and clinic-based measures of need. The most controversial application has been in the context of resource allocation. Problems of defining and assessing quality of life vary according to intended use.

Two contrasting types of evidence are discussed. Individuals who are actually ill provide reports of their quality of life which are, on the whole positive and indicate that substantial adjustment to illness occurs. In contrast, 'utility' or 'normative'-type survey studies draw on the evaluations of representative panels of healthy people who are asked to evaluate the desirability or severity of different health states. They produce quite different results, with a much wider range of positive and negative evaluations of quality of life. Fitzpatrick's essay examines the legitimacy and plausibility of quality of life assessments and the problems that arise from the contrasting judgements of health-related quality of life reported by prior 'normative' surveys, and that of patients actually experiencing ill-health.

After family and health, a third core quality of life domain is the experience of work. *Duncan Gallie's* chapter examines two broads strands of research into the quality of employment. The first—represented particularly by French neo-Marxian researchers—was concerned with the objective quality of employment. This claimed that the dominant trend was towards the deskilling and 'despiritualization of work'. It is suggested that this approach foundered through its adoption of an overly narrow conception of 'objective quality' that proved decreasingly relevant with the evolution of the nature of work in the post-war period. The second research programme focused on the subjective quality of working life, as expressed principally through job satisfaction and job stress. This has produced an impressively coherent set of research findings, which does not support the claim of a declining quality of work. Both of these approaches emphasize discretion and control as determinants of a satisfactory working life, but improvements in this regard are often also associated with greater stress as well. For all its success, this research programme has suffered from a conception of work that is primarily rooted in the experiences of manufacturing industry and we still lack any clear conception of overall trends of change.

Jonathan Gershuny and *Brendan Halpin* probe the boundaries of work and leisure, mainly through the allocation of time. According to neo-classical economic theory, the allocation of time between paid work and non-market production (which includes leisure), is determined by the productivity at the margin of different time uses. Reinforcing Gallie's observations, they point out that different activities are also enjoyable or unpleasant *in themselves*, quite apart from their instrumental value. Time-diary data have provided evidence of shifts in the allocation of time away from work and into leisure. Given that work is an important source of satisfaction, it is not clear that such reallocations are providing an increase in subjective well-being. New surveys of time use incorporate questions about the perceived benefit of different activities, allowing the intrinsic satisfactions provided by a range of activities to be added to their instrumental value. This opens the way to an economics of satisfaction based on the measuring rod of time, in place of the measuring rod of money.

If the market is our main source of goods and services, why has it been held in suspicion for so long? Why does the term 'consumerism' often carry a negative connotation? An abiding critique is that consumer choice is not entirely autonomous, due to the influence of marketing and advertising. *Avner Offer* attempts to evaluate whether the language of the market, advertising in particular, might not be generating unwholesome spillovers. It is easy to see how advertising could deface the natural environment. It is equally plausible that advertising has an effect on the *normative* environment. People value social norms and find it more difficult to function in their absence. Truth ranks high among personal and social norms, and is strongly associated with several others: with fairness, integrity, trustworthiness, authenticity. Advertising is hampered as a medium of communication by a pervasive doubts about its credibility. Advertisers are less truthful than they would like to be, owing to the difficulty of policing transgressors, who 'free-ride' on the majority's credibility. Market transactions, even when they benefit both sides, are adversarial and potentially stressful, and advertising attempts to conceal this with a simulation of intimacy, designed to promote trust. It uses effective cues of intimacy such as testimonial, non-verbal gesture and facial communication, which bypass the filter of reason. In consequence, advertising remains compelling even when it is not believed. When it draws upon the social, cultural, and personal sources of trust, does advertising also run it down? This has important social consequences, since trust is essential for co-operation and collective action at many levels, from the household up to the state. The chapter documents the process of symbolic degradation, and considers international comparative evidence on levels of advertising expenditure, levels of interpersonal trust, and levels of political trust, to determine whether the commercialization of the personal, the social, and the political is undermining the capacity for collective action. If advertising has such effects, it is not surprising that governments should seek to regulate it in the interests of both market efficiency and the quality of life.

Finally, *Robert Lane* considers the wider conceptual issues of well-being from the perspective of social and political philosophy. Quality of life, extensively treated by the social indicators movement, is here defined as quality of external conditions, sense of well-being, and the qualities of persons living those lives. Qualities of persons are at the same time elements of the quality of life, causes of that quality, and consequences of it. Quality of life implies the qualities of persons as 'receptors' and interpreters of external circumstances, as sources of value, as complements in attributional processes, and as the agents of psychic income. Because governmental policies promoting quality of life fail when they ignore qualities of persons, because human development cannot be exclusively a process of self-help, and because there is new knowledge on the processes of learning, governments should promote human development as part of the promotion of a better quality of life. But such promotion is opposed by dominant democratic, economic, and philosophical (especially utilitarian) doctrines. The accumulation of goods will fail to provide welfare in the absence of human development.

With a subject as broad as life itself, it is futile to attempt comprehensive coverage, but between them, the essays cover most of the main research approaches, albeit, in some cases, from a critical point of view. Despite the disparity of approaches, several common themes emerge. One central issue is the dichotomy of objective and subjective approaches. A second one arises from an implicit contradiction between the utilitarian, self-centred focus of most of the research paradigms, and the recurrent empirical findings about the importance of interpersonal relations to the quality of life. These issues are now explored in more detail.

OBJECTIVE MEASURES

The material resources available to construct the good life ought to be easy enough to measure. The subjective experiences that people manage to derive from these resources are less tractable to investigation. GNP measures of welfare are attractively concrete and theoretically tractable. If there was a price for everything, then the allocation of income to consumption choices would provide a complete measure of welfare for individuals and society. As it is, the market only measures 'affluence' in the narrow sense of access to market goods and services. Substantial production takes place within households, without leaving a trace in the market, except indirectly, through its effect on price levels. Even if one were able to capture *individual* well-being in consumption measures, there are serious problems of aggregation from the individual to society, for which there is no simple solution.[4]

But there is a case for putting these doubts to one side. Respect for 'revealed preference' in the market-place is urged strongly by Christopher Bliss, in his essay, and forms the basis of a good deal of policy. Important indices of well-being (like literacy and infant mortality) are positively correlated with income per head. That is not a great surprise: it is better to be rich than poor, and income per head is our best indicator of affluence. But it is no accident that the correlation falls well short of the perfect. What is the best use of affluence? And is further affluence the highest priority? The pursuit of the quality of life raises these questions. That is the reason why this book concentrates primarily on affluent societies.

[4] Dasgupta (1993: 32–7, 81, 182–3).

Other writers in this book regard market measures of welfare as incomplete and possibly misleading. One familiar critique is that not all GNP goods actually represent an increase in welfare: some of them, are really a measure of 'bads', like the cost of security guards or of commuting. Several scholars have constructed revised national accounts in which such 'defensive expenditures' are deducted rather than added. This procedure is problematic, since if the Garden of Eden is taken as a benchmark, then almost any expenditure might be regarded as 'defensive'.[5] It may also be possible to err the other way, and *underestimate* the benefits of GNP goods. For one thing, prices measure relative scarcity, and not subjective benefits. This is Adam Smith's paradox of water and diamonds, the one vital but cheap, the other optional but expensive. The concept of 'consumer surplus' also suggests that prices are not an accurate measure of welfare. Some purchasers derive much more utility than others from the same goods. Another aspect of the same issue is that price measures are poor at capturing quality. Moving from gaslight to electricity, for example, a unit of light might cost considerably less per lumen, and a fall in the recorded outlays on lighting might disguise a considerable increase in illumination.[6] If welfare were measured in physical units instead of price, it would show an enormous increase. Given the possibility of diminishing returns to illumination, or even negative returns when lighting is too powerful or ubiquitous, it is however less clear that physical quantities, or 'quality' measures, offer a big advantage over price. This indicates that (*a*) serious measurement problems affect even seemingly 'hard' data like GNP measures, and that (*b*) when it comes to the measurement of welfare, the objective is difficult to separate strictly from the subjective.

Revealed consumer preference is problematic in several other ways: it is not clear that the choices available in the market overlap with the prior preferences of the individual. Nor, as Offer argues in his essay, is it clear how autonomous an individual is when she makes a market choice, whether the goods deliver the satisfactions promised, and whether additional cost in the form of externalities and public bads can be evaluated by the chooser. Furthermore, market choice is made at a point in time which is usually prior to the use of the good. This affects its welfare value in several ways: (*a*) preferences do not remain consistent over time, and are sometimes affected by regret and remorse; (*b*) as Fitzpatrick demonstrates, the evaluation of outcomes is strongly

[5] Eisner (1988). [6] Nordhaus (1994).

affected by experiencing them. For many purchases, such experience is not available in advance.

One subjective aspect of the market is that goods may not be valued absolutely, but mainly for the social status they confer. When that is entirely the case, then even a doubling of income for everyone will not produce any increase in welfare. Indeed, this is almost precisely the experience that Easterlin detected in the United States since the Second World War, from the perspective of the 1970s.[7] A decline in growth (which took place in the early 1970s) was nevertheless experienced as loss of welfare (possibly because it increased insecurity). This process is captured by the concept of 'hedonic treadmill', in which continuous material improvement is required in order to maintain a constant state of subjective well-being.[8] This is also why countries with very different levels of income per head can have similar levels of reported subjective well-being. To improve one's subjective well-being it is not enough for everyone to be better off; it is necessary to improve one's position upwards *within* one's society.[9] Those at the top of society report moderately higher well-being scores than the others. Unfortunately, it is logically impossible for everyone to improve their relative position within society. Higher incomes thus provide access to 'positional goods'. These goods derive their value from scarcity, and lose it as they become more widely diffused.[10] Holidays in Majorca are an example. Another is good suburban locations, which combine a rural aspect with access to civic amenities. This problem of 'positional goods' is perhaps not sufficiently acknowledged by Bliss in his essay.

Stated differently, the value of goods can be affected by their distribution. Nor is the relation a simple one. Status comparisons are typically made with adjacent reference groups. On the face of it, increasing equality might paradoxically increase dissatisfaction by those whose position has improved materially, and who have thus come within the comparison range of more affluent reference groups. In principle, with assumptions no more onerous than those routinely made in economic analysis, it would be possible to work out a distribution which maximized satisfaction with positional goods, but I am not aware that such analysis has yet been undertaken. As economists would predict, there is some evidence of pragmatic adaptations in workplaces to maximize positional well-being, in which those with lower positional standing are

[7] Easterlin (1974). [8] Brickman and Campbell (1971).

[9] Easterlin (1974); Campbell *et al.* (1976: table 2-1, 28); but see a note of dissent in Diener *et al.* (1993). [10] Hirsch (1976).

compensated with money incomes. Robert Frank has identified such processes in environments as divergent as university departments, car dealerships, and real estate agencies. Where the prospects of positional mobility are limited, status competition is irrational. Frank also argues that such co-operative arrangements as minimum wages and maximum working hours are designed to limit futile positional competition, and there is some support for his argument in historical accounts of industrial relations.[11] Status appears to exercise a powerful effect on the state of health. In that respect, it mirrors the effect of growth on subjective well-being. In poor countries, health responds strongly to improvements in average income per head, but the effect disappears in affluent societies. In affluent societies it is *relative* income that counts. Expectations of death and illness are strongly related to occupational and social rankings, with those at the top, the managers and directors, experiencing better prospects even than professional workers just one rung below them in the hierarchy.[12]

Price itself, as an allocative mechanism is not costless to use, and for many goods, people are inclined to avoid it.[13] One reason is that the market relation is also an adversarial one, in which it is rarely possible to relax one's guard completely. Friendship, for example, with its norm of acceptance, is not a good that most people wish to purchase with money. Hence, the mere posting of a price can devalue some categories of goods, such as those that arise from interpersonal relations. Many of the goods in question are not trivial, and rank, like family, friendship, and acceptance, among the highest satisfactions.[14]

Some of them are best captured, as Gershuny and Halpin do, by considering the allocation of time, not money. Time resources can be allocated to market work, and to non-market work. For simplicity's sake, non-market work can be divided into housework and leisure. In Gershuny and Halpin's average British 'Great Day' only a little more than one-fifth of the time is allocated to paid work. When extended national accounts assign a money value to leisure and to housework, these two categories completely dominate estimates of national income.[15] This procedure would bring us closer to the real measure of welfare, but at a heavy cost in accuracy and objectivity. The money measure of income would no longer be derived from volumes and prices of traded goods, but from imputations of money values to goods which most people

[11] Frank (1985); Webb and Webb (1902: pt 2, ch. 5).
[12] Wilkinson (1994); Marmot (1994). [13] Frey (1986). [14] Offer (1996).
[15] Nordhaus and Tobin (1982: table A.17, 55).

deliberately choose *not* to value in money. If GNP goods is too narrow a measure of welfare, extended national accounts are too vague.

Another approach is to discard the straitjacket of prices altogether, and to find something else to measure. Many such measures are possible, and a good collection can be found, e.g. in the annual *Social Trends*, published by the British government. Measures of health, housing, education, literacy, transport, civic rights add a great deal to our conception of welfare, and provide targets for policy.[16] These *social indicators* are capable of objective and fairly precise estimation. But they do not add up to a *comprehensive* measure, do not present any self-evident priorities, and are not easy to integrate within a national accounts approach. Hence, after a surge of interest in the 1970s, they have fallen somewhat out of favour as an approach to well-being, and are not represented by any single essay in this book. In conditions of destitution, however, it is easier to specify priorities. Social indicators have found their most important recent applications in this field, and in particular in the Human Development Index and its variants, which measures a composite of poverty, literacy, and life expectations. It has gained considerable acceptance (see essay by Stewart, in this volume). It has also faced considerable criticism from two different quarters: from those who regard these priorities as distorting market-led liberal development policies (upheld in particular by the World Bank), which are supposed to maximize aggregate economic welfare in the long run; and from Amartya Sen's 'capabilities' approach, which regards such 'basic goods' as excessively narrow even for societies characterized by destitution (this is also discussed by Frances Stewart).

All of this suggests that the 'tough-minded' preference for objective measures of well-being, or the even 'tougher' belief in simple consumerism, are fraught with pitfalls, and cannot deliver, on their own, a single all-purpose measure of the quality of life.

Welfare economists are inclined to reject interpersonal comparisons of utility, on the grounds that people are the best judges of their own welfare, and that any external prescription is likely to reduce it. This view is contested by several essays in this book (especially by Stewart and Lane); their position is that such comparisons are done all the time, and that the ordering of preferences is far from random; that some wants are prior to others, and that this order of preference is widely acknowledged, if it is not actually 'wired in'. A common shorthand is Maslow's

[16] Erikson and Uuistalo (1987).

'hierarchy of needs', but this idea is also implicit in the notions of 'basic needs' and 'human development'.[17]

Given the limitations of objective measurement, it is clear that no single metric can be regarded as satisfactory. Dasgupta makes this clear: what is needed for such a metric is not market prices, but household-specific shadow prices. In other words, we need to know what people cherish *outside* the market. In the absence of such information, the best that can be done is to construct a multiplicity of indices of the constituents of well-being.

SUBJECTIVE MEASURES OF THE QUALITY OF LIFE

As we have seen, objective measures of welfare already involve assumptions about mental states. Those who seek to examine these mental states directly, face obstacles which are equally formidable. There are simple problems of access and measurement. The mental economy does not generate statistical yearbooks. Mental data have to be teased out by means of questionnaires and contrived experiments, and to a lesser extent by ethnographic observation or historical research. Survey research, the source for much of these data, is prone to errors, 'noise', and even deliberate deception. On the other hand, as Argyle, Gallie, and Gershuny and Halpin indicate here, many results are consistent with each other and are fairly robust.

Economic measures of utility assume a straightforward and simple psychological mechanism, one that is essentially consistent, rational, and well ordered. But this model is axiomatic rather than empirical. Actual psychic states diverge systematically from it. Hedonic experience is affected by well-documented mental biases which arise from the temporal dynamics of this very experience. Such is the process of adaptation: novelty wears off and arousal provides diminishing, then negative returns. Adaptation has two aspects: goods may lose their appeal, while bads lose their bite, leading, ultimately, to the 'happy slave' syndrome, or to Ivan Denisovich, Solzhenitsyn's labour camp inmate who looks back with satisfaction on a good day, in which nothing worse than the usual deprivations took place.

Other biases cause losses to count for more than gains; available

[17] Also acknowledged recently by Dasgupta (1993), 8.

and proximate goods to count much more than remote ones. Time-inconsistency is not in itself a cognitive bias, but raises the possibility of a 'multiple self', whose preferences are not consistent over time, and who might be prone to regret. As Argyle shows, more direct examination of mental states suggests a variety of dynamics, ranging from the positive dynamic of 'flow', which maintains subjective well-being at optimal levels, through the personality cluster of extraversion, which raises the probability of subjective well-being, to varieties of negative affect, from the 'pursuit of unhappiness' and all the way to mental disturbance and mental illness.

The links between objective and subjective measures are, on the whole, positive but weak. If measurement in each of these two domains is problematical, measuring their interactions is more difficult still. Rather than ordinal and cardinal measures of abundance such as income, education, and housing, other equally real states, processes, and relationships, e.g. in work, leisure, domestic activity, and interpersonal relations, may be more promising as proxies of subjective satisfaction. Several essays stress the importance of discretion, autonomy, or control as a strong determinant of satisfaction with work, with other life domains and with life in general. Another measure which has attracted considerable discussion (though not much in this book) is the idea (which complements the 'hedonic treadmill' hypothesis), of 'aspiration level'—that satisfaction is determined by the dynamic relationship between aspirations and outcomes, in which the best experience is that in which outcomes conform to aspirations or surpass them.[18]

INTERPERSONAL RELATIONSHIPS

We depend on others for the quality of our life; that is a recurrent result: not in the trivial connotation that goods and services come out of the division of labour; but in the sense that our well-being depends on the acknowledgement, attention, and approbation of others, on their affirmations, confirmations, and gifts. The number and configuration of personal relationships is an objective measure, and the quality of these relations is a subjective one. This has already been hinted by the way in which status affects economic measures of well-being. Status is an interpersonal relationship, in which some measure of deference from

[18] Michalos (1986).

others, implicit or explicit, is vital. To the extent that the 'relative income' hypothesis is valid, then what counts is not absolute affluence but relative wealth: even the GNP economy is a set of personal relationships. Argyle stresses the concentric circles of approbation and interaction, from intimate love, married life, kinship, friendship, and outwards, whose quality is strongly related to social distance. Finch reinforces this finding, but points out that intensity and reciprocity, even *within* families, have to be earned. From another angle Joshi underlines the gradual drift of women away from the domestic goods of marriage and children, towards the market ones of paid work and vocational careers. The slowness of this shift, and the continued primacy of marriage and child-rearing in the life of most women indicates the intensity of aspiration and satisfaction bound up in the family. Both Gallie and Lane stress the social benefits of work, the satisfactions of social interaction at the workplace. Offer argues that a good deal of advertising and marketing is an attempt to simulate intimacy in an impersonal market-place. A measure of welfare restricted to market transactions thus fails to capture a vital aspect of the quality of life, namely an explicit choice expressed in individual preferences, in culture and in social institutions, to *avoid* the market altogether.

Several issues are raised repeatedly by different writers. Arguments about the quality of life typically proceed from effect to cause. A pervasive feature of this field of enquiry is that the direction of causation is difficult to determine. Is marriage a source of happiness, or are those of a happy disposition more likely to marry? Work is only beginning on methods to identify cause and effect. But the knowledge is useful: to establish causation we first need to be certain about the association. Another issue, is the distinction between utilitarian and other approaches to the quality of life. Utilitarians regard the quality of life almost entirely as a matter for individuals, and are inclined towards a hedonic view of welfare. Non-utilitarians identify life-goals that transcend the individual, and non-hedonic motivations, such as justice, equity, and virtue. This is discussed extensively by Robert Lane.

The essays preserve some of the variety and immediacy of seminar presentations, and are pitched at different levels: this sometimes reflects the state of the art, sometimes an author's preferences. I have chosen, as editor, not to force them all into a common mould. The questions raised in the pursuit of the quality of life are too vast, too varied, to be contained within any single book, so this one is not comprehensive. The implicit claims of finality, implicit in philosophical discourse, are inappropriate. Our pursuit of well-being is blinkered: at the level of policy, by simplistic measures of welfare; at the personal level by cognitive biases, by the difficulties of co-operation with others and with our future selves. A true economics will not merely seek to maximize measures chosen for their simplicity, but will attempt to query what our real maximands ought to be, and whether the notion of 'maximizing' captures the nature of the quality of life. This is not a rejection of reason. Economic rationality may be inadequate, but the search for quality of life, both conceptually and in practice, is eminently reasonable. No mere book can meet the Aristotelian demand for action in place of talk. These essays break away from reflection and towards action, by reporting on the achievements and contradictions of the efforts to enhance and understand the quality of life.

REFERENCES

ARISTOTLE (1976), *The Ethics of Aristotle: The Nicomachean Ethics*, trans. J. A. K. Thompson, rev. H. Tredennick, introd. J. Barnes. Harmondsworth: Penguin Books, rev. edn.

BRICKMAN, P., and CAMPBELL, D. T. (1971), 'Hedonic Relativism and Planning the Good Society', in M. H. Appley (ed.), *Adaptation-Level Theory: A Symposium*. New York: Academic Press.

CAMPBELL, A., CONVERSE, P., and RODGERS, W. L. (1976), *The Quality of American Life: Perceptions, Evaluations, and Satisfactions*. New York: Russell Sage Foundation.

DASGUPTA, P. (1993), *An Inquiry into Well-Being and Destitution*. Oxford: Oxford University Press.

DIENER, E., SANDVIK, E., SEIDLITZ, L., and DIENER, M. (1993), 'The Relationship Between Income and Subjective Well-Being: Relative or Absolute?', *Social Indicators Research*, 28: 195–223.

EASTERLIN, R. (1974), 'Does Economic Growth Improve the Human Lot? Some Empirical Evidence', in P. David and M. Reder (eds.), *Nations and Households in Economic Growth: Essays in Honor of Moses Abramowitz*. New York: Academic Press.

EISNER, R. (1988), 'Extended Accounts for National Income and Product', *Journal of Economic Literature*, 26/4: 1611–84.

ERIKSON, R., and UUISTALO, H. (1987), 'The Scandinavian Approach to Welfare Research', in R. Erikson *et al.* (eds.), *The Scandinavian Model: Welfare States and Welfare Research*. New York: M. E. Sharpe, 177–93.

FRANK, R. (1985), *Choosing the Right Pond: Human Behavior and the Quest for Status*. New York: Oxford University Press.

FREY, B. (1986), 'Economists Favour the Price System—Who Else Does?', *Kyklos*, 39/4: 537–63.

GRIFFIN, J. (1986), *Well-Being: Its Meaning, Measurement and Moral Importance*. Oxford: Clarendon Press.

HARSANYI, J. C. (1994), 'A Case for a Utilitarian Ethic', in H. Siebert (ed.), *The Ethical Foundations of the Market Economy*. Tübingen: J. C. B. Mohr, 3–13.

HIRSCH, F. (1976), *The Social Limits to Growth*. London: Routledge.

MARMOT, M. (1994), 'Social Differentials in Health within and between Populations', *Daedalus*, 123/4: 197–216.

MICHALOS, A. C. (1986), 'Job Satisfaction, Marital Satisfaction, and the Quality of Life: A Review and a Preview', in F. M. Andrews (ed.), *Research on the Quality of Life*. Ann Arbor: Survey Research Center, Institute for Social Research, University of Michigan, 57–83.

NORDHAUS, W. D., and TOBIN, J. (1982), 'Is Growth Obsolete?', in J. Tobin, *Essays in Economics: Theory and Policy*, I. Cambridge, Mass: MIT Press.

NORDHAUS, W. D. (1994), 'Do Real Output and Real Wage Measures Capture Reality? The History of Lighting Suggests Not', Cowles Foundation Discussion Paper no. 1078, Yale University.

NUSSBAUM, M. C., and SEN, A. (eds.) (1992), *The Quality of Life*. Oxford: Oxford University Press.

OFFER, A. (1996), 'Between the Gift and the Market: The Economy of Regard'. University of Oxford Discussion Papers in Economic and Social History, no. 3, Jan.

ORMEROD, P. (1994), *The Death of Economics*. London: Faber.

WEBB, S., and WEBB, B. (1902 edn.), *Industrial Democracy*. London: Printed by the Authors.

WILKINSON, R. G. (1994), 'The Epidemiological Transition: From Material Scarcity to Social Disadvantage?', *Daedalus*, 123/4: 61–78.

2

Subjective Well-Being

MICHAEL ARGYLE

There is an obvious case for assessing subjective well-being (SWB), or happiness, as well as—or instead of—objective well-being. The list of possible *objective* indicators is endless—wealth, health, employment, education . . . rainfall, alcohol consumption, literacy, etc.[1] But how do we decide which of these many variables is worth including? One solution is to see which of them increases the *subjective* quality of life; perhaps it is no use making people richer if it doesn't make them happier; we shall see later whether it does or not.

THE MEANING AND MEASUREMENT OF SWB

One way to find out the meaning of happiness is to ask people. If this is done, they give two main kinds of answer: (1) it is a state of joy or positive emotion; or (2) it is satisfaction with life as a whole, or with work, leisure, and other parts of it. Each of these components is usually included in measures of happiness, and it is found that they correlate at about .50.[2] In other words they are partly independent of each other. However, there is a third component—the absence of unhappiness, i.e. of depression or anxiety. It is important to know whether unhappiness is the opposite of happiness. If it is not research is not then needed on happiness—the extensive research on depression would tell us all we need to know, and normal individuals could be treated in the same way as depressed patients to make them happier. It is found that the frequency of positive and negative emotions correlate at about −.50, so that the two are sufficiently independent for it to be necessary to measure them separately, which is usually done.

To measure SWB requires that all three parts of it be measured, it

[1] Jordan (1993). [2] Argyle (1987).

needs three questions, not one. However, psychological measures are far better if they have not just one question, but sample over the whole domain, like intelligence tests and personality tests. Happiness measures that are like this are found to have greater validity against other criteria, and to be affected less by irrelevant factors, such as the mood of subjects.[3]

Research carried out by Schwarz and Strack[4] found that factors such as the weather and if a football team had won or lost affected not only the mood of subjects but also their reported satisfaction with their lives, casting doubt on the value of such measures. However, we now know two ways in which such effects can be minimized: first the use of a series of items, not just one, and secondly by phrasing the questions as 'trait', rather than as 'state' questions, i.e. by asking about the respondent's condition over the past few weeks, rather than 'now'.[5]

A number of SWB measures include scales for these three components, though they can also be analysed to show a single general factor. Examples are the Oxford Happiness Inventory,[6] the Affectometer,[7] and a number of American scales like those of Andrews and Withey.[8] This may not be the last word on the subject, however. Ryff[9] found additional factors of purpose in life, personal growth, positive relations with others, and continued development. Waterman[10] distinguished between 'hedonic' measures, asking about pleasure and enjoyment, and 'eudaimonia' based on questions about 'feeling really alive' and 'this is who I really am'; although the two correlated at about .73, the second related more strongly to challenge, competition, concentration, and assertion. I shall describe later research on the benefits of serious leisure; we found evidence for a dimension of depth of positive emotions, experienced in situations such as close relations with others, powerful music, and the joys of nature.[11] On the other hand we shall also show later that quite ordinary measures of happiness, even with single items, are very responsive to some of these variables.

SWB scales like those described have been found to have very satisfactory properties. They are reliable over time: over a period of six months this is typically .8, or .6 over two years, and .45 over seven years.[12] There is also quite good evidence of validity, against ratings

[3] Pavot and Diener (1993). [4] Schwarz and Strack (1991).
[5] Kozma *et al.* (1990). [6] Argyle *et al.* (1989); Argyle *et al.* (1995).
[7] Kammann and Flett (1983). [8] Andrews and Withey (1976).
[9] Ryff (1989). [10] Waterman (1993). [11] Argyle and Crossland (1989).
[12] Horley and Lavery (1991).

by friends, at about .45.[13] There is of course a serious possibility that subjects will exaggerate their happiness, perhaps some more than others. Could some other measure of SWB be devised, not dependent on self-report? One possibility is the sampling of facial expression, but no practicable way of doing this has yet been found.

THE RELATION TO OBJECTIVE WELL-BEING

It is of great interest to know how far SWB relates to objective indices of well-being. In early studies correlations were studied, but more recent, longitudinal analyses have been able to establish the direction of causation as well.

Early studies such as that of Bradburn[14] found quite a strong relationship between income and happiness. In an American survey with nearly 7,000 subjects Diener *et al.* (1993) found a clear relationship with income, but it was stronger for lower incomes and levelled off at higher levels. The same has been found in Britain, and in international comparisons. However there is no evidence from the repeated surveys in the USA that there has been any historical increase in happiness, despite massive increases in economic prosperity. And, some poor people are quite satisfied with their lot; this has been called the 'paradox of poverty'.[15] At the other end of the scale Diener[16] found that a sample of American millionaires were distinctly happier than a control group: they said they were happy 77 per cent of the time compared with 62 per cent for the others.

There have been many studies of the relationship between health and happiness. A meta-analysis of many studies found an overall correlation of .32, though it was more than this if subjective measures of health were used.[17] Indeed subjective measures of health have been found to reflect negative emotions more than actual illness.[18] Research in gerontology has found that health and happiness are quite strongly related for the old. Feist *et al.*[19] in a longitudinal study using causal modelling, and a thirty-six-item measure of self-reported symptoms, found that both directions of causation operated.

A number of other objective conditions of life have been found to be

[13] Argyle *et al.* (1989); Pavot and Diener (1993). [14] Bradburn (1969).
[15] Olson and Schober (1993). [16] Diener *et al.* (1985).
[17] Okun *et al.* (1984). [18] Watson and Pennebaker (1989).
[19] Feist *et al.* (1995).

associated with happiness, and these will be examined later. Individuals who have jobs are happier than those without jobs, and people are happier if they have 'good' jobs, i.e. jobs that are more interesting, have higher status, or greater skill. People who are married and have good supportive networks of various kinds are happier than those who are more isolated. All this is as might be expected.

DEMOGRAPHIC DIFFERENCES

Gender

Meta-analysis of many studies shows that women are slightly happier overall. On the other hand women are twice as likely to be depressed. Part of the explanation of these apparently conflicting results is that women experience both positive and negative emotions more intensely.[20] A number of explanations have been put forward for female depression—women are more willing to admit it, and use less effective methods of coping, for example.

Age

The separate components of happiness are affected differently by age. Satisfaction increases, quite markedly, probably because the gap between aspirations and attainments becomes smaller. (The goal-achievement gap theory is expounded later.) Affect—both positive and negative—declines with age, as the intensity of all emotions decreases. The sources of happiness are also affected differently by age; older people are often richer, but in worse health; old people have less sex life, but may have supportive spouses and families.

Social class

We saw above that there is usually a small positive relation between income and happiness. The same is true of other social class indicators, such as education and occupational status. There are several possible reasons, including having more interesting jobs, and receiving more respect from others, which would affect self-esteem; self-esteem increases with class.

[20] Fujita *et al.* (1991).

National differences

There have only been surveys using single questions, which, as we have seen, are not good measures of SWB. However, Veenhoven[21] reported an interesting international study of twenty-eight countries. The happiest countries were the Scandinavian ones, followed by Britain, North America, and Australia; the least happy were Asian. Veenhoven found that the results could be explained partly by national differences in political freedom ($r = .67$), economic equality ($r = .45$), and economic prosperity. There are still some problems—Italy, France, and Japan come out very low on these surveys, and this may be because the questions in some way have a different meaning there. Another possible explanation is that each of these three countries is low in extraversion and high in neuroticism while the happy countries are the reverse,[22] and as we shall see below these traits are strongly related to SWB.

COGNITIVE SOURCES OF SATISFACTION

The low correlations often found between, for example, income and satisfaction, even satisfaction with income, have led to a search for cognitive processes that might explain such findings.

Social comparison

This is the theory that satisfaction depends on pay, for example, in relation to that of others, rather than on actual pay. This theory was tested recently by two economists, Clark and Oswald,[23] who found that job satisfaction had no relation to salary, but was higher for those who earned more than the 'expected' salary, obtained from equations showing income as a function of job, education, age, etc. This may show the effect of social comparisons, but there is a problem that people are selective over whom they compare themselves with. Runciman[24] found that better-paid manual workers were more satisfied with their incomes than many non-manual workers, because the manual workers compared themselves with other manual workers, most of whom were worse off, and many seemed to be unaware of doctors, lawyers, etc. and their

[21] Veenhoven (1990). [22] Lynn (1982). [23] Clark and Oswald (1993).
[24] Runciman (1966).

salaries, while the non-manual workers were discontented because they compared themselves with other non-manual workers, most of whom were better off than they were. Michalos[25] proposed the 'Michigan model' that satisfaction is a function of the 'goal-achievement gap', which in turn depends on comparisons with past life and with 'average folks'. In a number of studies it was found that about 40 per cent of the variance in satisfaction could be explained in this way. However, it is found that such comparisons are less important in private spheres such as love life than in public ones such as housing and attractiveness.[26] And there are limits to the importance of comparisons: it is not the case that 'if everyone has a pain, then mine doesn't hurt.'[27] Satisfactions due to sex or food probably do not depend on beliefs about what others are doing.

Adaptation

This is the theory that people become used to a certain level of stimulation, which comes to be regarded as normal. It received some support in the field of SWB from evidence that those who had become para- or quadriplegic became after a short time as satisfied with life as they were before.[28] However, in a study of 100 such patients it was found that after twenty years they were still somewhat lower than the population average on a number of measures.[29] The experience of lottery winners has been used in a similar way, and it is true that their satisfaction returns towards normal, but partly because their life is so disrupted by the advent of sudden wealth, often not in a favourable way, e.g. by giving up jobs and moving house. And it is obvious that depressed people have not adapted to whatever was bothering them.

The Polyanna effect

The majority of people say that they are very satisfied with their life, the great majority say they are very happy with their marriages (68 per cent at point 7 on a 7-point scale). Could this be due to 'social desirability bias', the feeling that one ought to give certain answers? It is found that there is almost no correlation between reported satisfaction and social desirability,[30] so there must be some other explanation of this upward bias. Headey and Wearing[31] found that most people thought

[25] Michalos (1986). [26] Fox and Kahneman (1992). [27] Diener (1984).
[28] Brickman *et al.* (1978). [29] Schulz and Decker (1985).
[30] Russell and Wells (1992). [31] Headey and Wearing (1992).

that they were above average in a number of respects, e.g. 86 per cent thought that they had better jobs, 73 per cent thought they were better parents. These authors suggest that this may be because each of these roles has several sub-roles and it is possible to think of the sub-role that one does best. It is also possible to make use of comparison with those who are worse off rather than with those who are better.

Though these cognitive biases seem like 'errors', those concerned really do feel satisfied, whether they 'ought' to feel satisfied or not.

THE CAUSES OF JOY

Positive emotions are produced in a number of different ways, some of which can be explained by psychologists, while others as yet cannot. Surveys of the causes of joy, mainly with young people, find that the main sources are contacts with friends, especially being in love, exercise and sport, success and achievement, eating, drinking, sex, and music, reading, religion, and other cultural and aesthetic experiences. Being or falling in love seems to be the most intense source of joy, time spent with friends the most common.[32]

Joy can be produced experimentally in the laboratory. The first method to be used was the 'Velten' technique, which consists of reading aloud and trying to believe a list of positive statements such as 'I really do feel good'. Perhaps surprisingly this works, but only for about 60 per cent of subjects, and the effect lasts only for about 10–15 minutes. Listening to cheerful music is a little more successful, in that it affects most subjects, but doesn't last much longer.[33] Many other methods have been used—funny films, 'succeeding' at tests, finding coins, and hypnosis. Thayer[34] found that brisk walks of ten minutes produced a positive mood, together with more energy, less anxiety, depression and tiredness, for two hours.

Strack *et al.*[35] used another method, asking subjects to spend twenty minutes thinking about recent happy events; this was very successful, especially if concrete images were called up. We thought that this effect might be enhanced if subjects talked to someone else about the happy events, but we found that the effect was very similar. On the other hand asking people to talk about recent unhappy events was only half as

[32] e.g. Scherer *et al.* (1986). [33] Clark (1983). [34] Thayer (1989).
[35] Strack *et al.* (1985).

TABLE 2.1. *Relationship of domain satisfactions with well-being and psychological distress: correlations*

Domain satisfaction	Life satisfaction index	Positive affect	Anxiety	Depression
Leisure	.42	.28	–.29	–.29
Marriage	.39	.17	–.29	–.32
Work	.38	.26	–.27	–.36
Standard of living	.38	.20	–.18	–.26
Friendships	.37	.19	–.15	–.12
Sex life	.34	.17	–.19	–.33
Health	.25	.11	–.23	–.14

Source: Headey and Wearing (1992).

depressing as thinking about them alone—'a trouble shared is a trouble halved'.[36] It is interesting to note that it is better to do neither.

What about real-life events that produce longer-lasting positive moods? Lewinsohn *et al.*[37] drew up a list of positive events, and asked subjects to keep diaries for a month of which events they had experienced each day, and their mood by the end of the day; computer analysis then showed which activities had most effect for each person; 'pleasant activities therapy' involves persuading people to engage in the successful ones more often, and has been found to increase SWB. Out of the long original list, 49 pleasant activities were often found to be successful in this way, mostly forms of social life and leisure.

THE CAUSES OF HAPPINESS

I turn now to the main causes of happiness, or SWB—that is all three components as described above. Table 2.1 gives some of the findings of the study in Australia by Headey and Wearing,[38] with 600 subjects; this shows the correlations of the various components with the main sources of satisfaction.

It can be seen that there are strong correlations for marriage and sex, and for friendship, and for work and leisure. Similar results were

[36] Argyle *et al.* (1989). [37] Lewinsohn *et al.* (1982).
[38] Headey and Wearing (1992).

TABLE 2.2. *Happiness of the married, single, and divorced*

	Percentage 'very happy'	
	Men	Women
Married	35.0	41.5
Single	18.5	25.5
Divorced	18.5	15.5

Source: Veroff *et al.* (1981).

obtained in the earlier American study *The Quality of American Life* by Campbell,[39] though they had a longer list of variables. In the next three sections I shall describe more detailed research on the effects of relationships, work, and leisure, and deal with the effect of objective conditions, rather than with ratings of satisfaction. Standard of living and health have been mentioned above, so no more will be said about these since they are really the domains of medicine and economics rather than psychology. There is a fourth cause of happiness not mentioned in Table 2.1, the effect of personality. As we shall see there are happy people just as there are depressed ones.

SOCIAL RELATIONSHIPS

In many studies these come out as the greatest single source of happiness.[40] The effects are often quite large; for example, look at the findings by Veroff in *The Inner American* shown in Table 2.2.[41]

These effects are found for each of the three components of SWB.

Joy is greater when with other people. Larson[42] bleeped subjects on many random occasions, and they reported being in the most positive mood when with friends, followed by family, followed by being alone; the effect of friends was strongest for subjects in their 20s and for old people. There are a number of possible explanations of the joys of being with friends: they do enjoyable things together; Argyle and Furnham[43] found that the most characteristic activities shared with friends in an Oxford adult sample were dancing, playing tennis, drinking sherry, and

[39] Campbell *et al.* (1976). [40] e.g. Cooper *et al.* (1992), and see Table 2.1.
[41] Veroff *et al.* (1981). [42] Larson (1990).
[43] Argyle and Furnham (1982).

TABLE 2.3. *Effects of life-events and social support on depression (%)*

	Spouse who is confidant	No such confidant
Stressful life-events in last 6 months	10	41
Few stressful events	1	4

Source: Brown and Harris (1978).

other joint leisure activities. (It was a *North* Oxford sample.) These may seem frivolous activities, but they may also bind those involved into a powerful supportive social network. A second explanation of the joys of friendship is that friends smile and send other positive non-verbal signals, which are reciprocated. This is a powerful source of positive affect.

Satisfaction, the second component of SWB, is particularly strong in marriage. There are several reasons for this: Argyle and Furnham[44] found three factors of satisfaction in relationships, and that marriage was the greatest source of all of them, especially by means of material help and emotional support, but also because of shared interests and companionship. Marriage is the most intense of all relationships. It is a kind of biological co-operative in which the partners share food, bed, and much of the rest of life, and can be the source of the most powerful benefits.

Relationships also prevent distress, and can lead to lower rates of illness and mental illness. Brown and Harris[45] showed that women who had experienced recent stressful life events were often depressed, but were much less likely to be so if they had a supportive spouse with whom they could discuss their problems, as shown in Table 2.3.

This is known as a 'buffering effect', i.e. the social support only operates when there is stress; buffering rather than main effects is found particularly for close relationships like marriage. Social relationships are also good for bodily health. Berkman and Syme[46] followed up 7,000 people in California over a nine-year period; 30.8 per cent of men in their 50s who had weak social networks died, compared with 9.6 per cent of those with strong networks. This result has also been widely replicated, though the differences have often been weaker.[47]

[44] Argyle and Furnham (1983).
[45] Brown and Harris (1978).
[46] Berkman and Syme (1979).
[47] Schwarzer and Leppin (1989).

Marriage has been found to be good for health in two different ways; first married people look after each other and engage in better 'health behaviour', e.g. drink and smoke less, take exercise, do what the doctor says, and secondly being in a close relationship is found to activate the immune system.[48] The result is that married people are less likely to catch colds or other diseases.

However, relationships can have bad effects as well as good ones. Argyle and Furnham[49] found that marriage was the greatest source of conflict as well as of satisfaction. It was also found that having rows was one of the most characteristic marital activities; the reason is obvious when people are living at such close quarters, there are many things that have to be decided and a lot of scope for disagreement. To avoid such conflict requires some social skills, especially the ability to negotiate disagreements in a constructive way, as well as keeping the rules of marriage, of which being faithful is the most important.[50] Marital satisfaction is reduced when children are babies, and when they are teenagers; otherwise children are a great source of satisfaction.[51] Marital satisfaction is high after the children have left home.

JOB SATISFACTION

SWB is strongly correlated with job satisfaction (see Table 2.1). But which causes which? Several longitudinal studies have been carried out in which different causal models could be compared. Headey and Wearing[52] concluded that the main influence is from life satisfaction to job satisfaction; Schmitt and Bedeian[53] concluded that causation went in both directions. But it is hard to make sense of some of the results reported below unless there is *some* effect of job satisfaction on SWB.

There are large differences in the job satisfaction obtained in different jobs; in an American study 93 per cent of university teachers were very satisfied, compared with 16 per cent of unskilled car workers (Table 2.4).

This is far greater than any difference in SWB between these groups. The job satisfaction differences are partly due to greater intrinsic satisfaction for certain jobs: those with more autonomy, and use of a

48 Kennedy *et al.* (1990).
49 Argyle and Furnham (1983).
50 Argyle and Henderson (1985).
51 Walker (1977).
52 Headey and Wearing (1992).
53 Schmitt and Bedeian (1982).

TABLE 2.4. *Occupational differences in job satisfaction, coronary heart disease, and social status*

	% satisfied	Coronary rate	Social status
University teachers	93	71	84
Biologists	89	69	80
Physicists	89	69	80
Chemists	86	100	79
Farmers	84	66	14
Lawyers	80	124	93
Managers	69	116	79
Sales	52	126	50
Skilled printers	52	110	49
Clerical	42	103	44
Paper workers	42	73	19
Skilled car workers	41	68	21
Skilled steelworkers	41	85	15
Textile workers	31	120	3
Unskilled steelworkers	21	125	4
Unskilled car workers	16	176	13

Source: Sales and House (1971).

variety of skills for example.[54] The same jobs usually have higher status and pay and better working conditions as well. A second important component of job satisfaction is social satisfaction, with co-workers. It is found that quite a lot of the time at work is spent on games, gossip, and fooling about. This is more important than it might seem, since it is a major source of job satisfaction, and also produces bonds between workers, which result in greater help and co-operation over the work.[55]

Not being at work is a great source of unhappiness, as well as of clinical depression and ill health. Again we need to know which causes which. Banks and Jackson[56] followed up 600 school leavers, who had been tested with the General Health Questionnaire before leaving school. When they were tested again two and four years later, it was found that those with jobs were in better mental health than before, but those without jobs were in worse mental health, which shows that work is good

[54] Hackman and Oldham (1980). [55] Argyle (1989).
[56] Banks and Jackson (1982).

TABLE 2.5. *Unemployment and mental health: self-reported mental health using the 30-item GHQ*

	Before leaving school	6–15 months after leaving school	16–23 months after leaving school
Unemployed			
Boys	11.4	13.6	
Girls	11.2		13.4
Employed			
Boys	10.6	8.4	
Girls	10.5		7.7

Source: Banks and Jackson (1982).

for mental health, unemployment bad for it (Table 2.5). There was a smaller effect that those who didn't get jobs were a little more mentally disturbed at the time of the first testing. That is, poor mental health makes unemployment a little more likely.

Retirement makes an interesting contrast with unemployment, since the retired are also technically unemployed. But while the unemployed are much less happy than those at work, most of the retired are happier, though some of them miss their work-mates or the work itself. The reason for this difference is that the unemployed feel rejected, that they have failed, while the retired feel they are enjoying a well-earned rest.[57]

LEISURE SATISFACTION

Leisure is a very important source of SWB: 34 per cent of people in jobs find leisure equally as satisfying as work, 19 per cent find it more satisfying,[58] and of course many people are not at work at all. Different kinds of leisure produce different benefits. We shall see that leisure groups are a great source of joy and social support, that exercise is good for both physical and mental health, holidays and other forms of relaxation can reduce stress, anxiety, and depression, and we have seen that happiness can be enhanced by finding which kinds of leisure produce the most positive moods.

What I mean by leisure is those activities that people do simply

[57] Campbell (1981). [58] Veroff *et al.* (1981).

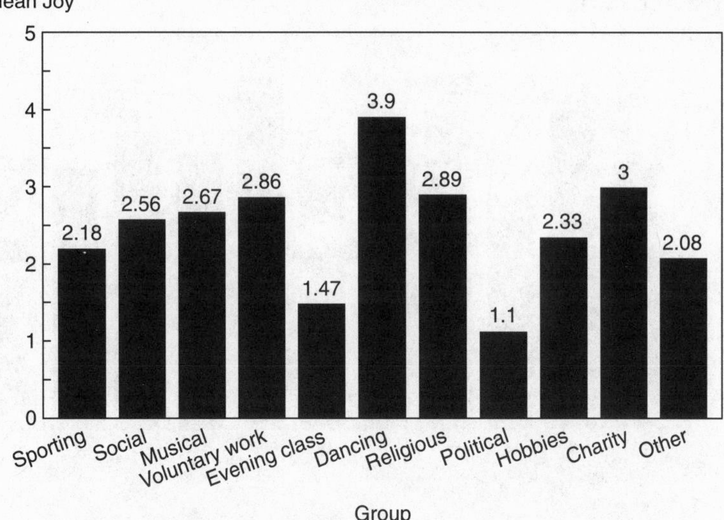

FIGURE 2.1. *Levels of joy reported after meetings of leisure groups*

Source: Argyle (1996).

because they want to, for their own sake, or for goals of their own choosing, but not for material gain. There are many kinds of leisure, social and non-social, arousing and relaxing, serious and non-serious. No one psychological theory can encompass all of them. In this section I shall look at the psychological basis of some of the main types of leisure in this section, in order to explain their benefits.

A lot of leisure is carried out in groups such as choirs, teams, clubs, voluntary groups, and churches. We carried out a study of thirty-nine leisure activities, and found that they grouped into several factors; one factor was going to teams and clubs, another was going to dances, parties, and debates and meeting new people. We found that extroverts were happier than introverts because they took part in both of these kinds of activity more often.[59] In a second study we asked members of different kinds of leisure groups to rate their mood at the end of a typical meeting, with the results shown in Figure 2.1.

It can be seen that dancing produced the most joy, followed by church and sport. We also asked about the amount of social support received, and as Figure 2.2 shows, church and voluntary work produced the most.[60]

[59] Argyle and Lu (1990*a*). [60] Argyle (1996).

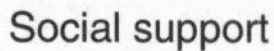
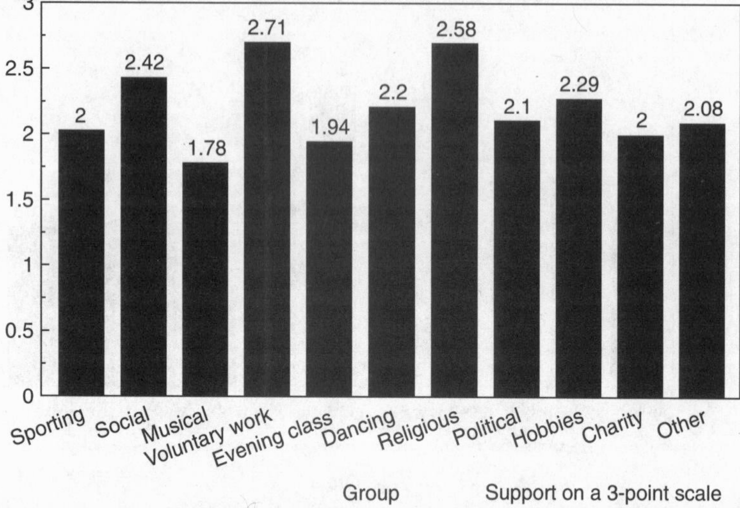

FIGURE 2.2. *Levels of social support from different leisure groups*

Source: Argyle (1996).

In the same study we found that 19 per cent of people said that their relationships with other club members were closer than their other friendships. The explanation for these powerful effects of leisure groups is not known. Partly no doubt it is the regular experience of shared and highly rewarding activities; in most kinds of sport, dancing, and music for example, the co-operation of others is essential.[61] There is often a lot of intimacy, such as self-disclosure in church groups, bodily contact in sport and dancing. In addition there may be a special effect of groups that have shared ideals, a shared desire for better performance, as is found in sporting, musical, church, and voluntary groups, for example. In this way the group contributes not only to the self-image, but also to the ideal self.

Csikszentmihalyi[62] produced evidence that engaging in serious, deeply demanding activities, such as serious chess or rock climbing, produced an experience of 'flow' or 'absorption', i.e. a deep level of satisfaction. We compared individuals who did and did not have a seriously committing leisure activity. We found, as predicted, that those who did

[61] Argyle (1991). [62] Csikszentmihalyi (1975).

were happier, and found their leisure more satisfying, though it was also more challenging and stressful than that of the others. Csikszentmihalyi thought that the basis for this satisfaction was the use and development of skills. We could add that it is rather like intrinsic job satisfaction, which is enhanced by autonomy, and the effect of work on others, as well as the use of varied skills. In leisure, almost by definition, there is a very high degree of autonomy.

However, a lot of leisure in the modern world is not at all demanding or serious, such as watching TV, which on average is done for 3–4 hours a day. It must be satisfying, presumably, though a number of surveys have found that it is rated quite low as a source of satisfaction, below housework in one, and producing a 'weak, drowsy, and passive state' in another. One of the most popular forms of TV is 'soap opera'. We compared individuals who were frequent or infrequent watchers of soap opera, and found that the frequent watchers were happier, though we had found that those who watch a lot of TV overall were less happy. The soap opera watchers reported high levels of various kinds of satisfaction, including 'educational satisfaction'.[63] Other studies suggest that this is because some inexperienced people watch in order to find out how to cope with everyday situations—almost a kind of social skills training by modelling. Another explanation of the popularity of soap opera is the theory of 'parasocial interaction', that viewers think that they actually know the characters, that they almost belong to the group themselves, thus gaining a kind of imaginary social network.

Sport and exercise provide some special benefits. Vigorous exercise, like swimming and running, produces an elevated mood for some time afterwards, and even before, in anticipation. It is now known that this is due to the release of endorphins in the bloodstream. Exercise is very beneficial for health: Paffenbarger[64] followed up 17,000 Harvard alumni for 6–10 years. The number who had heart attacks fell as the amount of regular exercise increased up to the level of about thirty minutes a day. Exercise is also good for mental health, and a number of firms have introduced exercise programmes for their employees. It has been found that this leads to less anxiety, tension, and depression, especially on exercise days, to reduced absenteeism, and to improved work performance.[65] This is probably because of the good moods produced, together with enjoyable activity in the company of other people. People

[63] Argyle and Lu (1992).
[64] Paffenbarger *et al.* (1978).
[65] Falkenburg (1987).

go on holidays for a variety of reasons, including 'self-discovery', and sexual adventures, but the most common reason given is the need to relax. Surveys show that when on holiday people report being much less tired, irritable, anxious, and constipated, and less often have headaches, insomnia, and stomach trouble, and have more interest in sex.[66] On the other hand there is also a small proportion of workaholics who enjoy holidays less, and are happier when the can get back to the office.

HAPPY PEOPLE: THE EFFECTS OF PERSONALITY

In addition to the effects of social relations, work, and leisure we must look at the effects of personality. There are 'happy people', with those other factors held constant, just as there are depressed people. This is shown by the high test-retest reliability scores for happiness scales shown above, and also by the strong correlations of happiness with personality traits. So if there are happy people, who are they?

Many studies have found a correlation between happiness and extroversion, typically of .30 to .40. The relationship is strongest with positive affect, and with the sociability part of some extroversion scales. In one study extroversion predicted happiness seventeen years later.[67] What is the explanation of this relationship? Headey and Wearing[68] found that extroversion predisposed people, particularly young people, to have favourable life events, especially in the domains of friendship and work, which in turn led to subjective well-being, as shown in Figure 2.3.

Argyle and Lu,[69] as described above, found that extroverts belonged to teams and clubs, and went to parties and dances, which in turn were sources of joy. We also found that extroverts have certain social skills, which produce favourable results for them. In a longitudinal study Argyle and Lu[70] found that part of the reason for the happiness of extroverts is they are more assertive, and found that this is a source of happiness, probably because it enables people to control their social life better; the causal pattern is shown in Figure 2.4.

In this study assertiveness was the social skill which was the strongest source of happiness. In another study we found that self-reported co-operative skills were also important.[71] A number of other personality

[66] Rubenstein (1980). [67] Costa, McRae and Norris (1981).
[68] Headey and Wearing (1986). [69] Argyle and Lu (1990*a*).
[70] Argyle and Lu (1990*b*). [71] Argyle and Lu (1991).

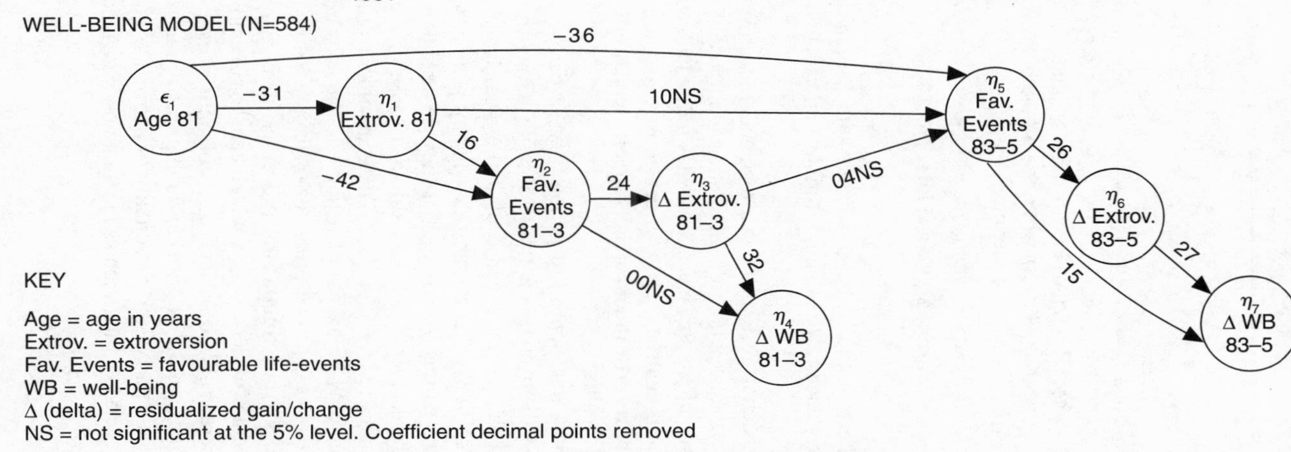

FIGURE 2.3. *Extroversion, life-events, and SWB*

Source: Headey and Wearing (1986)

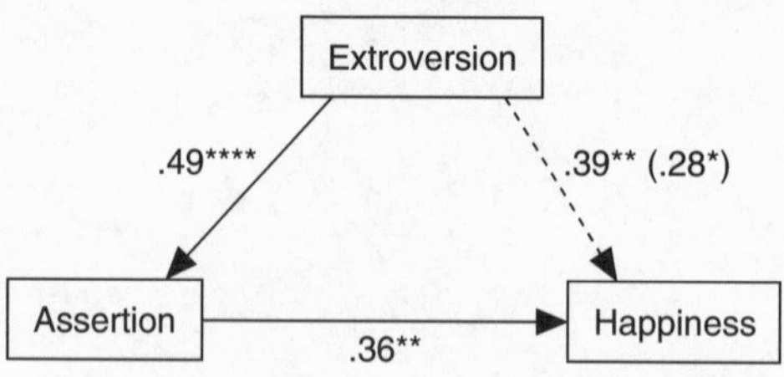

Note: The figure in parentheses is the reduced coefficient when the mediator is present.

FIGURE 2.4. *Assertion as a mediator of the extroversion–happiness relation*

Source: Argyle and Lu (1990*b*).

variables have been found to be correlated with happiness, including sense of humour, concern for others, religious beliefs, and resolution of inner conflicts.[72]

While extroversion leads to positive affect, neuroticism leads to negative affect: it is a major source of the distress component in SWB.

Research on social support has shown that individuals who are hostile, unfriendly, self-centred, negative, pessimistic, etc. are likely to be lonely and do not receive much social support, which in turn can lead to worse mental health.[73]

It is well known that depressed people have a certain attributional style: they blame themselves for things that go wrong; however, it is now known that this is not a cause of depression, but a result of it, or perhaps part of it. We have found that happy people do not blame themselves for things that go wrong, but they do attribute good things that happen to themselves.[74] Whether this is a cause or a consequence of happiness remains to be established. There are other cognitive factors in personality that may be causes of happiness. We showed above that the 'goal-achievement gap' is a predictor of happiness, and that this is partly a result of various comparison processes. This gap can also be looked at as a feature of personality, which can, for example, be modified by psychotherapy. We described the 'Polyanna principle' above—the tendency to look on the bright side. Doing this is part of the happy personality; it is also part of the personality of extroverts, since they are optimistic about social events, such as meeting new people; they assume

[72] Argyle (1987). [73] Sarason *et al.* (1990). [74] Argyle *et al.* (1989).

that they will like the others, will get on with them, and will enjoy themselves;[75] this can become a self-fulfilling prophecy.

What are the origins of the happy personality? Twin studies have found evidence for a genetic component; this is supported by family studies that have shown correlations between the happiness of parents and children, but not for adopted children. Happiness is correlated with extroversion and (negatively) with neuroticism, both of which are about 50 per cent inherited.[76] However, the greater component of the happy personality is environmental. Early childhood experience is almost certainly involved, since extroversion, co-operativeness, and related traits are all partly a product of a warm relation with mother during the first two years of life.[77] However, later experiences may be even more important. Headey and Wearing,[78] as was shown above, found that extroversion causes happiness, via the experience of positive events with friends and at work; but they also found that extroversion was a *dependent* variable too, i.e. it was in turn affected by these positive social events. This is important since it means that it may be possible to make people happy and to have happy personalities, not only by psychotherapy, but by experiences at work and leisure, and with friends.

THE EFFECTS OF HAPPINESS

Happiness has correlations with a number of other variables. In some cases we now have evidence from experimental or longitudinal studies that these show a causal effect of happiness. I can do no more than summarize some of the main findings here; others can be found in the report of a recent conference on this subject.[79]

Health

A Dutch study of over 3,000 subjects found that men who were of average health, but 1 standard deviation above average on happiness, lived on average 10 months longer, with health variables held constant; here and in other studies the effect was less for women. As was said earlier there is a correlation of .32 between health and happiness; it is at least partly due to happiness affecting health, as shown by the study above and by other studies in which it has been found that happy people

[75] Thorne (1987). [76] Argyle (1987). [77] Sroufe *et al.* (1983).
[78] Headey and Wearing (1992). [79] Veenhoven (1990).

survived longer after operations or illnesses. It is widely believed that happiness buffers stress, and thus contributes to mental health, but a recent careful study failed to find this effect.[80]

Help and altruism

Here the evidence is clear: put people in a good mood and they are more helpful; waitresses get bigger tips when the sun is shining, many more people in one experiment offered to give blood after being put in a good mood.[81] Individuals who are rated by their acquaintances as happy are also thought to be unselfish. However, the explanation is less clear; it has been described as an 'overflow of goodwill', which could be described as the wish for others to share one's good fortune, though there a number of other explanations.

Sociability

Again the experimental evidence is clear: put people in a good mood and they talk more, disclose more, like others more, and evaluate them more, favourably, say they want to be with friends or go to a party.[82] And again, the explanation is far from clear.

Work

This is the most heavily studied effect of happiness. A meta-analysis of 217 studies found that the overall correlation between job satisfaction and productivity was .15, though for supervisors and those above it was .31. As yet, attempts to show a causal effect of happiness here have failed, though it does have an effect on general helpfulness at work in a variety of ways.[83] Job satisfaction also has a modest causal effect in leading to lower levels of labour turnover and absenteeism.[84]

Problem-solving

When subjects are put into a good mood in laboratory experiments they tackle problems differently. These subjects move more quickly, accept the first solution, and solve the problem more often. They also make unusual and diverse word associations, and accept more fringe items as members of categories; this makes for greater creativity.[85]

[80] Van der Werff and Sanderman (1989). [81] Batson *et al.* (1979).
[82] Cunningham (1988). [83] George and Brief (1992). [84] Argyle (1989).
[85] Clark and Isen (1982).

CAN HUMAN HAPPINESS BE INCREASED?

We shall look at this problem by considering how each of the domains of causes of happiness could be manipulated.

Social relationships

How could relationships with friends, spouses, etc. be improved? Many individuals are unhappy because they cannot establish or sustain these relationships, and some of them are already being helped by social skills training. We saw above that assertiveness skills have a direct causal effect on happiness. However, more specific training may be needed for particular relationships; for example, marriage needs skills of both rewardingness and negotiation. Those who lack a supportive network are sometimes helped by social workers who create a special group for them. For example, those who share a certain problem can be organized into mutual-help groups, like Alcoholics Anonymous and many other similar groups. An alternative is to join existing leisure groups, whose benefits were shown above.

Work

The causes of job satisfaction are now well known, and there have been a number of movements to increase it, such as the Quality of Working Life movement. Some young people are given vocational guidance, to steer them towards work that they will find satisfying. Intrinsic job satisfaction can be increased by job enlargement, or by other changes that increase the skills used and make the work more interesting. The introduction of automation and computers can do this, though it can also make things worse, depending on how it is set up. Social satisfaction at work can be increased by keeping working groups intact, increasing the skills of supervisors and managers, and introducing industrial democracy.[86] The physical conditions of work are appalling for many manual workers; there is enormous scope for improvement.

Leisure

This is not more important than work as a source of happiness, but it is far easier to do something about it. Individuals can find out which

[86] Argyle (1989).

leisure activities give them the most satisfaction and joy, and be encouraged to practise them more often. We saw earlier that some leisure groups provide very high levels of positive affect and social support. 'Pleasant activities therapy', described earlier, is one way of achieving this. Another is to seek 'leisure counselling', now available in the USA. The public provision of leisure could enhance the general happiness, and needs to include training in the relevant skills as well as the facilities.

Personality

How could the number of happy people be increased? One solution is psychotherapy, and the findings about cognitive processes in happy people suggest how this could be done. Clients could be persuaded not to blame themselves for things that go wrong, and to reduce the size of the goal-achievement gap, as well as using other aspects of cognitive therapy. This has in fact been found successful in increasing happiness.[87] However, psychotherapy is very time-consuming and expensive, and unlikely ever to be available on a large scale. As was shown above, relevant personality variables such as extroversion are affected by positive experiences at work and with friends, so that successful manipulation of our first three variables may also succeed in altering personality.

Another aspect of 'personality' is social skills, which was mentioned in connection with establishing relationships. This is perhaps the one area of personality that it is worth while trying to do something about on a large scale. The most important social skills here appear to be assertiveness, co-operativeness, and other skills associated with extroversion, such as rewardingness.

Finally use can be made of mood induction techniques to produce positive moods twice a day, and individuals can choose the activities or combination of activities which do most for them, whether these consist of exercise, prayer, music, or just reading the paper.

REFERENCES

ANDREWS, F. M., and WITHEY, S. B. (1976), *Social Indicators of Well-Being*. New York and London: Plenum.

[87] Lichter *et al.* (1980).

ARGYLE, M. (1987), *The Psychology of Happiness*. London: Methuen.

—— (1989), *The Social Psychology of Work*. 2nd edn., London: Penguin Books.

—— (1991), *Cooperation, the Basis of Sociability*. London: Routledge.

—— (1996), *The Social Psychology of Leisure*. London: Penguin.

——, and CROSSLAND, J. (1989), 'The Dimensions of Positive Emotions', *British Journal of Social Psychology*, 26: 127–37.

——, and FURNHAM, A. (1982), 'The Ecology of Relationships: Choice of Situation as a Function of Relationship', *British Journal of Social Psychology*, 21: 259–62.

—— —— (1983), 'Sources of Satisfaction and Conflict in Long-Term Relationships', *Journal of Marriage and the Family*, 45: 481–93.

——, and HENDERSON, M. (1985), *The Anatomy of Relationships*. Harmondsworth: Penguin Books.

——, and LU, L. (1990*a*), 'The Happiness of Extroverts', *Personality and Individual Differences*, 11: 1011–17.

—— —— (1990*b*), 'Happiness and Social Skills', *Personality and Individual Differences*, 11: 1255–61.

—— —— (1991), 'Happiness and Cooperation', *Personality and Individual Differences*, 12: 1019–30.

—— —— (1992), 'New Directions in the Psychology of Leisure', *New Psychologist*, 3–11.

——, MARTIN, M., and CROSSLAND, J. (1989), 'Happiness as a Function of Personality and Social Encounters', in J. P. Forgas and M. Innes (eds.) *Recent Developments in Social Psychology*. Amsterdam: Elsevier.

—— ——, and LU, L. (1995), 'Testing for Stress and Happiness: the role of Social and Cognitive factors', in C. D. Spielberger *et al.* (eds.), *Stress and Emotions: Anxiety, Anger, and Curiosity*. New York: Taylor and Francis.

BANKS, M. H., and JACKSON, P. R. (1982), 'Unemployment and Risk of Minor Psychiatric Disorder in Young People: Cross Sectional and Longitudinal Evidence', *Psychological Medicine*, 12: 789–98.

BATSON, D., *et al.* (1979), 'Generality of the "Glow of Goodwill": Effects of Mood on Helping and Information Acquisition', *Social Psychology Quarterly*, 42: 176–9.

BERKMAN, L. F., and SYME, S. L. (1979), 'Social Networks, Host Resistance, and Mortality: A Nine Year Follow-up Study of Alameda County Residents', *American Journal of Epidemiology*, 109: 186–204.

BRADBURN, N. M. (1969), *The Structure of Psychological Well-Being*. Chicago: Aldine.

BRICKMAN, P., COATES, D., and JANOFF-BULMAN, R. (1978), 'Lottery Winners and Accident Victims: Is Happiness Relative?', *Journal of Personality and Social Psychology*, 36, 917–27.

BROWN, G. W., and HARRIS, T. (1978), *Social Origins of Depression*. London: Tavistock.

CAMPBELL, A. (1981), *The Sense of Well-Being in America.* New York: McGraw-Hill.

——, CONVERSE, P. E., and RODGERS, W. L. (1976), *The Quality of American Life.* New York: Sage.

CLARK, A. E., and OSWALD, A. J. (1993), 'Satisfaction and Comparison Income', *Discussion Paper Series*, no. 419. University of Essex Dept. of Economics.

CLARK, D. M. (1983), 'On the Induction of Depressed Mood in the Laboratory: Comparison of the Velten and Musical Procedures', *Advances in Behavior Research and Therapy*, 5: 24–49.

CLARK, M. S., and ISEN, A. M. (1982), 'Toward Understanding the Relationship between Feeling States and Social Behavior', in A. Hastorf and A. M. Isen (eds.), *Cognitive Social Psychology.* New York: Elsevier.

COOPER, H., OKAMURA, L., and GURKA, V. (1992), 'Social Activity and Subjective Well-Being', *Personality and Individual Differences*, 13: 573–83.

COSTA, P. T., MCRAE, R. R., and NORRIS, A. H. (1981), 'Personal Adjustment to Ageing: Longitudinal Prediction from Neuroticism and Extroversion', *Journal of Gerontology*, 36: 78–85.

CSIKSZENTMIHALYI, M. (1975), *Beyond Boredom and Anxiety.* San Francisco: Jossey-Bass.

CUNNINGHAM, M. R. (1988), 'What to Do When You're Happy or Blue? Mood, Expectancies, and Behavioral Interest', *Motivation and Emotion*, 12: 309–31.

DIENER, E. (1984), 'Subjective Well-Being', *Psychological Bulletin*, 95: 542–75.

——, HOROWITZ, J., and EMMONS, R. A. (1985), 'Happiness of the Very Wealthy', *Social Indicators Research*, 16: 263–74.

——, SANDVIK, E., SEIDLITZ, L., and DIENER, M. (1993), 'The Relationship between Income and Subjective Well-being: Relative or Absolute?', *Social Indicators Research*, 28: 195–223.

FALKENBURG, L. E. (1987), 'Employee Fitness Programs: Their Impact on the Employee and the Organisation', *Academy of Management Review*, 12: 511–22.

FEIST, G. J., *et al.* (1995), 'Integrating Top-down and Bottom-up Structural Models of Subjective Well-being: A Longitudinal Investigation', *Journal of Personality and Social Psychology*, 68: 138–50.

FOX, C. R., and KAHNEMAN, D. (1992), 'Correlations, Causes and Heuristics in Surveys of Life Satisfaction', *Social Indicators Research*, 27: 221–34.

FUJITA, F., DIENER, E., and SANDVIK, E. (1991), 'Gender Differences in Negative Affect and Well-Being', *Journal of Personality and Social Psychology*, 61: 427–34.

GEORGE, J. M., and BRIEF, A. P. (1992), 'Feeling Good Doing Good: A Conceptual Analysis of the Mood-Organisational Spontaneity Relationship', *Psychological Bulletin*, 112: 310–29.

HEADEY, B., and WEARING, A. (1986), 'Chains of Well-being, Chains of Ill-being', unpublished paper, International Sociological Conference, New Delhi.

——, and WEARING, A. (1992), *Understanding Happiness*. Melbourne: Longman Cheshire.

HORLEY, J., and LAVERY, J. J. (1991), 'The Stability and Sensitivity of Subjective Well-being Measures', *Social Indicators Research*, 24: 113–22.

JORDAN, T. E. (1993), '"L'Homme Moyen"; Estimating the Quality of Life for British Adults, 1815–1914, An Index', *Social Indicators Research*, 29: 183–203.

KAMMANN, R., and FLETT, R. (1983), 'Affectometer 2: A Scale to Measure Current Level of General Happiness', *Australian Journal of Psychology*, 35: 259–65.

KENNEDY, S., KIECOLT-GLASER, J. K., and GLASER, R. (1990), 'Social Support, Stress, and the Immune System', in B. R. Sarason, I. G. Sarason, and G. R. Pierce (eds.), *Social Support: An Interactional View*. New York: Wiley.

KOZMA, A., *et al.* (1990), 'Long- and Short-Term Affective States in Happiness: Model, Paradigm and Experimental Evidence', *Social Indicators Research*, 22: 119–38.

LARSON, R. W. (1990), 'The Solitary Side of Life: An Examination of the Time People Spend Alone from Childhood to Old Age', *Developmental Review*, 10: 155–83.

LEWINSOHN, P. M., SULLIVAN, J. M., and GROSSCUP, S. J. (1982), 'Behavioral Therapy: Clinical Applications', in A. J. Rush (ed.), *Short-term therapies for Depression*. New York: Guilford.

LICHTER, S., HAYE, K., and KAMMANN, R. (1980), 'Increasing Happiness through Cognitive Training', *New Zealand Psychologist*, 9: 57–64.

LYNN, R. (1982), 'National Differences in Anxiety and Extroversion', *Progress in Experimental Personality Research*, 11: 213–58.

MICHALOS, A. C. (1986), 'Job Satisfaction, Marital Satisfaction, and the Quality of Life: A Review and a Preview', in F. M. Andrews (ed.), *Research on the Quality of Life*. Ann Arbor: University of Michigan Survey Research Center.

OKUN, M. A., *et al.* (1984), 'Health and Subjective Well-Being: A Meta-Analysis', *International Journal of Ageing and Human Development*, 19: 111–32.

OLSON, G. L., and SCHOBER, B. I. (1993), 'The Satisfied Poor', *Social Indicators Research*, 28: 173–93.

PAFFENBARGER, R. S., WING, A. L., and HYDE, R. T. (1978), 'Physical Activity as An Index of Heart Attack in College Alumni', *American Journal of Epidemiology*, 108: 161–75.

PAVOT, W., and DIENER, E. (1993), 'The Affective and Cognitive Context of Self-Reported Measures of Subjective Well-Being', *Social Indicators Research*, 28: 1–20.

RUBENSTEIN, C. (1980), 'Vacations', *Psychology Today*, 13, May: 62–76.

RUNCIMAN, W. G. (1966), *Relative Deprivation and Social Justice*. London: Routledge and Kegan Paul.

RUSSELL, R. J. H., and WELLS, P. A. (1992), 'Social Desirability and the Quality of Marriage', *Personality and Individual Differences*, 13: 787–91.

RYFF, C. D. (1989), 'Happiness is Everything, or is It? Explorations on the Meaning of Psychological Well-Being', *Journal of Personality and Social Psychology*, 57: 1069–81.

SALES, S. M., and HOUSE, J. (1971), 'Job Dissatisfaction as a Possible Risk Factor in Coronary Heart Disease', *Journal of Chronic Diseases*, 21: 861–73.

SARASON, B. R., SARASON, I. G., and PIERCE, G. R. (eds.) (1990), *Social Support: An Interactional View*. New York: Wiley.

SCHERER, K. R., WALBOTT, H. G., and SUMMERFIELD, A. B. (1986), *Experiencing Emotion*. Cambridge: Cambridge University Press.

SCHMITT, N., and BEDEIAN, A. G. (1982), 'A Comparison of LISREL and Two-Stage Least Squares Analysis of a Hypothesised Life-Job Satisfaction Reciprocal Relationship', *Journal of Applied Psychology*, 67: 806–17.

SCHULZ, R., and DECKER, S. (1985), 'Long-Term Adjustment to Physical Disability: The Role of Social Support, Perceived Control, and Self-Blame, *Journal of Personality and Social Psychology*, 48: 1162–72.

SCHWARZ, N., and STRACK, F. (1991), 'Evaluating one's Life: A Judgment Model of Subjective Well-being', in F. Strack, M. Argyle, and N. Schwarz (eds.), *Subjective Well-Being*. Oxford: Pergamon, pp. 27–47.

SCHWARZER, R., and LEPPIN, A. (1989), 'Social Support and Health: A Meta-Analysis', *Psychology and Health*, 3: 1–15.

SROUFE, L. A., FOX, N. E., and PANCAKE, V. R. (1983), 'Attachment and Dependency in Developmental Perspective', *Child Development*, 54: 1615–27.

STRACK, F., SCHWARZ, N., and GSCHNEIDINGER, E. (1985), 'Happiness and Reminiscing: The Role of Time Perspective, Affect, and Mode of Thinking', *Journal of Personality and Social Psychology*, 49.

THAYER, R. E. (1989), *The Biopsychology of Mood and Arousal*. Oxford: OUP.

THORNE, A. (1987), 'The Press of Personality: A Study of Conversation between Introverts and Extroverts', *Journal of Personality and Social Psychology*, 53: 718–26.

VAN DER WERFF, J., and SANDERMAN, R. (1989), 'Does Happiness Buffer Stress?' in R. Veenhoven (ed.), *How Harmful is Happiness?* Rotterdam: University of Rotterdam Press.

VEENHOVEN, R. (1990), *World Database of Happiness*. Dordrecht: Reidel.

VEROFF, J., DOUVAN, E., and KULKA, R. A. (1981), *The Inner American*. New York: Basic Books.

WALKER, C. (1977), 'Some Variations in Marital Satisfaction', in R. Chester and J. Peel (eds.), *Equalities and Inequalities in Family Life*. London: Academic Press.

WATERMAN, A. S. (1993), 'Two Conceptions of Happiness: Contrasts of Personal Expressiveness (Eudaimonia) and Hedonic Enjoyment', *Journal of Personality and Social Psychology*, 64: 678–91.

WATSON, D., and PENNYBAKER, J. W. (1989), 'Health Complaints, Stress, and Distress: Exploring the Central Role of Negative Affectivity', *Psychological Review*, 96: 234–54.

3

Basic Needs, Capabilities, and Human Development

FRANCES STEWART

The 'dethronement' of GNP per capita as the exclusive objective of development was announced by Dudley Seers in 1970. Since then various objectives have been suggested to replace it. Among these are basic needs, capabilities, and human development. 'Basic needs' came first with the ILO conference of 1976, to be followed up by Streeten *et al.*, Stewart, van der Hoeven, etc. In a parallel move, not systematically incorporated into development thinking, Rawls suggested that certain primary needs should have primacy. In analysing famine, Sen focused on 'entitlements', subsequently developing the concept of 'capabilities'. In more recent years, the United Nations Development Programme's (UNDP) *Human Development Report* has put 'human development' at the centre of development objectives.[1]

Each of these alternative approaches leads to rather similar assessments of country performance and conclusions on policy recommendations. The aim of this note is to clarify the relationships between the various approaches—to assess how far the differences are merely terminological, and identify any important differences.

All three approaches—BN (Basic Needs), C (capabilities), and HD (Human Development)—share dissatisfaction with GNP per capita as a measure of societal well-being. The reasons for this dissatisfaction are both theoretical and empirical.

Utilitarianism provides the theoretical basis for using GNP per capita as a measure of societal well-being. But to provide such a basis, it is necessary to go well beyond minimal assumptions of utilitarianism. The following assumptions are needed, all of which present some problems:

[1] ILO (1970); Seers's contribution in Robinson and Johnston (1971); ILO (1976); Streeten *et al.* (1981); Stewart (1985); van der Hoeven (1987); Sen (1981) (on entitlements); Sen (1985) (on capabilities); UNDP, *Human Development Reports* (various).

(*a*) that people's choices maximize their utility; Sen has pointed out that in many circumstances choices are influenced by social norms and individuals' expectations about others' behaviour, so that choices often do not indicate individuals' first best position, but are rather constrained. He concludes: 'the perfectly rational man is close to being a social moron'.[2]

(*b*) that maximization of individual utility leads to maximization of social well-being—i.e. society is no more than the sum of the individuals in it;[3] yet there are societal features (communal activities; criminality; cohesion; culture) which are important for individual well-being, but are not necessarily optimized as a result of individuals' uncoordinated maximizing behaviour.

(*c*) that externalities among consumers are insignificant and can be ignored; public goods are absent.

(*d*) that income distribution (or utility distribution) among consumers is regarded as satisfactory or irrelevant to assessment of social progress.

(*e*) that those who make the choices (spend the money) are those who use the goods and get the utility. Yet here the family intervenes between spender and consumer; children, especially, rarely make their own choices. Strange models of the family (the glued-together family/the benevolent dictator) are necessary to rescue utilitarianism.

(*f*) that all types of consumption are potentially equally valuable—pornographic videos are as valuable as bread, water, or Mozart so long as consumers choose them.

(*g*) that prices reflect marginal social costs.

Every one of these assumptions can be challenged; some for their accuracy as an empirical description of the way the world works—(*a*), (*c*), (*e*), (*g*) in particular; and some for the value judgements they embody—(*b*), (*d*) and (*f*). The use of GNP per capita as a measure of welfare or well-being is thus without a well-founded theoretical base.

The more pragmatic motivation for replacing GNP per capita by some human-based indicators was that growth in per capita incomes—which did occur to an unprecedented extent in developing countries in the quarter of a century after 1950—appeared often to have led to

[2] Sen (1977).

[3] 'There is no such thing as society,' said Thatcher in the most extreme presentation of this position.

an unsatisfactory situation from a humanitarian perspective. In many countries it was accompanied by high, and sometimes rising, levels of poverty and a growing employment problem; income distribution was unequal and often became more so; although life expectancy and literacy improved significantly on average, some high-growth countries (e.g. Pakistan or Brazil) did poorly, while some very low-income countries had high achievements on 'human' indicators, such as life expectancy (e.g. Sri Lanka).[4]

The first reaction to the evident problems with GNP per capita as a measure of well-being was to place emphasis on employment creation as an overriding objective of development (for example, in the ILO Employment Missions starting with Colombia in 1970). But it was soon recognized that employment was not wanted for itself alone as much as for the income it would generate, the output it would create, and the recognition it would confer.[5] Emphasis then moved to the need to generate income among the poor—i.e. redistribution with growth.[6] This strategy 'failed' before it started because the political conditions needed in highly unequal societies were not present. But it was also unsatisfactory from a theoretical perspective because it continued to place emphasis on *income*, albeit income of the poor, so that all the theoretical defects attached to GNP as a measure of well-being remained apart from that concerning income distribution. Income, including that of the poor, was seen to be a means rather than an end from the perspective of well-being. But means to what? The three approaches being considered here all provide answers to this question.

BASIC NEEDS

The basic needs answer is 'means to the basic goods and services necessary for a decent life'. The objective of the BN approach is a minimally decent life;[7] defined in terms of levels of health, nutrition, and literacy. The BN goods and services (food, health services, water, etc.) constitute a *means* to achieve this. The relationship between the

[4] See the survey of developments by Morawetz (1977) and that by Turnham (1971).

[5] To use Sen's threefold terminology (see Sen 1975).

[6] ILO Kenya Mission (ILO 1972); Chenery *et al.* (1974).

[7] In Fei, Ranis, and Stewart (1979; 1985) we described it as the 'full life', but the terminology is unfortunate since what we are describing/aiming for are normally very minimal standards.

end (the decent life) and the *means* (the goods and services consumed) has been described variously as a 'metaproduction function' (Fei, Ranis, and Stewart) and a 'human production function' (UNDP, Human Development Report). Formally this relationship may be represented as:

$$L^* = f(B_{\mathrm{i}}, B_{\mathrm{ii}}, B_{\mathrm{iii}} \ldots)$$

where L^* is the quality of life achieved, defined in terms of health, nutrition etc, and B_{i}, B_{ii}, B_{iii} . . . are the basic needs goods and services which lead to its realization. We shall call this relationship the metaproduction function. It represents a complex empirical relationship which can be observed at many levels—world, country, household, or individual level. To give it meaning, the first necessity is to define the elements which constitute L^*, or the decent life.

The basic goods approach has defined the characteristics rather minimally as health, nutrition, and some indicator of educational achievements. These three are included on the grounds that these are 'basic' characteristics which (*a*) would probably achieve universal consent as universal human needs; (*b*) have some claim to priority as being necessary preconditions for other aspects of a full life, such as enjoyment of art or sport; and (*c*) are relatively easy to measure. Measurement problems remain, however. In most studies, life expectancy is used as the measure of health, literacy rates as measures of educational achievement, and, if the variable is included, child malnutrition as an inverse measure of nutrition. But using three indicators to capture three characteristics of L^* presents problems of weighting in arriving at a composite index. This arises also in connection with the Human Development Index to be discussed below.[8] If the metaproduction function is applied at any level of aggregation greater than the individual, problems of weighting the distribution of achievements among individuals also arise. Typically, L^* is presented as a simple average of the group covered. This could conceal varying disparities among individuals, similar to those associated with averages of per capita income, though the potential dispersion is less with these variables than with income.[9] Some distribution-sensitive measure would then be preferable (e.g. by weighting the

[8] Broadening the characteristics included in L^* would greatly increase measurement and weighting problems, and there would also be problems about reaching agreement on which additional characteristics are 'basic'.

[9] Strictly, the dispersion possibilities arise with respect to life expectancy, but not the on/off variables of literacy and malnutrition, although alternative continuous measures of nutrition and educational achievements would also lead to dispersion.

variable by $(1-G)$, where G is the Gini coefficient representing the distribution of the variable across the population.[10]

In this approach income is seen as a means of acquiring the BN goods and services necessary to achieve a decent life. At a national level, the relationship between average per capita income and L^* varies, depending on the distribution of income among individuals and their expenditure patterns, government expenditure priorities, and the historical circumstances which determine the nature of the metaproduction function.

The BN approach does not claim to provide a full account of social well-being—but it does sidestep some of the problematic assumptions associated with GNP per capita as a measure of well-being in poor societies. In particular:

1. Income distribution is taken into account in so far as it affects the ability of each member of society to gain access to the goods and services necessary for a decent life. However, beyond that, once everyone has access to enough BN goods and services, the BN approach says nothing about income distribution. Income distribution, like income, is treated as an instrumental variable.

As societies get richer the amount of income needed to achieve a minimally decent life is likely to rise, while what constitutes a 'minimal decent life' may also be redefined upwards so that the BN approach may have relevance to income distribution over a quite large range of income. For example, assuming that social intercourse is an essential aspect of decent life, then transport (e.g. buses or even cars) may be needed to participate as societies become more dispersed, while some goods (e.g. TVs) may be needed to achieve a minimally satisfactory level of social intercourse in higher income societies that in poorer societies could be realized without them.

While the BN approach has relevance to income distribution only in a limited range of situations, this range is precisely the one that appears most unsatisfactory with a GNP approach; i.e. there is much more agreement over the proposition that a high average income per capita accompanied by severe destitution is unsatisfactory, a situation that the BN approach does deal with, than about income distribution once extreme poverty has been eliminated.

BN relates to individuals not families, and thereby avoids the problem associated with GNP (assumption (*e*) above) of maximizing well-being

[10] See Fei *et al.* (1979, 1985); Streeten *et al.* (1981).

at a household level while ignoring intra-household distribution. It is necessary to explore intra-household distribution theoretically and empirically to plan effectively for BN.

2. A fundamental assumption of BN is that some goods are more important ('basic') than others, thereby departing radically from assumption (*f*) of the GNP approach. Why? Because the 'basic' goods are essential for a minimally decent life—i.e. for conditions in which there is enough food, health is good enough, and education sufficient to permit people to enjoy the other good things of life. It is for this reason that these goods are described as *basic*: they come first, and without them other goods have less (or even no) use. Of course there is no hard and fast rule which makes this definition clear and easy to apply. People can enjoy drinking and smoking when hungry; Maslow's hierarchy of wants turns out to be only broadly correct. The concept of a 'decent' life or a 'minimally decent life' used above is not well defined and may be culturally and historically specific. Moreover, even if we agreed on what a decent life was, the actual goods and services necessary to bring it about can vary between societies and individuals for a variety of reasons, as noted earlier with respect to social intercourse. For all these reasons, the goods and services to be described as 'basic' may not form a well-defined set. But despite this, a hierarchy remains; so that irrespective of the problems of definition, and the fact that the precise categorization may be fuzzy, some subset of goods and services can be classified as more basic than others in the BN approach in contrast to the GNP approach.

3. The BN approach emphasizes supply as well as demand, and in particular focuses on the supply of public goods ((*c*) above). For BN to be realized the basic goods and services have to be available; some are supplied by the market, some by the public sector, some by the household. Because of the nature of the BN goods and services, a larger than average proportion comes from the public sector (most of basic health care; primary and secondary education; water services) and the household (food in many poor economies, and informal health and education). The GNP approach does not focus on supply except in aggregate terms: supply must grow in aggregate if GNP grows. But this is consistent—certainly in the short term—with totally inadequate public sector expenditures on BN goods, as for example, in Peru where 5.9 per cent of GNP is spent on health and education compared with 10.2 per cent in Costa Rica. It can also be consistent with problems with food supply (as for example, in Nigeria in the 1970s when oil production

raised GNP and also indirectly lowered food supplies); more generally, the household supply of inputs into education and health can be very weak despite high incomes, with the result that the BN expenditures have limited effectiveness in terms of improving human indicators, which often is the case when levels of female education are very low.

The BN approach has been accused of 'commodity fetishism' on the grounds that it focuses only on the goods and services, not the quality of human lives which should be the ultimate objective (Sen 1988; Anand and Ravallion 1993). This is an incorrect criticism in relation to the BN approach presented here, since the metaproduction function takes the quality of life as the objective, and BN goods and services as the means to bring about an improvement in the quality of life.[11] 'A basic needs approach to development attempts to provide the opportunities for the full physical, mental and social development of the human personality, and then derives ways of achieving this objective.'[12]

Capabilities

Sen's capability approach to the objectives of development 'is based on evaluating social change in terms of the richness of human life resulting from it'[13] where human life is seen as made up of 'beings' and 'doings' (together defined as 'functionings'). The fundamental objective of development is argued to be to enhance people's capabilities to function. Capabilities are the various combinations of functionings a person can achieve. The emphasis is on *capability* as the objective rather than functionings themselves because of the importance Sen attaches to people's freedom to choose among functionings.[14] Being educated or being well nourished are examples of 'beings'; the corresponding capabilities would then be the capability to be educated or well nourished. Examples of 'doings' are riding a bicycle or playing tennis. In so far as income is worth having in this approach, it is as a means of enhancing capabilities. Income is one (but only one) of the conditions necessary to confer these capabilities. Some capabilities may not need income at all: e.g. the capability of being well exercised.

At any time, given an individual's entitlements and constraints, he or

[11] Streeten *et al.* (1981: 33).

[12] To calculate a Gini for a non-income variable such as years of schooling or life expectancy would require one to add the total societal achievement with respect to the variable, and then calculate a Lorenz curve showing the proportion of this total 'enjoyed' by different sections of the population.

[13] Sen (1988).

[14] Human freedom is seen as 'a central feature of living'(Sen 1988: 15).

she faces a capability set which represents that 'person's freedom to achieve various functioning combinations'.[15] But in practice only the chosen functionings can be observed so for practical purposes most assessments are made in terms of *functionings* (i.e. beings or doings) rather than capabilities.

The capability approach is thus potentially much richer than the BN approach since it includes all sort of 'higher-level' capabilities and functionings which people may have after they have realized the BN level of living. However, there is a subset of functionings, which correspond to 'basic capabilities' which is identical to the characteristics of the decent life in the BN approach (L^* above). In practice, Sen himself has tended to confine his empirical work to the same set of functionings as in the BN approach (see e.g. Appendix A of *Commodities and Capabilities*).

The capability approach, like the BN approach, avoids many of the problems associated with the utilitarian assumptions behind GNP as a measure of well-being. It does not infer welfare from behaviour, but rather from objective conditions as indicated by observed functionings. In principle, communal activities can be incorporated as well as individual (e.g. capabilities may include the capability to vote and to live in a peaceful society). Capabilities, like BN, are related to individuals not households, avoiding 'stopping' at the level of the household as the income approach tends to do.

Sen is ambiguous about whether the capability approach in itself says anything more about income distribution, or about ranking the capabilities/functioning of a particular individual, than the utility-based approach. On the one hand, he distinguishes the specification (or description) of functionings from their valuation.[16] But he does differentiate 'basic capabilities' which 'separate out the ability to satisfy certain crucially important functionings up to certain minimally adequate levels',[17] and suggests that 'equality in the fulfilment of certain "basic capabilities" provides an especially plausible approach to egalitarianism'.[18] The 'basic capabilities' approach comes extremely close to the BN approach.

Suppose there are two situations:

A—where all BN are fulfilled at a low level of income with egalitarian distribution;

[15] Sen (1988). Note the parallel between the capability set with income which represents the person's freedom to consume various combinations of goods. But a big difference is that income can be observed, while the capability set cannot.

[16] Sen (1985: 30). [17] Sen (1993: 41). [18] Sen (1993: 40–1).

B—where many enjoy a wide range of functionings, and some have unfulfilled BN.

The BN approach unambiguously favours A over B, since the approach combines description with valuation (the only possible ambiguity arising if over time BN in A were likely to decline and those in B to rise). The capability approach as such would not involve a preference between A and B; this would depend on the valuation made.

Similarly, suppose there are two consumption sets possible for the same individual given their income/entitlements:

C—where all BN are fulfilled;
D—which allocates more consumption to drink and tobacco than C and leaves some BN unfulfilled.

Again the BN approach prefers C to D, while the capability approach would depend on a valuation exercise which could go either way.

But in each case, a 'basic capabilities' approach, combined with the valuation that priority should be given to achieving basic capabilities, would come to similar conclusions to the BN approach.

The BN approach is thus more robust about ranking alternatives than the C approach in situations where more or less BN are met since it incorporates a strong element of valuation. But the BN approach says nothing about ranking where BN fulfilment is similar, while the C approach offers the same potential for a theoretical valuation and ranking in this as in the other situations and comes close to the BN ranking if a basic capabilities approach is adopted.

Similarity between capability/functioning and BN is only close for that subset of capabilities/functionings which correspond to the BN characteristics of a decent life (L^*). Here the two approaches are very similar as elucidated in Figure 3.1. As shown there, both approaches start with individual claims over resources (entitlements) and end with quality of life characteristics (L^*). But there are important differences in emphasis. The BN approach strongly emphasizes public provision of goods and services (one reason for the 'commodity fetishism' critique); this emphasis is justified because in the set of basic goods and services a large proportion (especially health and education, but also often water) are supplied by the public sector. In contrast, Sen puts little emphasis on the public sector in his theoretical writings, though in his policy work he emphasizes the need for public action. The C approach places great emphasis on personal characteristics as a determinant of

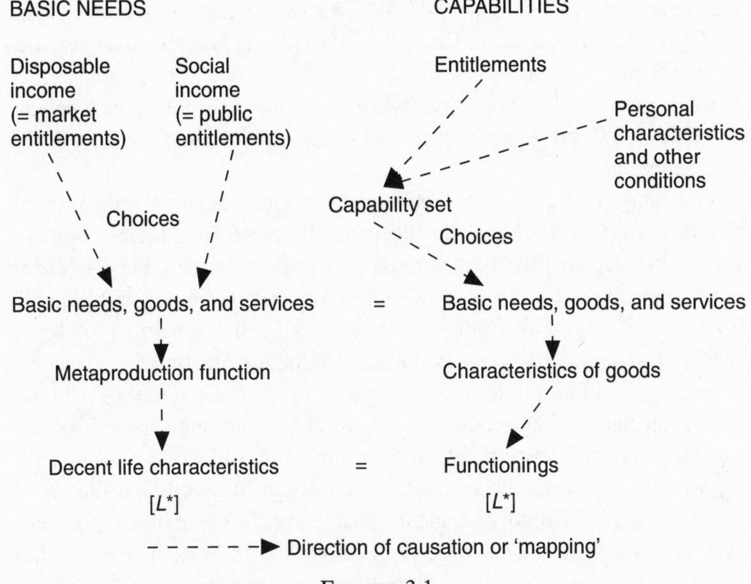

FIGURE 3.1.

how a given set of entitlements maps onto a set of capabilities (e.g. the need for more resources to achieve a given C level among handicapped people). The BN approach tends to neglect differences in personal characteristics other than those of age and gender. In the C approach, Sen explicitly adds the characteristics of goods and services (following Lancaster) as a stepping stone between consumption of goods and services and functionings. These do not form an explicit step in most BN writings. However, the BN approach gives a major role to the metaproduction function, the relation between the BN goods and services and the quality of life characteristics. This function is determined by a variety of factors including the location, age, gender, personality, physique, and education of the individual, the nature of the household in which the individual lives, the combination of BN goods and services available and their characteristics. The metaproduction function is regarded as of central importance to a BN approach, and in urgent need of empirical investigation. The function appears implicitly also in the C approach in the jump from the BN subset of basic goods and services to functionings, but is given less emphasis.

Empirical work has to be confined to observables (or elements that can be inferred from observables). The two approaches come closer together in empirical work, since the capability set and the characteristics of goods and services are difficult to observe. Hence both approaches mostly confine empirical observations to incomes, public and private provision of basic goods and services, and functionings, or decent life characteristics.

One important difference between the approaches in theory (though not in empirical work) is the ultimate objective: in the BN approach this is the decent life characteristics, or 'basic' functionings, while in the C approach the ultimate objective is not functioning but capability (i.e. not being well nourished, but having the capability of being well nourished). This is an important distinction for two reasons: first, it gives individual choice a prime position, in the sense that it builds the requirements that people are able to choose among capabilities into the objective. In contrast, in the BN approach, choice is not normally regarded as a decent-life characteristic (though it could be a feature of L^* if desired). Secondly, it means that people's capabilities for being well nourished (or some other capability) could be met even if they were actually malnourished, if they had the possibility of being well nourished and chose not to be. In the BN approach, malnutrition is regarded as a failure irrespective of the reason for it (i.e. even if it arose because individuals chose to be malnourished). The problem about emphasizing capabilities as the objective rather than functionings in relation to basic functionings like nutrition is that an observed functioning failure may be due to choice, or it may be due to some hidden constraint (including e.g. anorexia due to physical or psychological disease, or to failure of the household to allocate food in such a way as to enable the whole family to be well nourished). In the BN approach the functioning failure would ring immediate alarm bells and a search for a cause and cure; but a functioning failure in the C approach apparently accompanied by a C fulfilment may be attributed to choice and accepted as such. In my view, a more satisfactory way of dealing with choice, therefore, would be to regard it as a functioning which should be pursued along with other basic functionings. This would have the advantage, also, of permitting trade-offs to be considered between choice and other functionings.

A more pragmatic objection to giving capability the ultimate position as the objective of development is that capabilities cannot normally be observed directly whereas functionings can. For this reason, in practice most of Sen's empirical work is concerned with functionings.

HUMAN DEVELOPMENT

The *Human Development* approach (developed in successive *Human Development Reports* of the UNDP) shares elements of both BN and C approaches.[19] The central ideas of the HD approach are that human well-being is central to the goal of development and that human beings form the major economic resource: 'People are the real wealth of a nation. The basic objective of development is to create an enabling environment for people to live long, healthy and creative lives . . . Human development is a process of enlarging people's choices. The most critical ones are to lead a long and healthy life, to be educated and to enjoy a decent standard of living. Additional choices include political freedom, guaranteed human rights and self-respect.'[20]

In this statement, one can see elements of the C approach (especially the emphasis on enlarging choice) and the BN approach (with the list of things people need, including both the usual BN list and also more adventurous ones such as 'creative lives' and political freedom.)

The contribution for which the HD approach is best known is the Human Development Index (HDI). This represents an attempt to arrive at a national index of well-being reflecting the goals of BN and C approaches, which neither approach had previously attempted.

The HDI, in its initial formulation, was made up of three elements —a measure of life expectancy for the society as a whole, a measure of literacy and an index of average per capita income for poor societies, using Purchasing Power Parity (PPP) adjustments and also making some adjustments for lower weights to be given to income at higher national levels. There is no weighting of income within nations.[21] The three indicators were weighted together in a complex and essentially arbitrary fashion.[22] Since 1990 major changes to the index have been to

[19] Perhaps not surprizing in view of the fact that the main authors responsible for BN and C approaches have acted as consultants to the UNDP in this exercise.

[20] UNDP (1990: 9, 10).

[21] The construction of the HDI has changed over time, partly in response to criticisms. In the initial (1990) formulation national income per capita was measured correcting for Purchasing Power Parity. The raw index was the log of income per capita for countries whose PPP per capita income fell below a developed country poverty line; countries above this line all received a weighting of one.

[22] For each country, each of the three indicators was transformed into an index which represented the difference between the achievements of the country and the minimum achievement on that indicator expressed as a percentage of the difference between the maximum and minimum performance on the indicator for countries as a whole. The three indices, transformed in this way, were then averaged.

include average years of schooling as well as literacy in the educational variable, and to alter the way income is treated.[23]

The HDI index thus lies between the utility (as measured by average incomes) and the BN measures.

Despite the fact that the HD objective shares elements of both BN and C approaches, the HDI is not an accurate indicator either of societies' BN achievements or of their capabilities/functionings. Two of the elements in the HDI—life expectancy and literacy—are important decent-life characteristics. The problem, from a BN perspective, arises with the income variable which does not capture people's ability to meet BN because it is a societal average and not sensitive to income distribution. Hence it could be high when many people were unable to meet their BN.

The HDI is not an index of C achievements as it measures functionings not capabilities. The arbitrary weighting of the three variables in the HDI cannot be justified by the C approach any more than the BN approach. Moreover, the capability approach explicitly rejects income as an objective, arguing that it is a means to capability and functioning rather than an objective itself. Average income per capita for a country is a very clumsy proxy for other basic functionings since the nature of functionings possible depends critically on the distribution of income. A measure of nutritional achievements would be preferable as a third variable for both BN and C approaches, since being well nourished is an important characteristic of a decent life and an important functioning. However, it was excluded from the HDI largely because of lack of data.

The HDI is thus unsatisfactory as a measure of either BN or C achievements. Its great merits, however, are that it is comprehensive across countries and has come to be recognized internationally as an alternative measure of well-being, beginning to displace GNP per capita in some situations. Although its theoretical justification is weak, so is that of GNP per capita, and the HDI does shift attention towards BN and C achievements where these differ significantly from GNP per capita.

SOME EMPIRICAL ASPECTS OF THE ALTERNATIVE APPROACHES

The significance of these differences in approach depends partly on how they differ empirically. If, in reality, countries which maximized incomes

[23] The most recent formula allows some weighting for income per capita above the developed country poverty line, but with progressively diminished weighting.

also maximized capabililities and basic needs, then the debate between the approaches would be of less practical significance than if there were substantial differences in performance. In order to be able to assess this, the first requirement is to arrive at an appropriate measure of the various approaches. This is difficult, as noted above, for each of the three approaches we are discussing—utility, basic needs, or capabilities.

For *utility*, incomes are the appropriate measure, but only where prices are competitive and income distribution is the desired one. In practical terms, incomes can be adjusted to PPP, which corrects for some distortions in exchange rates, but data are not available for adjustment for income distribution for many countries, while the precise adjustment made would in any case be arbitrary. Below we use PPP-adjusted income, but do not adjust for income distribution.

For *basic needs*, the 'decent life' approach suggests that life expectancy is a good single indicator; some weighted average of life expectancy and literacy might be better, and other characteristics of the quality of life might also be included (e.g. nutrition, employment, participation). But the more variables that are added, the more data deficiencies appear and the greater the difficulty of choosing appropriate weights.[24] Below we use life expectancy, as the single BN indicator. This is an average indicator for a nation as a whole; it would be preferable to incorporate some system of weighting for differentials among groups, but data deficiencies prevent this. However, the potential disparities in life expectancy are limited because the upper end is bounded with a maximum life expectancy of around one hundred.

Capabilities incorporate a complex set of potential 'beings' and 'doings'. Since potentials can rarely be measured, assessing performance requires some translation into actuals or 'functionings'. Here too there are a very large number of possible functionings which might be included, and considerable variations among different groups within a nation. Possible alternative measures would be to accept the arguments advanced in relation to BN and use life expectancy as the indicator, or to adopt the more complex HDI as the indicator of the capability approach. Neither indicator does justice to the capability approach. It might be argued that life expectancy would be the better measure of capability at low levels of development and HDI at higher levels.

[24] Hicks and Streeten (1979) provide a full discussion of some of the difficulties of arriving at an appropriate yardstick for the BN approach. Moon adopts the 'Physical Quality of Life Index' (PQLI) as a measure of BN—this includes life expectancy, under-one mortality, and literacy.

TABLE 3.1. *Correlation between measures of different approaches*

	Life expectancy (BN; C at basic levels)	HDI (HD; C at higher levels)
Life expectancy (BN)	1	0.954 [0.836]
HDI (Cap.)	0.954 [0.836]	1
Income per capita (utility)	0.697 [0.442]	0.768 [0.683]

C = Capabilities, BN = Basic Needs, HD = Human Development. Unbracketed data is for 173 countries for 1992. Bracketed data is for 55 low human development countries, 1992.

Source: UNDP, *Human Development Report, 1994*.

The HDI index has, of course, been explicitly adopted by UNDP as the HD indicator.

The correlation matrix shown in Table 3.1 shows how the three indicators were related in 1992. The unbracketed figures show the relationships for the whole world, the bracketed figures for the fifty-five least developed countries. As can be seen, there is a very high correlation between the BN and HD approaches, as measured here, for the whole world, though the correlation is less for the least developed group.[25] The correlation is less between income per capita and the other two measures, being least between life expectancy and incomes for the least developed group of countries. An assessment of the correlation over time, 1960–92, between the percentage change in life expectancy and the percentage change in real per capita income showed virtually *no* correlation (correlation coefficient of .06), which is surprising in view of the quite high correlation between the two indicators in 1992.

We can conclude, therefore, that there are considerable differences in country performance according to whether it is assessed with respect to BN or utility, while differences between HDI and utility are smaller, according to the indicators used here. Hence which approach adopted is of practical as well as theoretical significance. Since the HDI is an imperfect measure of capabilities and the differences are greatest between life expectancy and incomes, we shall focus on differences between these variables in looking at the performance of particular countries.

Table 3.2 shows the countries whose differences between BN, as measured by life expectancy, and the utility approach, as measured by average

[25] Life expectancy forms part of the HDI so a positive correlation would be expected.

TABLE 3.2. *Countries with greatest difference between life expectancy and per capita incomes, in ranking*

	HDI—GNP rank	Growth rate, % 1980–91	S/GNP[a] 1990	Income disparities 1980s[b]	% in poverty around 1980s	Fuels/& miner. % export 1990–1
Good life expectancy						
China	49	7.8	4.4	6.5	9	10[d]
Guyana	44	–4.5	4.7[c]	n.a.	n.a.	n.a.
Colombia	41	1.2	4.7	13.3	42	29
Sri Lanka	38	2.5	4.5	11.5	39	7[d]
Costa Rica	36	0.7	10.2	12.7	2.9	1[d]
Lithuania	35	n.a.	n.a.	n.a.	n.a.	n.a.
Vietnam	34	n.a.	1.1[e]	n.a.	54	n.a.
Nicaragua	33	–4.4	6.5[e]	n.a.	20	2
Madagascar	31	–2.5	1.3[e]	n.a.	43	14[d]
Poland	30	n.a.	10	3.9	n.a.	20
Poor life expectancy						
Gabon	–72	–4.2	8.4	n.a.	41[f]	
Oman	–54	4.4	5.6	n.a.	6[f]	
UAR	–52	–6.3	10.9	n.a.	n.a.	
Seychelles	–44	3.2	8.5[c]	n.a.	20[f]	
Guinea	–44	n.a.	2.3[e]	n.a.	70[f]	
Namibia	–43	–1.2	9.7	n.a.	n.a.	
Iraq	–41	n.a.	n.a.	n.a.	30[f]	
Lib. AJ	–38	n.a.	n.a.	n.a.	n.a.	
Djibouti	–38	n.a.	5.6	n.a.	70[f]	
Algeria	–37	–0.7	14.5	n.a.	23	
				n.a.		
Least dev.		0.2	5.0	n.a.	64	20[g]
All dev.		3.6	6.1	n.a.	31	20[h]

[a] S = expenditure on health and education.

[b] Ratio of incomes of top 20% households to incomes of bottom 20%.

[c] Education only.

[d] 1988.

[e] Health only.

[f] Rural only.

[g] Low-income countries, 1990.

[h] Middle-income countries, 1990. Source of income and exports.

per capita incomes, are greatest. The ten countries which do relatively better on BN, show a variety of characteristics. Some have had positive growth (China, Sri Lanka, and Colombia) while others show negative growth, where the relatively good performance on BN may be due to failure on economic growth rather than particular success on BN (Nicaragua, Guyana, for example). These countries do not show a uniformly high ratio of social expenditure (health and education) to GNP: only Costa Rica, Nicaragua, and Poland have notably high social allocation ratios. Data is incomplete on income distribution. Two countries—China and Poland—have unusually low disparities between the top and bottom 20 per cent of households. In the remaining countries for which data are available, the disparities appear to be moderate. Poverty rates vary, some showing low rates (China, Nicaragua), and others quite high (Madagascar, Vietnam, and Colombia).

Countries which have had particularly weak performance on BN, relative to incomes, appear to have one characteristic in common. They all rely heavily on minerals (mainly oil) as a source of income and exports. This appears to lead to a distribution of income and resources which is unfavourable for BN. Social expenditures are, nonetheless, relatively high in many of these countries. Data is lacking on income disparities, but the high levels of poverty indicate unequal income distribution.

Table 3.3 records the countries whose *improvements* in life expectancy were greatest between 1960 and 1992; again they vary in other characteristics with high income growth a feature of some (China, Indonesia) but not others (Saudi Arabia, Jordan, Honduras) and few countries (Saudi Arabia, Tunisia, for example) showing notably high social expenditure. The limited evidence produced here points to the same conclusions as more in-depth research: there are a variety of ways of improving performance on basic needs or basic capabilities. Some countries succeed through egalitarian economic growth; others by lavish state expenditure; others by well-targeted state expenditure; and some through a combination of these alternatives.[26]

CONCLUSIONS

The capability and functioning approach of Sen is richer than the BN approach in having deeper philosophical foundations and in potentially

[26] See e.g. Stewart (1985); Dreze and Sen (1989); UNDP (1990).

TABLE 3.3. *Countries with largest improvement in BN (life expectancy) 1960–1992*

	Change in life expectancy 1960–92 years	Per capita incomes 1991 ratio of 1960	Social allocation ratio, 1960[d] %	Social allocation ratio, 1990[d] %	Income disparities, 1980s[e]	% in poverty 1980s	Adult literacy 1970[a]
Oman	29	4.52	n.a.	5.6	n.a.	6[r]	n.a.[28]
China*	23.5	4.07	3.1	4.4	6.5	9	n.a.[50]
Saudi Arab.	22.3	1.43	3.3	9.3	n.a.	n.a.	9[36]
Indonesia	20.8	5.57	0.3[h]	0.7[h]	4.9	25	54[51]
Jordan	20.3	2.18	3.6	7.7	n.a.	16	47[75]
Solomon Isles	19.7	n.a.	n.a.	5.0[h]	n.a.	60[r]	n.a.
Vietnam	19.2	n.a.	n.a.	1.1[h]	n.a.	54	n.a.[52]
Tunis*	18.7	3.36	4.9	9.4	7.8	17	31[50]
Honduras	18.7	2.02	3.2	6.9	23.5	37	53[47]
Bahamas	18.7	n.a.	n.a.	3.5[h]	n.a.	n.a.	n.a.[70]
Med. human dev.[b]	15	2.38	3.2	7.1	n.a.	37	60[52]
Low human dev.[c]	10.5	1.62	3.0	5.5	n.a.	53	28[33]

* also among the top ten increases in HDI, 1960–91.

[a] Figures in brackets are total enrolment ratios, 1980.
[b] Excludes China.
[c] Excludes India.
[d] Public expenditure on education and health % GNP.
[e] Ratio of highest 20% to lowest 20%.
[h] Health only.
[r] Rural only.

being applicable to a much greater range of situations. In contrast, the BN approach is concerned only with fairly severe deprivation and has little to say for richer societies, though the approach could be further developed in the direction of defining BN for better-off societies. The BN approach is based on a simple moral imperative—that everyone should have access to a minimally decent condition of life and that this objective should be given priority over other objectives. It thus represents a quite robust political philosophy for poor societies, which has implications for income distribution and desirable patterns of consumption, and suggests strong policy conclusions.[27] While the capabilities approach is more sophisticated and has a wider potential relevance, it actually says less about real situations in poor countries; it states that the objective of development should be to enhance capabilities, but it does not say whose capabilities should be given priority, nor whether some capabilities are of more importance than others. In practice, something very close to a BN approach has to be adopted to yield policy conclusions in poor countries. When this is done, the two approaches give very similar results.[28]

REFERENCES

Anand, S., and Ravallion, M. (1993), 'Human Development in Poor Countries: On the Role of Private Incomes and Public Services', *Journal of Economic Perspectives*, 7: 133–50.

Chenery *et al.* (1974), *Redistribution with Growth*. Oxford: OUP.

Dreze, J., and Sen, A. K. (1989), *Hunger and Public Action*. Oxford: OUP.

Fei, J., Ranis, G., and Stewart, F. (1979), 'A Macro-economic framework for basic needs', background paper for World Bank, Washington, DC: World Bank.

—— —— —— (1985), 'A Macroeconomic Framework' in Stewart (1985).

Hicks, N., and Streeten, P. (1979), 'Indicators of Development: The Search for a Basic Needs Yardstick', *World Development*, 7.

ILO (1970), *Towards Full Employment: a Programme for Colombia*. Geneva: ILO.

—— (1972), *Employment, Incomes and Equality: A Strategy for Increasing Productive Employment in Kenya*. Geneva: ILO.

—— (1976), *Employment, Growth and Basic Needs: A One World Problem*. Geneva: ILO.

[27] These are elucidated in e.g. Streeten *et al.* (1981) and Stewart (1985).

[28] See e.g. Dreze and Sen (1989).

LANCASTER, K. (1966), 'A New Approach to Consumer Theory', *Journal of Political Economy*, 74.

MASLOW, A. H. (1970), *Motivation and Personality*. Rev. edn. London: Harper and Row.

MOON, B. E. (1991), *The Political Economy of Basic Needs*. Ithaca, NY: Cornell University Press.

MORAWETZ, D. (1977). *Twenty-five Years of Economic Development, 1950 to 1975*. Washington, DC: World Bank.

RAWLS, J. (1971), *A Theory of Justice*. Cambridge, Mass.: Harvard University Press.

ROBINSON, R., and JOHNSTON, P. (1971), *Prospects for Employment in the Nineteen Seventies*. London: HMSO.

SEN, A. K. (1975), *Employment, Technology and Development*. Oxford: Clarendon Press.

—— (1977), 'Rational Fools: A Critique of the Behavioural Foundations of Economic Theory', *Philosophy and Public Affairs*, 6, repr. in A. K. Sen (1982), *Choice, Welfare and Measurement*. Oxford: Blackwell.

—— (1981), *Poverty and Famines: An Essay on Entitlement and Deprivation*. Oxford: Clarendon Press.

—— (1985), *Commodities and Capabilities*, Amsterdam: Elsevier Science Publishing.

—— (1988), 'Development and Capabilities', duplicated.

—— (1993), 'Capability and Well-Being', in M. Nussbaum and A. K. Sen (eds.), *The Quality of Life*. Oxford: Clarendon Press.

STEWART, F. (1985), *Planning to Meet Basic Needs*. London: Macmillan.

STREETEN, P., BURKI, J., UL HAQ, M., HICKS, N., and STEWART, F. (1981), *First Things First: Meeting Basic Human Needs in Developing Countries*. Washington, DC: World Bank and OUP.

TURNHAM, D. (1971), *The Employment Problem in Less Developed Countries: A Review of the Evidence*. Paris: OECD.

UNDP (1990), *Human Development Report 1990*. Oxford: OUP.

VAN DER HOEVEN, R. (1987), *Planning for Basic Needs: A Basic Needs Simulation Model Applied to Kenya*. Amsterdam: Free University Press.

4

Economics of the Environment

CHRISTOPHER BLISS

INTRODUCTION

An economist who dares to talk about the environment cannot fail to be aware that for many environmentalists economics is not the solution to the problem—economics, especially in the form of cost–benefit analysis, *is* the problem. No surprise that I do not support that view, although I do believe that cost–benefit can be, and has been, dreadfully abused. My argument, however, will not follow the lines of the usual punch-up between economists and environmentalists. In the worst examples of that type of debate, both sides, it seems to me, pretend to certainties to which they have no rightful claim. To summarize an important subtext in my argument: the world is bigger than humanity. Not only is it likely to make fools of those who think they can dominate it and subdue it by means of technology; it is also capable of making fools out of those who believe that they know it so well that they can forecast what will happen, up to and including disaster.

If our world includes everything which affects humanity, then it also includes humans with their actions and choices. This raises two issues. One is predictability again. Predicting how humans will behave is specially difficult, and the inability to do it correctly accounts for many grand failures of prognosis. Moreover, even when we neglect prediction, and simply observe human decisions as they are taken, there remains the problem of how to interpret decisions and what value to attach to them.

One does not have to maintain that what people choose is coterminous with what gives happiness, or with the good life, to maintain that choices, properly interpreted in terms of what options are really available, constitute highly informative data—more informative sometimes than the actors' own accounts of what they are concerned with. We can learn from the careful examination of what people vote for with their feet, to borrow a phrase, and it is extremely perilous to ignore such information. Moreover, those committed to discrediting such information are sometimes motivated by a dislike of what this messenger may be telling them.

ECONOMIC CATASTROPHE

If the title, 'Economics of the Environment' brings to mind the possibility of future environmental catastrophe, it is simply because some very influential economic, and broadly environmental, viewpoints have pointed to catastrophe. The Club of Rome extrapolations were certainly catastrophic.[1] They were never influential with mainstream economists. The methodology was plain silly, even in comparison with what economists normally do when they attempt to forecast. And even forecasting based on good technique is typically unsuccessful. It would be a mistake, however, to assume from economists disdain for crude forecasting efforts that they are congenitally optimistic. Indeed the dismal science in its 200-year history has very often been just that—dismal.

In discussing the quality of life we should not think exclusively in terms of environmental catastrophe, which is after all only the limiting case of a poor quality of life. I doubt that any form of environmental pessimism can be proved to be wrong, simply because, for reasons which I shall indicate, almost nothing can be proved wrong or right with any degree of confidence when we stare into the future.

Yet it must be easier to throw doubt on catastrophic extrapolations than to demonstrate that the future which awaits humanity will not constitute increasingly wretched existences in economies appallingly ineffective at the provision of a good way of life, because weighed down by external diseconomies of production and pollution and high population density.

It is obvious that the world cannot go on the way that it is carrying on now, but then it never has done. Things always change. In the past they have sometimes changed fairly inarguably for the worse. The historian who tells you that the Middle Ages in Western Europe were not as bad you think, is talking about the later Middle Ages. Unless you have studied them, the early Middle Ages were worse than you think. Declining cities, the complete breakdown of large-scale agricultural systems, famine, population decline, and the replacement of centralized

[1] See Meadows *et al.* (1972).

law and order by warlordism. We would have to be extraordinarily arrogant to believe that similar decline and degradation cannot possibly await our children or grandchildren.

'I have seen the future and I know it works', remarked Lincoln Steffens returning from the Soviet Union in 1919. Our problem is that we have not seen the future, and are unable readily to imagine it. This makes a proof that it cannot work inherently difficult. Tom Schelling pinpoints the problem beautifully in his American Economic Association presidential address when he speculates about predicting the consequences for the future of a possible global warming.[2] The length of the quotation is justified by the effectiveness of the argument:

> Even if we had confident estimates of climate change for different regions of the world, there would still be uncertainties about the kind of world it is going to be in 50, 75, or 100 years from now. Imagine it were 1900 and the climate change associated with a three-degree average temperature increase were projected to 1992. On what kind of world would we superimpose either a vaguely described potential change in climate, or even a specific description of changes in the weather in all seasons of the year, even for our own country? There would have been no way to assess the impact of changing climates on air travel, electronic communication, the construction of skyscrapers, or the value of California real estate. Most of us worked outdoors; life expectancy was 47 years (it is now 75); barely a fifth of us lived in cities of 50,000 or more. Anticipating the automobile we might have been concerned about whether wetter and drier weather would bring more or less mud, not anticipating that the nations roads would become thoroughly paved. The assessment of the effects on health would be without antibiotics or inoculation. And in contrast to most contemporary concern with the popular image of hotter summers to come, I think we would have been more concerned about warmer winters, later frost in autumn, and earlier thaw in the spring.
>
> If the world, both North America and the other continents, is going to change as much in the next 90 years as it has changed in the 90 just past, we are going to be hard put to imagine the effects of climate changes.

Therefore, the conclusion cannot be that because environmentalist disaster descriptions are fairly dubious as prognoses there is unlikely to be environmental disaster. Other civilizations besides our own ran out of luck in the past, why should we be immune? We cannot, however, rely on an essentially cyclical view of history because history is certainly not wholly cyclical. Some 12,000 years ago humanity invented Agriculture. No doubt the hunter-gatherer quality of life seminars at the

[2] See Schelling (1992: 4–5).

time concluded that these trends would disastrously deteriorate the quality of life. They managed to write their views into Genesis 3: 19 and perhaps they were right. Agriculture could be the worst thing that ever happened to the quality of life, at least of those who have to do the work. It was a punishment fitting for an angry God.

My serious point is that no breakdown of civilization in the future, however awful, is likely to involve the uninventing of agriculture. We cannot forget it and we cannot return to the state of affairs that existed before we needed it. So not everything can be cyclical. Now consider the seventeenth-century invention of Science. Should that turn out to be as irreversible as was the invention of Agriculture, the long future may be qualitatively different from the long past for that reason alone.[3]

Science and scientific inventiveness, along with other varieties of adaptation, are central to the difficulty which faces predicting future problems and their likely impact. This is what made previous predictions of early disaster completely wrong, just as it is what would have faulted the hypothetical attempt by our forefathers to assess the consequences of global warming depicted by Tom Schelling.

I am here following the main stream of environmentalist thought, and of earlier economists' pessimism, in locating the question of the quality of future life in the area of mankind's relations with Nature broadly conceived. Human beings' relations with each other are not so amenable to mastery by the technical and have much more potential for catastrophic effects. I am definitely a pessimist, for instance, in finding it nearly inconceivable that the shattered ex-Soviet Union's abundant stock of nuclear warheads will not in time find its way into exchange for desperately needed dollars, resulting in widespread nuclear proliferation by early next century, with very probably several nuclear bombs exploded in anger by that time. Economic sustainability is not the only problem for our futures. It was not, after all, economic problems as such that undermined the Western Roman Empire. It was problems of government, taxation, and military effectiveness.

THE POWER OF GOVERNMENT

Note an important corollary of the observation that human beings' relations with each other are not amenable to mastery by the technical, which

[3] There is no implicit suggestion of inevitable progress here. Obviously the future may be particularly horrible just on account of what Science may make possible.

seems to me often under-emphasized. The recognition of an environmental problem and its solution are connected, of course, but they are not the same thing. There may be serious environmental problems about which, in effect, real life governments can do very little. Excessive population growth, of which more later, may be one of these.

In such cases governments can often be shown to be making things worse. Yet even in that case, actual governments have to get elected or survive, or both so just telling them to stop may not have much effect. While some green thinking has tended towards advocating an autocratic form of government for that kind of reason, government by the philosophers is neither achievable nor desirable in this connection. The Bolshevik revolution may well have been one of the worst environmental disasters of the twentieth century. While it may be clear, on the one hand, that democracy is no guarantee of environmental protection; autocracy, on the other hand, seems nearly to guarantee severe environmental neglect.

ECONOMIC GROWTH

Leaving aside war and peace, or the decline of the Roman Empire, let us consider a narrower focus on economic growth. That might mean the ending of growth, and what might be called the battle between diminishing returns and technical progress. The subtleties of this battle play a role in explaining the tendency among economists to regard environmental issues with what environmentalists can easily see as breathtaking complacency.

Economists have been here before. Indeed the history of economics since it first took its modern form in the eighteenth century has included substantial periods characterized either by a pessimistic view of the environmental question, or of grudging retreat from such pessimism. True, we started optimistic. Adam Smith believed that population growth would allow finer division of labour and greater productivity, and also that the sweeping away of archaic interference by governments, and other bodies, would release pent-up productivity, in which he included better use of the land and higher agricultural productivity.

It happened that economics grew deeply pessimistic at the same time as it became more abstract. The classical economists discovered diminishing returns, and Mill turned that into a stationary state in which society had run out of ways round the environmental block. Malthus famously developed older pessimistic views of the population question into a mathematical law which said that the technical-progress tortoise stood not a chance against the demographic hare. If economists irritate you, take pleasure in the fact that we were going on and on about diminishing returns while the industrial revolution was burying the concept. Economic historians still debate about how long it took for these changes to increase the standard of living of workers, and, yes, trade and the opening up of distant regions played an important role. Yet economists learnt the lesson that a naïve pessimism had once made them look foolish.

The second half of the nineteenth century brings a period of qualified optimism, with the exception of Marx, whose optimism is unqualified (and not just where the environment is concerned). Even economists, such as Marshall, who believed in the possibility of technical progress, held that only virtue and hard work will earn its benefits. Wicksell was a fanatical Malthusian, and Stanley Jevons did the first resource extrapolation and concluded that Britain would cease to be an industrial power by 1920 because by that time it would certainly have exhausted its coal reserves.[4] Jevons's extrapolations were not the absurd outpourings of some cranky nit-wit. Here was one of the very finest minds of nineteenth-century economics. All his assumptions were wholly reasonable. He looked at known reserves, assumed then-available mining technology, did his sums and did them right. This goes some way to explaining why economists are often uncomfortable with simple projections to a disaster point.

THINKING ABOUT THE UNTHINKABLE

Obviously the fact that important people have been wrong to project disaster in the past does not prove that disaster will not eventually happen. Rather the lesson seems to be that if it does happen we cannot count on foreseeing it far ahead and in sharp focus. Indeed problems which we do not foresee are likely to be worse for us. If only AIDS had left us its calling card a few decades before presenting itself at our door, we might have been in a better position to entertain it now.

I have argued that we cannot depict our disastrous future with any plausibility, but that does not deter me from attempting the task. The

[4] See Jevons (1865).

point of doing so is not that I stand any chance of being even approximately correct. Rather, attempting the exercise is highly illuminating in itself. One can see where the argument does not look secure. Take the traditional workhorse of the UN, and old-style environmental pessimism right back to Malthus, the relation between human population and food availability.

At a global level, and the most rapid rate of growth in human numbers which our planet has ever seen notwithstanding, food production has been keeping up. The distribution of the total available, however, has been getting worse in some—though not all—respects. For instance India has substantially decreased its dependence on imported grains, while Egypt has increased it to an extent which it is hard to see as viable. I am not making an arbitrary assumption here that countries should be self-sufficient in food production. It is obvious, however, that a heavily food-importing country must either export something else, or resign itself to client-state status.

Despite global balance, we still experience famines in the modern world. That is real famines, not statistical hunger produced by researchers with electronic calculators and dubious estimates of nutrient-intake requirements.[5] Unfortunately, misgovernment, or even government actively malevolent to some of the peoples in its charge, plays a large role in contemporary famine, as does war and its aftermath. Once again, man's relation to man is a worse problem than man's relations with nature.

For global balance between food availability and demands we have got by more or less, so far. That does not mean we can keep on winning. Borlaug argued long ago that there is a biochemical maximum to the tonnage of wheat that an acre of land can produce, however much varieties may be improved and agricultural technique optimized. Surely best practice agronomy for wheat cultivation is already close to that ceiling, while less effective cultivators are rapidly improving their techniques and getting as close to that ceiling as they are ever going to be. As rapid population growth makes the proportion of huge populations which are at childbearing age increase, and thus feeds into more population growth, what next?

More population means higher population densities which brings problems of its own. Some of these are political governmental again, but even ignoring those, high population density imposes considerable economic

[5] On nutrition requirements, see Dasgupta (1993: part IV).

costs (for instance, but only one instance, the disposal of human waste). For those who like catastrophic prognosis, the possibility of what I call biological strikeback will be compelling. The history of the last fifty years has consisted to an extraordinary extent of our successfully pushing back the biological frontier on expansion of human populations (and their density) and on the intensity of exploitation of land for growing crops. It is a battle against a resourceful adversary: natural selection.

New crop varieties, chemicals, and (for humans and animals) new antibiotics, have played an essential role in the huge expansion of population and in the growth of wealth. Having rushed nature with a mass of ideas and knocked it back, we may have become accustomed to winning. But diminishing returns may apply in this case. The game gets harder and we constantly make our own side tougher to play—for instance by travelling more and in larger numbers, relying more exclusively on a small number of plant varieties, abusing antibiotics, etc. We could start to run into serious difficulties soon, in a manner which the AIDS epidemic only illustrates. In any case, even if we keep on winning in the West, we may prove unable or unwilling to expend effort to enable the poor of the world to keep up with us. Some of this is happening already with cholera epidemics in South America and the rise of TB in New York city.

This constitutes some good scary prognosis but also runs an evident risk of being proved ridiculous. We are currently experiencing a remarkable revolution in our biological understanding and command. Who knows where it may take us? What we can do with wheat may be better than even Borlaug supposed if recombinant DNA designer wheats punch holes in his biochemical ceiling. Or grains may become less important if we develop the fermentation of biomass to produce edible protein and carbohydrates directly. And these are only technologies which already exist on the drawing board, which is what allows me to talk about them.[6]

The principle of diminishing returns says that there comes a point at which one cannot go on winning. But diminishing returns is an assumption not a theorem. It is surely possible that future historians will record that the early twenty-first century was the time when the great late eighteenth-century breakthrough which was the industrial revolution finally began to prove itself unable to support the massive human

[6] If this seems most unappetizing, note that we are never asked to like the future. We never will, just as our ancestors would mostly hate our present.

populations which it had generated; that is generated and supported for a long time even in countries little influenced directly by the industrial way of life. Yet, equally, future historians may laugh at our pessimism as we now laugh at Jevons.

POLICY CHOICES

Economics is meant to be about the design of policy. What can we say about policy? This raises several issues which need to be considered separately. Let us note, however, that policy design is not only about solving problems in the sense of disposing of them. Many Greens believe that if only they could convince people, the right policy would be able to solve the problem. It may not be that simple. It may be misleading to suppose that we either do nothing and perish, or adopt the right policies and solve the problems. Policy does not have to be designed for the regulation of the economy by an all-powerful administration to achieve an ideal end. It can be made for the use of weak administrations to address decline. So we need good policy even if the pessimistic view of our future should be correct.

To many Greens the standard economics way of looking at a problem is singularly inappropriate for environmental issues. An economist is trained to think roughly as follows:

(*a*) What objective function is to be maximized?
(*b*) What are the constraints of resources and technology?
(*c*) What constraints do institutions and policy instruments impose?
(*d*) Which policies maximize the objective function subject to the constraints?

Properly understood that is a very general framework, but obviously habitual assumptions about what specifications are appropriate tend to creep in. In the context of our present concerns, for instance, the objective function may be too narrowly 'economic' for the Green taste. In particular, the idea that man can orchestrate the world environment to maximize an objective function defined by him (no problem with the maleness of the pronoun here) would be rejected by some Green philosophers.

Some of the resulting philosophy would be of a kind from which economics, which after all is a product of eighteenth-century Enlightenment thought, instinctively shrinks. Having fought against overbearing principles—such as money is barren and should earn no interest—the economist is not going to be convinced easily that a forest or a way of life commands a status such that its protection is an absolute. Economics is a vulgarly practical discipline which thinks in terms of trade-offs and the aggregation and reconciliation of divergent individual values. If the preservation of a forest is an absolute and overriding value for every individual, one need not be at all concerned that it will be chopped down.

If that seems arrogant, note that the economics can be what might seem shamelessly compliant when values are being defined. Modern economics explicitly asserts its own uselessness in that connection. The idea that value judgements are something concerning which the economist has no special expertise or status is the basis of mainstream welfare economics. If the population be Jainists, and believe that the avoidance of any taking of life is an overriding absolute, economists can oblige with a Jainist economics. Plug Jainist assumptions into the objective function above and out will come good Jainist economic policies.[7]

While it is true that all sorts of exotic economics may be created in principle, most of what one is likely to encounter is much more narrowly focused on the objective of increasing the economic component of human welfare. Pigou's well-known definition says that economic welfare is 'that part of welfare which can be brought within the measuring rod of money'—surely an overrated definition. If an individual is willing to change his religion for £250,000, does that bring religious adherence within the measuring rod of money and make liberty of religious confession a part of economic welfare?

WHAT PROMOTES HUMAN WELFARE?

This large field encompasses issues which are often invoked when environmentalists talk to, or against, economists. I shall consider two by

[7] Jainism in this context refers particularly to the belief that all life is sacred and should not be sacrificed unavoidably. An offspring of this tradition is Buddhism, and one of the central ideas of Buddhism is that desires should be accommodated to what is available, not what is available made to conform to desire. Buddhism is still a major world religion, though not many Buddhists live according to its ideals. One might be tempted to say that there cannot be a Buddhist economics, because accommodating desires to what is available is too absolutely antithetical to what economics represents. Even so, the French economist Serge-Christophe Kolm, who is a Buddhist, has written several works attempting that seemingly impossible task, largely unnoticed by Anglo-Saxon academics. See, for instance, Kolm (1984).

way of illustration. One issue is how to take into account environmental bads, such as polluted air. Should the standard measure of national productivity, gross national product, be amended to reflect the environment, and if so, how?[8] Should we, for instance, subtract from GNP a measure of resources used up, such as oil extracted? Should we deduct from GNP an estimate of the harm done by noxious exhaust emissions from motor vehicles?

There is no question but that these are serious issues. Equally, the measurement problems are formidable. In particular, it is often the case that people do not vote with their purses where environmental bads are concerned, as they do routinely when they buy goods in markets. Many environmental bads are things that we suffer and against which we cannot readily purchase protection. This inclines me to think that we probably do not do well to mix together standard measures of GNP, which measure what they measure fairly usefully, with estimates of environmental bads which, important though they certainly are, can only be measured much more subjectively. If that reminds us that GNP is not by definition an objective to be pursued, so much the better.

Equally, there are serious problems in deducting from GNP an allowance for resources depleted. How is the deduction to be estimated? Consider the oil industry to illustrate the problems. At any time there is in principle a stock of proven reserves in the world, call it P. If all the oil ever to be discovered was already proven, then P would decline over time as oil is extracted. Environmental accounting would then deduct an allowance for oil sold from P, and the value added of the oil industry would consist entirely of oil extracted multiplied by the difference between the market value of reserves in the ground and the market value of crude oil at the surface. Plainly such accounting would vastly reduce the contribution of the world oil industry to world GNP.

On the other hand, additions to P, due to new discoveries, would raise GNP, sometimes in large discrete jumps. And in the long run it might make little difference, because the value of oil would be counted in GNP, it would just be that more weight would be given to it in the ground and less to its extraction as such. In the case of oil, at least, there are fairly good market valuations even of reserves. With many goods, and bads as well, that is not the case. The value of a low carbon-dioxide atmosphere remains controversial despite mounting evidence, suggestive if not decisive, that the costs of global warming will be considerable.

[8] Dasgupta (1993: chs. 4 and 5) addresses this issue.

Many environmentalist arguments directed at economists start from the assumption that economists are professionally committed to economic growth and GNP expansion *ad nauseam*. Environmental considerations aside, the standard position does identify growing income and wealth with a usefully expanded command over goods and services, which in itself is good. Yet many economists have noticed that the association between increased consumption and happiness, while inevitably subjective, and not necessarily absent, is not terribly impressive.

Also, for the sake of clarity, it is most important to recognize that environmentalism and anti-consumerism are not at all the same. Environmentalism may be defined as a concern with deterioration of the environment and with negative environmental externalities. Anti-consumerism is the belief that the ways of life of all or many people are too much concerned with consuming things to achieve happiness, goodness of living, define the ideal as you will. If our values are wrong and we are too consumerist for our own good, then there is an argument for reigning back our income generation and consumption, which is strictly independent of environmental issues.

While many Greens are by inclination anti-consumerist, the value issues involved are several and complex, and that they do not line up together by definition. While being logically independent they may yet connect. For instance, separate and logically independent cases may reinforce each other. If our consumption is not good for us, and it pollutes, we have two reasons for cutting back consumption. If when we give up consuming we will walk in the hills, our new way of life may make us more concerned about the environment. Consuming and the environment are substitutes in consumption, to use the economist's terminology.

COST–BENEFIT ANALYSIS

Cost–benefit analysis is a method for accounting for all the considerable effects of a development project, the direct and the indirect, weighting them appropriately, and thus arriving at an assessment of the total impact of the project which may assist the competent decision-makers in making up their minds.[9] Notice that I have not said that cost–benefit

[9] The economics of cost–benefit analysis is a large field which embraces some highly technical aspects. For a good survey supported by many references, see Squire (1989).

analysis chooses projects. My reason is that this does not happen. Politicians are never willing to surrender their administrative discretion to calculations done by technicians. Yet the World Bank used to promote the use of cost–benefit analysis partly with a view to making the process of assessing project investments more rigorous.[10]

Many Greens argued that cost–benefit analysis is a method particularly liable to neglect environmental and related considerations. The issues involved are several and would need more space than I have here. However, a hypothetical example captures several of the points of the type which make Greens hot under the collar.

Imagine a high valley in a poor country, surrounded by rain-forest-clad mountains and the home to an ancient people who live a simple and traditional way of life without greatly altering their natural environment. The government is promoting industry some distance away and needs more electric power. It considers damming the river which flows through the valley, flooding it, and using the pressure of water created by the dam to power turbines to generate electricity. Sounds like a good idea—send in the cost–benefit analysts.

I assume that the intentions of the cost–benefit analysts are the very best. They compute with care the resources required by the dam project and the social value of the electricity produced, and they notice, of course, that the indigenous people will have to be displaced. Now things get difficult. How are they to bring that within the measuring rod of money? The market value of the products produced by the local people is tiny, the value of their dwellings at sale is minuscule. The rest of the calculation is showing a large surplus of benefit over cost. The locals can all be set up on good farms somewhere else with their location costs generously reimbursed and still an excess of benefit over cost remains.

When this situation is explained to the government minister in charge of the project he asks why so much fuss is being made about relocating a few tribal people, and is delighted that his pet project passes the cost–benefit test. Meanwhile other commentators are highly critical of the scheme: new dam to destroy ancient way of life and biodiversity! scream the hostile headlines in the foreign press.

[10] More recently the World Bank has rather gone off cost–benefit analysis. The main reasons are similar to those illustrated in an example below. Cost–benefit analysis systems are highly manipulable. Hence making funding dependent on a favourable cost–benefit analysis finding encourages optimistic projections. Bank experience was that projects evaluated *ex post* underperformed relative to the *ex ante* projections.

How should cost–benefit analysis bring the measuring rod of money to bear on such questions? What money value should be put on a way of life or on biodiversity? Biodiversity is slightly easier in so far as it is partly claimed to confer economic benefits, to pharmaceutical research, for instance. And a consortium of developing countries at the Rio conference[11] was keen to bring biodiversity very much within the ambit of the measuring rod of money, so as to send a large bill to the industrial countries for the maintenance of biodiversity.

There are many problems of estimating the economic value of biodiversity. It is potentially an important source of the external diseconomies long recognized by economic theory as requiring intervention, including taxation or subsidy. An ideal cost–benefit analysis would take account of all such considerations. I doubt, however, that those concerned about biodiversity only have what one might call the economic value of biodiversity in mind. They surely see it partly as a good in itself, and that connects with the issue of the destruction of a way of life, already alluded to. Those who maintain that we have no right to destroy a way of life are really arguing that some things are outside the scope of the calculated trade-offs which economists are trained to undertake. Obviously these sort of considerations are at the boundary of the competence of technical economics, if not definitely outside it.

What I have to say is quite banal. An economic calculus has no trouble in principle with absolutes: no-go areas for the calculation, provided that there are not so many as to make any solution infeasible. If no trade-off between a way of life and standardly defined economic welfare is allowed, then no trade-off is allowed. But someone who wants to save a way of life from the dam-builder would be ill advised to concentrate exclusively on converting economists to the appreciation of its importance. Frankly they are not that powerful.

If the recommendations of, say a more humane, cost–benefit analysis are not appealing to governments, they will not find it difficult to ignore its recommendations, or even to employ other experts to 'get inside' the calculations, identify the fact that protection of a way of life played a large role in the rejection of the dam project, and impose their own different weights. Cost–benefit analysis is both science and art. Used well it is a valuable aid to sensible decisions, abused it misleads, it is never the key which opens every door.

[11] United Nations Conference on Environment and Development (UNCED), Rio de Janeiro 1992, 'The Earth Summit'.

THE INTERGENERATIONAL QUESTION

Many environmental effects are slow acting and irreversible and hence reach out across generations. Greenhouse gases are an obvious example. The standard economic model of what is called optimal saving is usually applied to the case in which our children will be richer than we are (though the theory is general and can apply to either case).[12] In that case a small consumption benefit which could be provided to each of the present generation should be preferred to the same benefit provided to the same number of members of a future generation. In other words we should discount the future. If the pessimistic environmentalists are right, however, our children will not be richer than we are. In that case, the logic of optimal saving theory would lead to the conclusion that we should apply negative discounting to projects of all kinds. An investment which not quite, but nearly, stops output falling, could be a highly desirable investment in a negative discounting world. It may come as a surprise to some people that economic theory already justifies expensive negative rate of return investments to protect the environment—yet such is the case.

The discount rate under discussion is the real rate of discount. In recent times the real rate of interest seems to have been moving the other way. The measurement of the real rate of interest, which is a forwardlooking concept, is a complicated exercise. If the long-run real rate of interest really has risen in recent years, this is bad news for the environment, because a high interest rate encourages use over preservation and tends to bring consumption forward.

I do not think that we can necessarily conclude that a high real rate of interest reflects a growth in the productivity of investment through technical progress. An important contribution may have been made by anti-inflation policies by governments which, while they may have pushed up the marginal productivity of investment, will have done so by depressing its level. A high rate of interest probably does explain the softness of the oil market in the 1980s. Oil prices tend to rise faster when interest rates are high, which means that when interest rates go up the oil price will often fall to rise subsequently at a more rapid rate.[13]

[12] See Broome (1992) and Dasgupta (1993: ch. *10).

[13] See Chichilnisky and Heal (1991).

UNCERTAINTY AND CATASTROPHIC POSSIBILITIES

I have stressed that the future is dreadfully uncertain. This is the case even where global warming is concerned, despite the fact that the fundamental physics is hardly controversial. How should we react to uncertainty, especially when catastrophic possibilities are involved? The standard economic model of rational choice under uncertainty concludes that low probability disaster outcomes should carry high weights in our calculations.

High weights but not infinite weights, a distinction to which I attach some importance. Take global warming produced by the release of greenhouse gases. Some economists have argued that the costs implied by even cautiously pessimistic projections of the effect of warming are considerable but not apparently massive in comparison with the costs that would attach to a huge global cut-back in fossil fuel burning.[14] Yet what about the possibility that climate change might trigger a discontinuous or uncontrollable shift of some kind to which a monumental cost might attach. An example would be a large redirection of the North Atlantic drift such as might make Northern Europe as cold as Northern Canada.

This is not quite such a crazy idea as may at first seem. True, the expansion of water around the equator will go on as long as the sun shines, some will inevitably come north, and the shape of the North Atlantic basin will continue to route it towards Europe. But Europe does not have to mean Scotland. In the geological past the Gulf Stream has been directed further south, playing roughly on northern Spain. If an increase in greenhouse gases were to result in the Gulf Stream flipping that way again, mankind would have triggered a simply horrendous climatic disaster. Of course this is all pretty speculative, but who cares? The tiniest tiniest risk that we might do that means that we must stop adding to greenhouse gases. We must stop at once, if not sooner, as my mother used to say.

There is no economic theorem which says that this type of reasoning is irrational and incorrect. If one attaches a utility nearly infinitely small compared with other possibilities to the catastrophic outcome, then a minuscule probability attaching to it happening still means we should do everything to avoid it. It is similar to the principles which apply to

[14] See Nordhaus (1991).

nuclear power station design, though even more extreme. Huge costs are paid to reduce the probability of very low probability events precisely because the costs attaching to those events (which might be associated with a serious nuclear accident) are extremely high.

Yet I am probably not alone in feeling uncomfortable with that type of reasoning. It seems to allow any discussion to be hijacked by the imagination of someone who can dream up a nightmare possibility, however improbable. Classroom examples can be quite like that, but the world is seldom constructed so as to make the 'anything to avoid the tiniest risk of disaster' type of reasoning at all sensible. Reality does not typically display precipitous discontinuities between the safe and the risky. If we stop doing X everything will be fine, but if we do not stop doing X, there is a small probability of extreme disaster. End of argument.

In reality downside risks attach even to environmental correctness. Suppose that fear of horrific consequences from global warming induces us to cut back carbon dioxide emissions drastically. What exactly will happen is uncertain, but many risks of harm to human populations caused by energy shortage will obviously be present. The good outcome is helpless when it comes to outweighing the appalling outcome, however more probable it might be. The not wildly improbable poor outcome stands up to the dreadful outcome on something more like equal terms.

POLICIES FOR ENVIRONMENTAL CARE

This is a huge area which I can hardly develop here. Yet it represents an important reason for the difficulties which economists and environmentalists sometimes experience when they try to talk to each other. The theory of economic policy design sees the economic system as something which responds to policy variables, sometimes in perverse ways. This is partly because it is complex, and is particularly because human beings are conscious maximizing agents whose actions are affected by policy variables.

I illustrate the point with a single example. Suppose that global warming is a serious problem, what should we do about it? Tax carbon emissions is a standard answer and one which played a leading role at the Rio meeting. Yet while the general adoption of carbon taxation by industrial countries is improbable at present, it should also be understood that the effect of general carbon taxation on the long-term build-up of carbon in the atmosphere would be complex. An understanding of it must take into account the effects of taxation on base energy prices.

Known world reserves of fossil fuels in the ground and cheap to extract are almost certainly going to be burnt sometime. At least simple taxation will not stop them being extracted. If taxation lowers demand, it may happen, as Peter Sinclair has shown, that producers will get a lower price, but no less will be burnt.[15]

As energy reserves are not fixed and known, a carbon tax would discourage exploration and the development of fossil-fuel energy generation, and through this route might have the eventual effect that less carbon would be burnt. Hence the main effect of a simple carbon tax would be to lower the price charged by the sellers of these fuels, including OPEC and other producers. That in turn would disadvantage energy producers selling at prices much closer to production costs than is the case for major oil producers, notably industrial country coal mines. The net contribution to the reduction of carbon burning might be disappointingly small.

Recognizing this, some environmentalists have advocated tradeable carbon permits.[16] That would take care of the problem that prices might fall. It is hard to believe, however, that such a system could be policed by a world community which cannot stop ethnic cleansing in Bosnia, or dreadful overfishing on the high seas—both cases in which the costs are incontrovertible, huge, immediate, and unambiguous. I think this says something interesting: that global warming is top of the pops in the environmental problem hit parade, not because it is the world's leading environmental problem, but for other reasons. It is global, it is mainly the rich countries' fault, and it is subtle, hence intellectually interesting.

FEET WITH VOTES

At the end the argument returns to revealed preference. That is a technical term for a technical concept. Yet at issue is something more simple and basic, to indicate which a rougher term serves well. On occasion environmental concern has kept company with a somewhat contemptuous view of ordinary people's choices concerning life-styles and ways

[15] See Sinclair (1994). Also Ulph and Ulph (1994).
[16] See Larsen and Shah (1994).

of existing and surviving. Sometimes these people are speaking and environmentalists and others are not listening, perhaps because we do not like what is being said. The issue is not what people themselves may or may not say, or what articulate individuals who claim to speak for them may declare. The question is what behaviour reveals, in particular what may be called voting with feet.[17]

We have looked at a critique of cost–benefit analysis which claims that particular ways of life are sacred things that need to be respected and preserved, argues that one can never put a price on such a thing, and criticizes cost–benefit analysis of dams for obtaining their favourable findings for dam building by putting footling little valuations on such precious resources as the life-styles of tribal people displaced by dams.

Certainly many traditional ways of living are under attack by wretchedly self-serving or inconsiderate decisions by governments (with or without the help of cost–benefit analysis). Others, such as fishing in many places, are threatened by environmental degradation or poor management of resources. And others, or the same ones, sometimes seem not to be able to command the commitment of those who live them.

The Alti Plano in the Andean Region, for instance, is home to a unique and tough way of life dependent on hard work and deep and subtly evolved ways of living in which the cultivator becomes almost one with the environment. Surely we should attach a massive weight to the preservation of such a life-style. Yet the fact is that the region is subject to heavy out-migration. People are voting with their feet against staying there. We need a method of reading meaning into such observation, particularly because the causes are several. It would be wrong, for example, to interpret the migration exclusively as a vote against the practice of agriculture in the high Andes. The policies of governments have been hostile to that region and its needs, and policies which worsen conditions in any region tend to encourage out-migration.

We need to understand closely why people are on the move. We need to decode their decisions and in that exercise we must respect their human worth and imperatives. They may be revealing a preference, if one likes to put it that way, but what preference they reveal is determined by their actual menu of choices.

[17] For a subtle discussion, see Sen (1973). Sen rests much of his case against the idea that behaviour reveals preferences on the famous Prisoners' Dilemma example. For that case I would say that, as always, the constraints under which a choice is made have to be understood and taken into account, and that with such understanding it is possible that a choice may be completely uninformative.

Similarly people in rich countries are voting with their feet, which is to say that they are selecting ways of living that can tell us something, whether we like the message or not. They are not, tiny minorities apart, voting for a simple, less consumerist life-style, or for minimal effects on their environments. They are voting for the suburbs, massively so, and for high consumption in the suburbs. Everywhere the city centres of rich countries are losing population. As are rural areas, incidentally, except where they provide essentially suburban living.

These choices, like all choices, are constrained by the menu of possibilities available, more of that below, but even constrained choices tell us something. In any case, it is not always honest to disregard choices just because they are constrained, for if people cared enough they could sometimes do something by themselves to create new possibilities. Anyone who commutes by car to a higher paid job who could settle for a lower paid job is voting for car use and for higher consumption. That they might travel by metro if one was available is irrelevant to that conclusion.

To claim that choices tell us nothing about what people want because people are like automatons, or that their consciousness is false, patronizes and insults them. No surprise then that such a view leads towards the government by philosophers which is the stuff of tyranny. On the other hand, to read choices correctly from behaviour, one has to look at what options people have available. If an individual is forced to choose between being hung and being shot, an election for the bullet does not reveal a ballistic death wish, only a preference for one horrible way of being killed over another. Similarly, the farm folk fleeing the 1930s dust bowl were not telling us that they wanted the horrors described by John Steinbeck, only that things can get so bad that feet vote for whatever may be outside.

Plainly for most people most of the time, the choices that they have are severely limited. That does not mean that the choices that they do make do not inform. An individual who excuses living a spiritually denuded life with the reason that no life inspected proved perfect, so just any life was selected, deceives no one. Often choices point in a direction itself unattainable within the choice set. We have all heard it said that because people drive cars it does not mean that they like cars: no public transport is available, they have no choice. Why not conclude that the choices that people do make, though dreadfully partial in their reach, still tell us something and they do not tell us that people hate the automobile. The flight to the suburbs is a case in point. When people elect for a way of life in itself inescapably dependent on heavy motor vehicle use, please do not say that they really hate the motor car. Until recently the signals that politicians receive from their electorates seemed to indicate that people strongly dislike roads in their immediate vicinity but like there to be more roads further away.

The feet that are voting, the directions in which they are pointing, tell us a lot about attitudes to Nature in our time. The mass movements out of rural areas into the cities in poor countries tell us that closeness to the soil does not effectively hold millions of people when the going is rough. Of course the reasons for that are complex, and surely those least close to the soil are those most likely to move. The landless flood into the shanty towns before those to whom the land offers a direct return. The people of the high Andes teach us that closeness to the soil is a relative thing, that a people and its life can be very close to the soil, or less close to the soil. But even great closeness does not necessarily hold, as Andean out-migration shows.

The draw of the suburbs also tells us about attitudes to Nature in the rich North. That the suburb is a metaphor for Nature has always been its attraction. But it represents Nature in a particular form; Nature in the sense that a garden is Nature, i.e. an extremely human-regimented encaged version of Nature. It is the very opposite of wilderness, although the skilled garden designer can make a garden allude to wilderness. The attraction of the suburb indicates that people *en masse* are at ease with the garden version of Nature. They like to see trees and flowers and to pick fruit but they do not love their soil as peasants might.[18]

To finish, consider the growth of human numbers. Much discussion of rapid population growth adopts a condescending attitude towards poor families which have large numbers of children, representing them, for example, as stupid or backward. Yet in the world people are acting, and what they do tells us something. Generally speaking, they are telling us that as individual groups they do not find the large family to be a problem. Some do of course, and some who do are cruelly denied access to a modern contraception, but often they are telling us that other things worry them more. They want jobs for their children, not fewer children.

In Palanpur village in Uttar Pradesh in India, I once showed a highly articulate farmer the growth of village numbers over a period of sixteen years.[19] Then I asked him what he thought would happen in the next

[18] See Ulrich (1986). Oddly, ecologists tell us that in Britain the suburban garden has become a wild-life resource of a kind, but only because it is territory treated less cruelly than farm-land, because it is used only marginally for production.

[19] On Palanpur, see Bliss and Stern (1982).

sixteen years. He said he did not know but he added that the numbers had been much smaller when he was a boy and yet more people had been really hungry. In that village, outside employment has grown over the years, which reflects both more factory jobs in the vicinity and feet voting for them when they are there. So the villagers know that higher incomes are possible beyond what the soil can provide. Yet they do not know what the future, will bring. Neither do we.

REFERENCES

Bliss., C., and Stern, N. H. (1982), *Palanpur: The Economy of an Indian Village*. Oxford: Clarendon Press.

Broome, J. (1992), *Counting the Cost of Global Warming*. Cambridge: White Horse Press.

Chichilinisky, G., and Heal, G. M. (1991), *Oil in the International Economy*. New York: Oxford University Press.

Dasgupta, P. (1993), *An Inquiry into Well-Being and Destitution*. Oxford: Clarendon Press.

Jevons, W. S. (1865), *The Coal Question*. London: Macmillan.

Kolm, S-C. (1984), *La Bonne Économie (La Réciprocité générale)*. Paris: Presse Universitaire de France.

Larsen, B., and Shah, A. (1994), 'Global Tradeable Carbon Permits, Participation Incentives and Transfers', *Oxford Economic Papers*, 46: 841–56.

Meadows, D. H., Meadows, D. L., Randers, J., and Behrens, W. H. III (1972), *The Limits to Growth*. New York: Potomac Association.

Nordhaus, W. (1991), 'To Slow or Not to Slow: The Economics of the Greenhouse Effect', *Economic Journal*, 101: 938–48.

Schelling, T. (1992), 'Some Economics of Global Warming', *American Economic Review*, 82/1: 1–14.

Sen, A. (1973), 'Behaviour and the Concept of Preference', Economica, 40 (Aug.): 241–59; repr. in Amartya Sen, *Choice, Welfare and Measurement*. Oxford: Basil Blackwell, 1982.

Sinclair, P. J. N. (1994), 'On the Optimal Trend of Fossil Fuel Taxation', *Oxford Economic Papers*, 46: 869–77.

Squire, L. (1989), 'Project Evaluation in Theory and Practice', in H. Chenery and T. N. Srinivasan (eds.), *Handbook of Development Economics*, vol. ii. Amsterdam: Elsevier Science Publishers.

Ulph, A., and Ulph, D. (1994), 'The Optimal Time Path of a Carbon Tax', *Oxford Economic Papers*, 46: 857–68.

Ulrich, R. S. (1986), 'Human Responses to Vegetation and Landscape', *Landscape and Urban Planning*, 13: 29–44.

5

Combining Employment and Child-Rearing: The Story of British Women's Lives[1]

HEATHER JOSHI

INTRODUCTION

Love and work are two major aspirations of the lives of both men and women. In a traditional stereotype, the gender division of labour would have the men doing paid work, winning the bread for their loved ones, and women busying themselves with unpaid labours of love within the domestic sphere. While this pattern may never have been as widely practised as aspired to, it certainly seems anachronistic now. This chapter examines some evidence about the increasing involvement of women in paid work in Britain over the post-war period, its conflict and conciliation with their domestic role, and its impact on the quality of British life. It focuses on employment at the crucial juncture at which women become mothers.

Motherhood and employment: the general context

We first set the scene by looking briefly at how the combination or conflict of employment and childbearing has appeared as an issue to other writers. Economic development has generally involved a decline in fertility and led to the eclipse of domestic activities by paid ones, transforming opportunities for both men and women in most countries. But the transformation usually affects them differentially.[2] Women's (not

[1] This chapter is part of an ESRC funded project (R000234600), 'Employment after Childbearing'. The assistance of Susan Macran is gratefully acknowledged, as is the permission, by Prof. M. E. J. Wadsworth, to use the MRC National Survey of Health and Development.

[2] See Folbre (1994), for a very wide-ranging survey, Fuchs (1988) and Goldin (1990) for studies of the USA and Stockman *et al.* (1995), for a comparison of China, Japan, Britain, and the USA.

men's) productive and reproductive activities are often regarded as being in conflict. Employment and childbearing have to be traded off, and may be mutually influential.[3]

In the earlier part of the century at least, paid work for women was something to be fitted in with, and inferior to, the roles of wife and mother. More recently, employment has come to be recognized as a lifelong source of identity for women as well as men, and a route to emancipation from women's traditional subordination. The transition is uneven and incomplete. Change has presented a set of tensions and dilemmas. If women

> devote themselves to housework and childcare they are likely to have to assume a subordinate role in a hierarchical marriage . . . and risk divorce leaving them with inadequate skills for earning a living at a paid job. On the other hand, if women seek to compete with men in the labour market, the evidence to date suggests they will have to make substantial sacrifices with respect to marriage and children.[4]

Such tension applies as much to the big decisions in the lives of British women as it does for their American sisters. As we shall see, the manner in which these dilemmas are resolved is far from uniform across countries.

Forms of female subordination have been more susceptible to change than elimination. Feminist ideas have produced a revolution of expectations, if not in the actual structure of social and economic relations between genders. The aims of the women's movement to establish equal rights with those of men have been approached by various strategies. Coote and Campbell state the goal as the elimination of subordination, rather than turning women into surrogate men.[5] Hence, an emphasis on women's rights in the workplace has been criticized as occupying too high a place on the agenda of the US women's movement.[6] It is becoming increasingly apparent that better terms for the combination of paid work and parenthood are needed to improve the quality of life.

It is in this context that the present focus on mothers' employment is an important issue. The spotlight is on the changing experience of British women after childbearing. Though the evidence about the quality of life is fragmentary, it has not so far been brought together with employment in a life-course perspective.

[3] A full review of the literature on social and economic determinants of fertility is not attempted here. See for example: Davis (1984), Willis (1973), Cramer (1980).

[4] Fuchs (1988: 74). [5] Coote and Campbell (1982). [6] Hewlett (1986).

The British context

The growth of the British economy in the twentieth century expanded options facing women as well as men, although in a differentiated fashion. As customers, women on the whole benefited from rising material standards of living, though for many their claim on resources depended at least partially on the recycling of purchasing power within the family. As producers in the paid economy, opportunities for earning cash and self-respect also expanded, though the notion that women's work should be separate from men's persists. Most of the increased female participation in the British economy was in predominantly feminized occupations. Men's jobs remained predominantly segregated as well, both in manual occupations and at the top of many white-collar hierarchies. Responsibility for reproductive, or caring activities also remain primarily with women. The advance of paid work into women's adult lives has had a more complex effect on the quality of those lives than a straightforward move towards prosperity and equality.

In pre-war Britain, marriage was typically the point at which women left paid work for good. In the post-war era it was the arrival of the first child which occasioned withdrawal from paid work, but not for good. Once returning to the labour market became established, the spell away from it tended to shorten. Increasingly, responsibility for younger children has been combined with employment, mostly part-time. Motherhood and employment have ceased to be mutually exclusive options.

While there have been other relevant changes—more education, especially for women; less paid work for men, perhaps some increase in their minor share of domestic work, and increased employment of older women—the employment of women with children is a key feature of the changing division of labour between British men and women, meriting the special focus of this chapter.

Whether or not a woman's employment is expected to be interrupted at motherhood has implications before and after that stage of the lifecycle. It will influence decisions about education and training beforehand, affect when and whether to become a mother, and earnings, promotion, and pension prospects thereafter. During the years when children are young the question arises of what other services provide for their care.

Plan of the chapter

The following section describes the main source of data used in the original analyses presented below—two national birth cohort studies.

Sections 3 and 4 provide information about the extent of employment after childbearing. Section 3 compares the incidence of employment after childbearing in Britain and other industrial countries, and Section 4 takes a closer look at the British life-histories to see how the experience of employment after childbearing has differed across the social spectrum. The quality of life appears in various aspects in Sections 5 to 7, as the consequences of women's employment trends. The impact of women's earnings on material standards of living and economic inequality is addressed in Section 5. The influence on women's health of their employment is reviewed in Section 6. Section 7 presents original data linking life satisfaction to employment status from the National Child Development Study. This study also provides evidence on attitudes and practice of gender equality. The changing role of women in the labour market has important implications for the formation and stability of families. These questions are briefly surveyed in Section 8. The evidence considered is quantitative. Qualitative evidence on the quality of life is beyond the present remit.[7]

To recapitulate, the expansion of educational and employment opportunities, and accompanying changes in attitudes about appropriate behaviour faced British women with choices about whether and how to combine the roles of mother and worker. This chapter attempts to evaluate how far these increased options have affected the quality of their lives.

DATA SOURCES

The main source of original evidence used is the National Child Development Study of the cohort born in a week in March 1958, supplemented with some comparable material on women's life histories from the Medical Research Council's (MRC) National Survey of Health and Development of the cohort born in 1946. The studies are unique to Britain, two out of three multi-purpose national follow-up studies of a week's births. The National Child Development Study (NCDS) cohort born in 1958 was aged 33 at the most recent sweep, in 1991. Further details about the study can be found in a collection of the first findings of the 1991 sweep.[8] Over 17,000 people have at some stage been in contact with NCDS, though the number taking part in the 1991 interview (NCDS5)

[7] For one example of eloquent testimony on the experience of motherhood, from an exceptional selection of women see Gieve (1989).

[8] Ferri (1993).

was 11,407, representing 73 per cent of the target population. Not all of these gave complete information. For example 11 per cent of the 5,799 women interviewed did not fill in the forms on employment and birth history. One-quarter of the remainder had not, by age 33, become mothers. This leaves a sample of 3,894 women born in 1958 known to have had children.

The MRC's National Survey of Health and Development follows up the legitimate singleton births in Britain during a week in March 1946. They are therefore exactly twelve years older than the NCDS cohort.[9] One in four of children from the urban working class, and all of the rest, were followed up, leaving a study size of 5,362 cases from 1946.[10] There have been periodic follow-ups across childhood and into middle age. At age 32 (the latest data available to us) the response rate for women in the target population was 77 per cent. 87 per cent of this cohort had become mothers by that date. This gives a sample of 1,543 women born in 1946 whose employment after childbearing can be followed. We were also able to follow the employment histories of nearly 4,000 mothers of cohort members, month by month over the period 1946 to 1961.[11]

EMPLOYMENT AFTER CHILDBEARING: GENERAL BACKGROUND

The cross-sectional perspective

The proportion of women with paid jobs at any one time has almost doubled in the post-war period.[12] Most of this increase has applied to part-time employment. Full-time employment rose little except at the end of the 1980s. Another closely related feature of the trend has been the disproportionate increase in the paid employment of mothers of dependent children. Their employment rate, probably not more than

[9] See Wadsworth (1991) for full details.

[10] In our analyses, cases have been weighted appropriately.

[11] Not only are dated longitudinal histories relatively rarely collected in large-scale surveys, they also present a challenge in data handling. The employment history data for the 1958 cohort used here depends entirely on the self-completed data reported retrospectively in 1991, as processed by a program written by Elias in 1993. The female employment histories in the NSHD were constructed from a number of instruments, coded and checked by a team working at the London School of Hygiene, using software developed by Ni Bhrolchain and Timaeus (1985).

[12] From around 42 per cent those under 60 in 1951 to 67 per cent in 1991: Joshi (1990*a*); Thomas *et al.* (1994) table 7.7.

one-fifth in 1951, was 26 per cent at the 1961 census and had reached 60 per cent in 1990—roughly a threefold increase over the forty-year period.[13] Fewer of these mothers than other women hold full-time jobs.

The longitudinal perspective

The longitudinal perspective is desirable as it helps to inform the demographic debate which has represented conflict between women's paid work and childbearing without resolving the issue of which causes changes in the other. In the longitudinal perspective the full range of women's work, paid and unpaid, can be considered, whether they are organized sequentially or simultaneously.[14]

It requires longitudinal data to fill out how the familiar statements about cross-sections have been distributed over the life course of individual women. They could in theory have been brought about, for example, by one group of women maintaining continuous full-time employment while an increasingly large group entered part-time employment instead of permanent domesticity. Longitudinal evidence suggests otherwise. By 1980 at least (the time of the Women and Employment Survey) virtually all women under 60 had been in paid work at some time (this was also true in 1990, see Table 5.1).[15] What differed between cohorts was the proportion of time they had been in employment. As the point of exit from the labour market moved forward from marriage to motherhood, it became increasingly common to return. The gaps became shorter, lowering the age of the last child on 're-entry', and closer to the birth of the first child. Employment between births became more common. On the whole the 'returners' took part-time work, from which they sometimes switched back to full-time. The extra experience of part-time work was collected by people who at other times had full-time jobs. The divide between full-time and part-time employment is not a gulf between women devoting an entire lifetime to one type of job or the other.

In the histories reported in 1980, continuous employment broken only by maternity leave was rare.[16] By the end of the 1980s such a pattern did emerge, for a minority, particularly the well qualified.[17] Until this development the practice of leaving employment when children are

[13] This dropped to 59 per cent in 1991. See Joshi and Owen (1988: table 2), Thomas *et al.* (1994: table 7.8).
[14] Kempeneers and Lelievre (1991).
[15] Martin and Roberts (1984).
[16] Dex (1984), Martin and Roberts (1984).
[17] MacRae (1991), Dale and Egerton (1995).

small and resuming on a part-time basis when they are at school seemed the normal experience for British women.

The 'terms of engagement'

Employment could be combined with child-rearing, but it was also severely constrained by it. The presumed responsibility of mothers to be at home whenever their children were entails an interruption of employment, a reduction of hours, status, and earnings on return. For over one-third of re-entrants (in studies spanning the 1950s to 1980) the new job represented a downgrading.[18] Taking a longer perspective, the reduction in gross lifetime earnings can be around half of potential earnings for illustrative cases.[19] Although such earnings opportunity costs to childbearing are substantial, they would be higher if motherhood and paid work were entirely incompatible. Part-time jobs in Britain were, largely, created in order to enable women to combine their domestic responsibilities with the demands of the labour market. The combination of employment and child-rearing is a compromise. Woman's place in the home has not been fundamentally challenged, her place in the labour market has been fitted around it.

An international perspective

The 'normal' pattern of the British compromise is not a universal arrangement. Part-time employment is more common for mothers in Britain than in many other countries, and in the Scandinavian countries where part-time jobs are also common, they are normally for longer hours and on better terms than those offered in Britain. A great variety of patterns of combining employment and motherhood are reported in OECD *Employment Outlook 1988*. In the USA, as in France and Belgium for example, women's employment histories have tended to polarize between those who stay in paid work more or less continuously and those who never, or seldom, take paid work.[20] In the history of American women's particiation, the marriage bar has dominated the motherhood bar.[21] The marriage bar also remained effective in Australia for longer than in Britain.[22]

Longitudinal summaries of women's life histories to date were collected in the then twelve countries of the European Community in

[18] Dex (1987), Joshi and Newell (1987), Joshi and Hinde (1993).

[19] Davies and Joshi (1995), Joshi (1990b).

[20] Dex and Shaw (1986), Dex *et al.* (1993).

[21] Goldin (1990).

[22] Heitlinger (1993).

1990.[23] Some features are presented in Table 5.1. The columns show respectively the cross-sectional employment rate of women across the age range 22 to 60, then the proportion who had ever entered paid work, generally rather higher. The third column reports those with roughly speaking continuous careers, interrupted by no more than twelve months at any one time, from which can be inferred the fourth percentage, that of women with a discontinuous employment record (including those who had left and had not, so far, returned). Among the latter, column 5 records those whose main reason for their longest employment interruption is given as bringing up children. Among mothers, the proportion who stayed out of employment while their first child was under school age is reported in column 6. The rows of the tables are arranged in groups of countries identified by the authors of the report. Denmark is the sole representative of Scandinavia, with high rates of participation throughout the child-rearing cycle. Eastern Germany represents the state of affairs in one of the formerly communist regimes of Eastern Europe. In this case too, participation is currently high, near universal (at some stage) and fairly continuous, though leave around childbearing is often taken for more than twelve months. France and Belgium are distinct as having relatively high proportions of women with continuous employment, but also as having appreciable numbers with no or minimal contact with the labour market, tending towards a bi-polar pattern. The same polarity is discernible in various guises in the countries of southern Europe, where current levels of participation are low and lifetime non-participation relatively common. Among the remaining countries in the north of the European Community, apart from Britain, participation at some point in the lifetime is high, but current rates are not. West Germany has above average incidence of interrupted histories, and the majority of mothers there, in the Netherlands, Luxembourg, and Ireland had not been employed while their oldest child was too young for school.

Against these patterns, the British experience stands in contrast. Employment at some point is near universal, as in Denmark and East Germany, but continuous employment is less common than in any other country. Employment interruptions associated with child-rearing are matched only in East Germany, where the gaps involved were much shorter. While children are given as the reason for interrupting employment by a majority of British women with a break, in most other countries other reasons (often employment or marriage related) account for

[23] Kempeneers and Lelievre (1991).

TABLE 5.1. *International comparisons of employment history summaries (women aged 22–60 in twelve European countries, 1990)*

	% of all women employed				% of breaks for child-rearing	% of mothers not employed 1st preschool child
	Currently (1)	Ever (2)	No gap over 1 year (3)	At least one gap (4)	(5)	(6)
Europe 12	50	83	49	33	44	52
Denmark	73	97	64	33	34	24
East Germany	78	99	42	58	60	19
Belgium	55	84	60	23	36	39
France	59	86	54	32	43	41
Greece	38	62	42	20	35	45
Spain	35	63	46	18	36	60
Italy	39	67	50	16	33	43
Portugal	47	63	51	12	22	29
West Germany	52	92	50	42	36	64
Luxembourg	38	88	63	25	*	71
Netherlands	38	86	63	23	48	76
Ireland	34	87	58	29	45	74
Great Britain	59	96	39	57	59	61

* small sample.

Source: Eurobarometer 34: Employment and Family within the Twelve (Kempeneers and Lelievre 1991); col. 1: table 6, cols. 2–4: table 23, col. 5: table 27, col. 6: table 34. Col. 5 reports the main reason given for their longest gap by those who have one; Col. 6 reports the proportion of mothers with no employment in pre-school years of first child.

Sample size 8,449 interviews in the twelve countries, less than 1,000 in any one. Percentages are based only on valid responses, which varied by question.

more than half the cases. In most countries other than the north European neighbours, mothers are more likely to have combined rearing a pre-school child with a paid job. The longitudinal data are essential to reveal the existence of employment interruptions. They also reveal that the link of the employment gap with childbearing is less well established in many countries than in Britain.

Public policies on social protection, employment rights, taxation, maternity leave, and, particularly subsidized day-care help, account for these differences, alongside cultural and structural features which they may reflect.[24] Such policies, in which there is no uniformity, facilitate mothers' employment, and reduce the earnings they forgo.[25] The state is not the only agency facilitating mothers' employment. In the USA, the private sector labour market is an important source of child care, while the extended family, particularly grandmothers, plays a role particularly in southern Europe. The nuclear family is also not unknown as a source of care. Fathers are officially encouraged to participate in the care of children, particularly in Sweden. Although Britain remains one of the few countries without some statutory allowance for parental leave, fathers provide an important, though limited, source of care for British children whose mothers work part-time.

Day care

The 'typical' British pattern is constrained by the day care available as a by-product of the school system (mothers are not expected to provide the midday meal, as in Germany). In contrast to most other European countries, there is little subsidized provision for children under five (or out of school hours). Given the low wages of most women, few can afford to purchase formal child care, e.g. from child minders or nannies. Most employed mothers make informal arrangements (e.g. with their partners, mothers, or neighbours), to supplement school care.[26]

Rates of pay

Evidence that mothers in the cohort were paid (even) more badly than other women was reported by Waldfogel and confirmed by Paci and Joshi.[27] Part of this penalty results from many mothers being confined

[24] Gustafsson (1994), Gustafsson and Stafford (1994), Heitlinger (1993), Folbre (1994).

[25] Joshi and Davies (1992).

[26] Ward and colleagues describe child-care arrangements made by the employed mothers in the 1958 cohort, and give further references (Ward *et al.* 1996).

[27] Waldfogel (1993); Paci and Joshi (1996).

to the low-paid part-time sector. Among those in full-time jobs, mothers were at a disadvantage compared to their childless equivalents unless they had taken advantage of maternity leave to maintain employment continuity.

VARIATION IN THE EMPLOYMENT GAPS OF THREE COHORTS OF WOMEN

The national cohort studies provide the opportunity to compare different experiences of the job gap after childbearing within three groups of women becoming mothers in different decades of the post-war era. Because they provide micro-data, differences between women at each point can also be compared, to look for influences of, for example, a woman's education or her partner's socio-economic status.

Dimensions of the data

The three groups of women are: the mothers of the 1946, birth cohort, women born in 1946, and women born in 1958. The first group, all giving birth to a child at the same time, March 1946, were followed until that child reached 15 in 1961. The second group, their daughters, themselves become mothers mostly in the late 1960s (in their early twenties), and faced the possibility of returning to employment mainly during the 1970s. Our information on their histories stops around the end of 1977, close to their thirty-second birthday. Typically we can follow their experience of combining motherhood and employment for about ten years. The third group of women are the female members of the 1958 birth cohort, followed to age 33. They tended to become mothers a bit later than the previous cohort. Half of the women born in 1946 had become mothers by age 23 (1969), compared to age 26 (1974) for the women born in 1958. This means just under nine years of follow-up available on average. By the last contact, fewer of the 1958 cohort had become mothers at all (75 per cent at 33) compared to the 1946 cohort (87 per cent mothers at 32), though it cannot be assumed yet that there will be a lower eventual level of parenthood. Some first births may still be postponed.

A very crude index of how the experience of employment after childbearing has changed on average for these groups of women is to measure how many had recorded any paid work at all during the period they can be followed as mothers. For the mothers giving birth in 1946 altogether, the proportion with any paid job over 15 years was 63 per cent; for those where the survey child was their last, the proportion was 69 per cent. For women born in 1946, returning to the labour market in the 1970s, the percentage ever employed since their *first* birth was 57 per cent (in around ten years), and for those born in 1958 the proportion who had ever had employment in around nine years of motherhood was 80 per cent.

Survival analysis

These indicators are unsatisfactory because they do not allow for the varying lengths of exposure. A more satisfactory technique is to measure duration in a life-table, which can allow for all exposure to be counted up to the point where follow-up ceases, whether this be at the latest interview, or, in the case of the NSHD at an earlier dropout.[28] The median gap given by a survival analysis of women having their last child in 1946 was 8 years 1 month, i.e. half these mothers had been in paid work at some time before April 1954 when their youngest child was just over 8.[29] For the next generation, themselves born in 1946, the median break after the first birth was 5 years 10 months, i.e. at a time when their eldest child had reached school age, but before any younger child did. For the women born in 1958, the median gap between first birth and next job was down to 2 years 5 months—an indication that employment while children are under school age is becoming the norm rather than the reverse. The typical British solution to the combining of employment and child-rearing may be becoming historically as well as geographically unique.

Social correlates

The histories also reveal that the speed of return to paid work varied substantially for different social groups, and that the experience of change in this respect was uneven. For mothers who bore their last child in 1946, differences were particularly marked by region and the occupation of the woman's husband. The median gap for women living in Wales or married to husbands who were employers, self-employed, or professional was fifteen years or more, in contrast to just over five years

[28] See Macran *et al.* (1996). [29] Joshi and Hinde (1993: table 2).

for those resident in the textile-producing North-west region or married to husbands with unskilled manual occupations.[30] Variations by the woman's own occupational status and educational status appeared to be counter to the expectation that women with higher earning power should take up employment sooner.

Analysis showed some positive effect of women's earning power, but a dominant effect of higher social class of husband inhibiting the propensity to resume employment. An analysis of the propensity to resume employment after a first birth and before a second was performed for the two generations in the 1946 cohort study. The second generation had an average probability of entry to employment three times as great as the previous one. The models accounted for about half the change. Part of it was due to a shift of composition towards women with attributes likely to raise their earning power, but the most striking result was the diminution in the inhibiting effects of living in certain regions or with higher status husbands. These results reflect the reduction, between the 1950s and early 1970s, in regional industrial specialization, and a weakening of the inhibiting effect of family income on female labour supply.

The latest evidence

The analysis, to date, on the third set of mothers, born in 1958, having children in the 1980s suggests that the importance of the woman's own earning power in accelerating employment after childbearing has continued to increase. The employment histories after childbearing of the previous, 1946, cohort varied little by their own educational attainment (at the bivariate level). The proportions having entered employment within five years are all within a few points of the overall 45 per cent. Similarly, with the exception of one subgroup (28 per cent A-level or higher non-degree), the proportions in employment after one year are all around 20 per cent. Because they tend to start childbearing later, those with better qualifications tend not to be followed for so long. This is more of a severe problem for the 1958 cohort, with their later pattern of childbearing. We focus on educational differentials after the first year. Nearly two-thirds (65 per cent) of the graduates had been in paid work within their first child's first year compared to little more than one-quarter (28 per cent) of the women with no qualifications. Each educational group in the 1958 cohort has a higher chance of having been

[30] Joshi and Hinde (1993).

employed at this stage than the women of equivalent attainment in the previous cohort, but the change is much greater for the highly qualified. In other words, alongside the upward trend, differentials by woman's education have opened up dramatically.

Qualifications and age at motherhood are highly correlated in the 1958 cohort, indeed many of the best qualified women had not yet even had a child by age 33. When we examined the patterns of entry to employment of women born into the 1946 and 1958 cohorts we found a similarly uneven distribution of the changed employment propensity. Women who had become mothers as teenagers, whether before 1966 or before 1978, followed a very similar pathway back into employment. Among those who became mothers at ages 20 to 24, the more recent cohort was less than a year ahead in the process of returning to employment. It was only among those who became mothers between age 25 and 30 that the gap opened up, or around five years at the median. For those who became mothers after age 30 in 1946, 14 per cent had been in employment one year later. For those who became mothers after a thirtieth birthday in 1988, the figure was 61 per cent. The 1958 cohort's employment records have been both genuinely and artificially boosted by the spread of maternity leave during the 1980s.[31]

This pattern in the trend by age at motherhood prompted us to ask whether the whole cohort had indeed taken up a shift differentiating them from their predecessors, or whether those in the 1958 cohort who had come late to motherhood just happened to get caught up in an economically propitious period. In the late 1980s the demand for female labour was running high, and there was some press speculation of an impending 'Demographic Time Bomb' due to the falling birth-rate. 'Family friendly' policies to retain mothers in jobs and attract them back were being pioneered by some leading employers. These included enhancements of statutory maternity leave, career break schemes, flexi-time, job-sharing, work-place nurseries, and child care vouchers.[32] To test this hypothesis we compared our results with those of the Policy Studies Institute Maternity Rights Survey taken in 1988.[33] This revealed similar age-at-motherhood effects within the 1988 period. Indeed we found that women who became teenage mothers in 1988 were less attached to the labour market than those from the 1958 cohort. Thus the age and educational differentials found within the 1958 cohort are not

[31] See McRae (1991), and Macran *et al.* (1996), for details.
[32] Brannen *et al.* (1994). [33] McRae (1991).

just an outcome of labour market trends during the 1980s. As MacRae also concurs,[34] there has been a growing polarization among families embarking on child-rearing: on the one hand highly educated couples, both employed full-time, and purchasing child care to maintain this life-style whenever they eventually have children, and on the other, women with no partners (or partners without jobs), and no qualifications, who start childbearing a lot earlier. Such women seldom maintain continuous full-time employment, and generally take part-time work when they do return to the labour market. For such women the labour market in the 1980s was not so very different from what it was in the 1970s, although the chances of belonging to a no-earner partnership probably increased for the age group of concern here, as it did among the population at large.[35]

IMPLICATIONS FOR INEQUALITY

The distribution of income between families

Both the analyses of employment patterns, around the 1950s and the 1970s, suggest that socially differentiated patterns in employment after childbearing would tend to bring disproportionately more second earners into families in the higher part of the income distribution. This is among the forces of polarization noted above. Whatever the changes in the distribution of income among families with children may have been, other changes have also occurred. Studies of the income distribution of the population at large have found a net equalizing impact of increased female earnings. Harkness and colleagues find that, over the period 1979–91, family income inequality growth among couples aged 24–55 would have been higher in the absence of female earnings.[36] They also find, along with others, that female earnings have an important impact in preventing poverty.[37]

Nevertheless women remain over-represented among the poor, at a rate which has fluctuated during the period 1971 to 1991.[38] On the question of where women are placed relative to men on the household income distribution, the conclusion is that there has been a move

[34] McRae (1993). [35] Gregg and Wadsworth (1994).
[36] Harkness *et al.* (1995). [37] e.g. Davies and Joshi (1994*a*).
[38] Jenkins and O'Leary (1994).

in the direction of income equality for women, but that the progress is limited.

Within-family distribution

Such statements about the income distribution depend upon the conventional assumption that couples pool their income.[39] The distribution of welfare within households remains a mystery to quantitative social science, but the individual sources of couples' incomes can be identified. This is of interest since it can be presumed that the greater a woman's contribution to cash income the greater her independence, subjectively and objectively speaking. In a detailed study of the women in the 1958 cohort who had partners in 1991, the concepts and evidence are reviewed.[40]

Women whose contribution to family finances was similar to or larger than their partners were a surprisingly small minority, around one-tenth of the sample each. Nearly half of those bringing in more cash than their partners had partners with no job. The 'equal contributors' were largely employed full-time, both with and without children. Part-time employment was seldom enough to put the woman on an equal parity with her partner, though half the part-timers earned enough to put them over the subsistence threshold represented by the Income Support Scale. Married mothers without jobs had the minimal resource of child benefit received in their own right. We concluded that the vast majority of these women were partially dependent on sharing income with their husbands for current and long-term financial security.

The presence of children did not automatically imply the women made a minor contribution to the family finances. Nearly half the mothers who worked full-time made a major or equal contribution. The 'equal contributors' among them were generally well qualified and used formal child care. Other correlations of high contributions to the couple's budget were having an uninterrupted employment record, not being formally married to her partner, or having had previous partners. In the analysis of employment after childbearing, those who had been cohabiting rather than legally married at the time of their first birth also showed a stronger attachment to the labour force than married or single mothers. Those whose relationships are arguably less secure appeared to be making

[39] Critically reviewed by Jenkins (1991).

[40] The vast majority (nine out of ten) of these were actually legally married. Joshi *et al.* (1995).

themselves less reliant on a domestic division of labour and a continuing commitment.

Lone mothers

Lone mothers in the 1958 cohort, both those who had no partner at the time their first child was born, or who had parted company with their children's father by 1991, had low participation in employment (around one-third in 1991 compared to nearly two-thirds of the partnered mothers). This comparison is typical of late 1980s and early 1990s, and low incomes are the consequence.[41] With no partners to 'depend' on most were dependent on state benefits to provide enough income to 'get by'.[42]

IMPLICATIONS FOR THE QUALITY OF LIFE: THE HEALTH OF THE 'WORKING MOTHER'

If earning her own income provides the typical British mother with vital though limited cash resources, what about non-pecuniary impact of employment on the quality of life? One hypothesis is that it is detrimental. The 'double burden' of paid and unpaid work creates 'role overload', stress harmful to health and life satisfaction. Another is that the accumulation of roles is life and health-enhancing. Reviewing the literature, Macran found that on the whole there was more evidence for the employment of mothers benefiting their health than harming it.[43] In empirical research there remain problems of sorting out cause and effect, the selection of women who would anyway have poor health out of paid work, and indeed motherhood.

Macran's review formed part of a research programme on social inequalities in the health of British women which also undertook its own empirical investigations into the health aspects of mother's employment. Weatherall looked for an association of the double burden with premature mortality, using the vital registration-census link in the OPCS Longitudinal Study.[44] Following married women with and without children and with and without paid jobs in 1971, we found each factor, taken separately, was associated with better survival prospects over fifteen years. The hypothesis of an effect of *combining* employment and motherhood was tested in our multivariate models by looking for an interaction of the two 'effects'. None was found. We concluded that there was

[41] Thomas *et al.* (1994). [42] Joshi *et al.* (1995). [43] Macran (1993).
[44] Weatherall *et al.* (1994).

no evidence in the mortality follow-up for an adverse effect of mothers' 'going out to work'. Other factors were much more important in generating mortality inequalities, factors connected with the household's material resources as a whole.

Similar conclusions emerge from our analysis of the health and morbidity of living women.[45] Of various dimensions of health recorded in the Health and Lifestyle Survey, we found an inventory of 'psycho-social' malaise and the respondent's assessment of her own health were most systematically associated with socio-economic factors including low household income.[46] Motherhood and employment taken separately were each again associated with better health. Tests for an intensification or reduction of the 'effects' when the two are combined found none among married mothers (as in the mortality analyses).

Among lone mothers, who were not numerous enough in 1971 to enter the mortality study, there was some indication of role strain. We found, all else equal, lower psycho-social health (e.g. greater tiredness) among lone mothers with full-time paid jobs. Being a breadwinner while bringing up children alone may present greater problems than those with which married mothers cope.

From these and other studies reviewed by Brannen and Graham, the dominant correlate of poor health is poverty.[47] This applies to the health of children and their fathers as well as mothers. To the extent that the employment of mothers keeps families out of financial hardship it is helping to maintain living standards and the quality of their families' lives. It does not look as if the unpaid time which has been diverted into the labour market by post-war trends has been diverted from essential human maintenance activities in the home.[48] These are maintained, even by mothers with full-time jobs, and perhaps more easily with than without the cash resources which the employment brings.

IMPLICATIONS FOR THE QUALITY OF LIFE: EVIDENCE FROM NCDS

The NCDS has not yet been put to full use in exploring the consequences of domestic and market work for health or the quality of life.

[45] Macran *et al.* (1996).

[46] This is not to say that such variables explained a very great deal of the variance in any of the health indicators examined.

[47] Brannen *et al.* (1994), and Graham (1993).

[48] This hypothesis would repay further investigation with time-budget data.

This chapter presents some preliminary analyses of material collected in 1991 about the cohort members' attitudes to life, work, and family, in relation to their current position as mothers, partners, and workers.[49] This is taken from a self-completion schedule entitled 'What Do You Think?' which was returned by nearly 11,000 men and women in the study. A more comprehensive report of the range of questions asked can be found in the NCDSV sourcebook.[50]

Gender equality in principle and practice

As might be thought to befit a generation who were still children in the 1960s, the cohort on the whole endorsed the idea of equality between men and women. There was near unanimous agreement about equality of access to labour market opportunities. Men were slightly less enthusiastic than women about the need to increase the number of women in top jobs. There was almost as strong endorsement for the principle of equal division of labour in the home, 69 per cent of the cohort agreeing that 'men and women should do the same jobs around the house'.

While opinion on traditional gender roles seems to have been fairly widely 'reconstructed', this was far less true of practice. The employed women in the cohort were worse paid than the men, even when similarly qualified and allowing for differences in labour market experience. This applies even to childless women in full-time jobs, but most strongly in the case of part-time jobs, mostly held by mothers.[51] The same study finds that the cohort experienced the prevailing pattern of occupational segregation. Especially if employed part-time, the women mostly did 'women's jobs'. Our parallel study of the hourly earnings of the 1946 cohort at age 32 indicate that unequal treatment within full-time jobs had been worse in 1978, but that this improvement for women was somewhat offset by deteriorating pay conditions for part-timers.[52] The differences in labour market opportunities for men and women underpinned the generally minor contributions made by women in couples to joint income even in the 1958 cohort.[53]

On the actual division of unpaid work in the home, those with partners were asked of a number of specified tasks whether they were shared

[49] A complete investigation should use multivariate techniques and data from more than one point in time.

[50] Wiggins and Bynner (1993).

[51] Paci and Joshi (1996).

[52] Dale and Egerton (1995) confirm gender inequality in the weekly earnings of full-timers.

[53] Joshi *et al.* (1995).

equally, mainly done by the cohort member, or by their partner.[54] Equal sharing of household chores, which had been endorsed by 93 per cent of the cohort for a hypothetical couple with two full-time jobs, was a minority practice, even for actual dual full-time earners. A gendered division of unpaid labour was clearly apparent, with women being mainly responsible for most tasks. Around three-quarters of women, survey members or survey members' wives alike, do most of the cooking, shopping, cleaning, laundry. Exceptions are that men are mainly responsible for house maintenance, and play a relatively less minor role in child-rearing. The minority of couples sharing their tasks equally is biggest where both have full-time jobs and roughly equal incomes.[55]

Life satisfaction

On the whole, most of the 33-year-old women in 1991 were doing most of the unpaid work in the home, even when they had full-time paid jobs. The question of the 'double burden' of domestic and market work does indeed arise. Does it harm or enhance mothers' quality of life? Tables 5.2 and 5.3 can begin to suggest the answer, though they cannot strictly unravel the direction of causation. As the data were all collected at the same time, an association could in theory reflect either a life-enhancing effect of employment (for whatever reason) or a greater difficulty of those who were unhappy (for whatever reason) in finding or retaining employment. The British Household Panel Study, with a measure of life satisfaction at two points in time,[56] suggests that there are genuine effects from employment on the 'happiness', and particularly an impact of becoming unemployed on morale.[57]

One representative source of evidence on the morale of the 33-year-olds surveyed in the fifth sweep of the National Child Development Study is the response to an overall rating of how they felt about their lives so far, summarized in Table 5.2. Characteristically, the question produces a fairly up-beat and positive response amongst most people. The average for all women, 7.5 out of 10, is just a shade ahead of the average for men. Among men, the lack of a job made a more than

[54] A fourth option, that they were mainly done by someone else, was offered, but seldom mentioned. The exceptions were very minor: 3 per cent for cleaning the home and 5 per cent for household repairs.

[55] See Joshi *et al.* (1995), and Dale and Egerton (1995).

[56] Life satisfaction was measured by the GHQ inventory of psycho-social health, an instrument similar to that in the Health and Lifestyle Survey used by Macran *et al.* (forthcoming). Although such a set of questions is also available in NCDS5, they are not included in the present analyses.

[57] Corti (1994).

TABLE 5.2. *How do you feel about the way your life has turned out so far? (Scores out of 10 (= completely satisfied): women and men aged 33 in 1991)*

	Women			Men		
	Mean	SD	N	Mean	SD	N
All	7.5	1.7	5,461	7.3	1.6	5,156
Employed	7.5	1.6	3,745	7.4	1.5	4,695
Not employed	7.5	1.8	1,716	6.2	2.3	461
Full-time job, no child	7.4	1.5	1,068			
Part-time job, no child	7.7	1.3	91			
Full-time job + child	7.5	1.8	909			
Part-time job + child	7.6	1.6	1,677			
Not employed + child	7.5	1.8	1,610			
Not employed + no child	6.8	2.0	106			
Employed + partner employed	7.8	1.5	2,852	7.6	1.4	2,505
Employed + partner not employed	7.2	1.8	157	7.7	1.4	1,337
Not employed + partner employed	7.9	1.6	1,254	7.1	1.9	55
Neither partner employed	6.9	2.0	203	6.5	2.3	165
No partner, employed	6.6	1.9	720	6.5	1.8	888
No partner, not employed	5.8	2.4				
Women with no partners						
job, no child	6.9	1.7	473			
job, child	5.9	2.3	247			
no job, no child	6.3	2.1	50			
no job, child	5.6	2.5	202			

Note: The third panel omits cases where a partner's employment status is not known.

Source: National Child Development Study.

just statistically significant difference (6.2 versus 7.4 in favour of the employed). There was no such marked contrast between women in and out of employment—if anything, it was those with part-time jobs who appeared the happiest.

The next panel of Table 5.2 looks for an interaction between parenthood, employment, and life-satisfaction for women. There was little noticeable variation among the men by whether or not they had children. Among the women, life satisfaction is marginally (and, given the

TABLE 5.3. *Selected responses about work: women and men aged 33 in 1991*

	Women			Men		
	Mean	SD	N	Mean	SD	N
A person must have a job to be a full member of society[a]						
All	3.5	1.0	5,516	3.0	1.2	5,217
Employed	3.4	1.0	3,787	3.0	1.2	4,747
Not employed	3.6	1.1	1,729	3.0	1.3	470
My work is monotonous because I always do the same thing[a]						
All	3.5	1.3	5,477	3.9	1.2	5,135
Employed	—	—	—	4.0	1.1	4,743
full-time	3.9	1.2	2,010	—	—	—
part-time	3.5	1.3	1,776	—	—	—
Not employed	2.9	1.3	1,592	3.5	1.3	392
children, not employed	2.9	1.3	1,592	—	—	—
no children, not employed	3.0	1.2	99	—	—	—
lone mothers, not employed	2.7	3.0	206	—	—	—
Number of skills rated good but unused in present work						
Employed	—	—	—	0.7	1.1	4,266
full-time	0.7	1.1	1,725	—	—	—
part-time	1.2	1.3	1,500	—	—	—
Not employed	1.7	1.3	1,412	—	—	—
Full-time job, no children	0.6	1.0	940	—	—	—
Full-time job + children	0.8	1.2	785	—	—	—
Part-time job, no children	1.0	1.2	74	—	—	—
Part-time job + children	1.2	1.3	1,426	—	—	—
Not employed no children	0.9	1.3	79	—	—	—
Not employed + children	1.8	1.3	1,333	—	—	—

[a] Average of scores 1 to 5. Strong disagreement = 5, uncertain = 3, strong agreement = 1.

Note: The sample size (N) varies with the numbers giving valid responses to each question.

Source: National Child Development Study.

large sample size, statistically significantly) higher, if they have a paid job rather than none, but the differences by parenthood are not significant. The small increment associated with employment is much the same whether or not the woman is a mother. As in the studies quoted earlier, both parenthood and paid work have positive associations with well-being, but there is little sign of their combination enhancing or overloading roles.

The large sample size of the NCDS also permits an exploration for different patterns within subgroups, and in particular mothers without partners, who are often too small a minority in national cross-sections to provide much evidence. When the above analysis was repeated separately for women with and without partners, the mostly married group displayed the same lack of pattern by motherhood and employment, but those for women without partners are shown separately. For them, like unpartnered men, life satisfaction scores are one point or more below their partnered counterparts, and the pattern of response by motherhood and employment status is different. There is no longer any (significant) positive association between paid work and life satisfaction, and the presence of children is associated with lower morale. It is perhaps no surprise that lone mothers report less satisfaction than single women without children or married mothers. Lone mothers are often living in poverty, and rearing their children single-handed. What is particularly noteworthy for present purposes is that here there does seem to be some sign of role overload: children more of a burden than a boon, and particularly for lone mothers with jobs. This finding corresponds to the particularly poor psycho-social health of employed lone mothers found in the Health and Lifestyle Survey.[58] Nevertheless the lowest life satisfaction reported by women was by lone mothers *out* of employment, who are almost entirely dependent upon Income Support. Their average score of 5.6 corresponds to that of unpartnered men with no job, also likely to be surviving on a minimal benefit income. Although the age at entry to motherhood did not in general show much difference in the average life-satisfaction scores, amongst non-employed current lone mothers, reported satisfaction rose with age at entry into motherhood, from 5.2 for those who had become mothers as teenagers to 5.8 to those whose first child was born since the mother was 28.

For the majority of women with partners, it was not so much their

[58] Macran *et al.* (1996). In the case of the Health and Lifestyle Survey, the interaction detected was with full-time employment, in this case part-time jobs were also involved.

own employment as that of these partners which showed variation in reported life satisfaction, as shown in the third panel of Table 5.2. Women with employed partners scored life satisfaction at 7.8, an average which was barely affected by their own employment status, but if their husband was not employed the average dropped to 7.0. Women who were in no-earner partnerships scored 6.9 and men 6.5. Men's satisfaction scores did not vary significantly by their partner's employment.

Doubtless life satisfaction is drawn from a number of sources, but these patterns in life satisfaction reveal the broad contours of the variation in the cohort in the earning of material resources, and their importance for the men and the single women. The insignificance of wives' earnings for men could reflect its relatively small revenue in most cases, or a reluctance of husbands to acknowledge whatever is brought in by their partner, but it could also reveal that a man's satisfaction is in being himself the earner. To explore this issue further, consider a few of the responses given by the NCDS cohort to questions about their orientation to work.

Attitudes about work

One of the items about the importance placed on employment was to ask the respondents whether they agreed that 'a person must have a job to be a full member of society' (Table 5.3). The men's average was 3.0, ambivalent on balance, despite the importance of employment for their own satisfaction alleged above. In support of employment being more important for men is the women's score, 3.5, half a point closer to disagreement. There was no difference on average between those who did and did not have jobs, nor by their parental or partnership status.

Questions about the intrinsic interest in work, may give a further clue to the link between employment, children, and life satisfaction among the cohort. Questions about 'your work' were not only addressed to those in paid work. Those who were out of employment but occupied full-time in housework or child care were asked to treat this as their job, but it is hard to say how far these instructions were actually heeded. Response to 'My work is monotonous because I keep doing the same thing', also recorded on the 5-point scale, is shown in Table 5.3. Men in jobs fairly definitely disagreed that the work was monotonous. Women in full-time jobs came close to their male counterparts, but women in part-time jobs were significantly less inclined to deny monotony. Women without paid jobs were closer to agreeing that their (unpaid) work was monotonous (2.9). Within the group whose work was in the domestic sphere, there was little difference by presence of children. Lone mothers without jobs tended most towards finding their unpaid work monotonous. Thus the work performed by mothers tends to be tedious particularly if it is a domestic routine, and also if it is a part-time job on the labour market. On the other hand cohort members in full-time jobs, be they mothers, other women, or men, tended not to find their work monotonous.

The relative lack of intrinsic interest in part-time jobs accords with their low occupational status.[59] Part-time employment is more frequently offered in low skill activities than in those of higher status and responsibility. Women frequently accept jobs below their qualifications and capabilities in order to work part-time, if only for a few years while responsibility for children dictates. The questions asked of the cohort about their skills and how well they were used in their current work (defined as above), are therefore relevant. They were asked about fifteen specified skills. We count skills which were rated good but not currently used (Table 5.3). The average for men and women employed full-time was 0.7, less than one per person. As expected, more underutilized good skills were reported by women in part-time jobs, 1.2 on average. The greatest occurrence of underutilized skills was 1.8 per mother not in paid work. Boredom and underutilization of skills appear to go together, and they appear to be more of a problem for mothers who stick to unpaid work than for those who combine it with employment, particularly full-time. The more remunerative work is also more likely to have non-pecuniary rewards.

Attitudes to marriage

Life satisfaction was associated with the existence of a partnership as well as a job. The security of the marital contract also affects whether it is wise or risky for a woman to specialize in the domestic role.[60] Wiggins and Bynner[61] report several themes amongst NCDS5 responses on marriage and the family: support for traditional values (e.g. 60 per cent agreeing that 'marriage is for life'), alongside permissiveness about family life (e.g. 85 per cent agreeing that people can have a satisfying relationship without children) and another vein which acknowledges advantages outside family life (this includes, for example, the item, 'being single

[59] See Paci and Joshi (1996). [60] See Joshi and Davies (1996).
[61] Wiggins and Bynner (1993).

provides fewer worries or responsibilities'—55 per cent agree). There was mild disagreement to the proposition that marriage gives you economic security.[62] On the whole the cohort feel that marriage ought to be a lifelong partnership, but deviations are often tolerated.

There was some, perhaps greater, commitment expressed towards children than partners.[63] There was, however, little variation by employment or partnership status in the family attitude items. This means that the women combining child-rearing and employment, whether full- or part-time, were not systematically different from those who stayed at home as far as their views about family obligations were concerned.

It therefore seems that attitudes about family relationships are formed by broader forces, not just formed, if at all, by individual experience. Some links are apparent between work, paid and unpaid, and life satisfaction.

IMPLICATION FOR FAMILY TRENDS

A complete review of the consequences of labour market change for mothers would trace the feedback from labour market opportunities into trends in family formation and dissolution, but this is not attempted here. As has been said, fertility decline, growing marital instability, and more employment of women are 'all of a piece'.[64] The trend in jobs could inhibit family formation and facilitate family fission. That motherhood is not entirely incompatible with employment, as discussed here, may help explain why fertility in Britain has not fallen as much as it has elsewhere, in Germany for example.

Fertility rates have nevertheless fallen, with the postponement of the first birth being a major element in the drop in births in the 1970s. As illustrated by the 1958 cohort, the deferring of childbearing has been socially selective, women with the highest earning power being most affected. Change in the terms on which employment and childbearing can be combined is likely to affect the number and timing of these

[62] Women in particular were marginally less likely to disagree. It may be that further analyses will yet bring a clear pattern to the surface from under the cross-currents, or it may be that the economic functions of marriage were not its salient feature, or at least that it is not respectable to emphasize them.

[63] In response to the statement, 'people should consider the needs of children as more important than their own', cohort members who were themselves parents on the whole agreed (on the 1 to 4 disagreement scale, mothers scored 2.5 and fathers 2.3).

[64] Ermisch (1990).

births. The full analysis of the fertility behaviour of the cohort has yet to be carried out, and also that of their family dissolution.

For all the opportunities theoretically offered by the labour market to facilitate family break-up, and single parenthood, in practice few women seemed to be reaping great advantage. Typically, the lone mothers were living on the breadline, trapped by the rules of the state benefit system, the lack of affordable child care and possibly deterred by the practical and health problems encountered by breadwinning sole mothers. Their low standards of living were reflected in low life satisfaction, but had not as yet acted as much of a deterrent to the formation of more lone mother families.

CONCLUSIONS

The standard way British women reconcile employment and child-rearing is to take them in sequence. This characteristically British broken employment pattern is internationally, and perhaps historically, unique. Its development over time has also been socially differentiated, convergence giving way to divergence as middle-class mothers overtook the rest in speed of 'return to work'. By the 1990s, we see social polarization between continuous careers among the most advantaged women, and exclusion from the labour market of the least. Between a mass of ordinary folk entering childbearing in their twenties, sharp distinctions emerge between teenaged mothers, seldom employed, and 'elderly primagravidae', coming to motherhood after 30, utilizing maternity leave and maintaining full-time employment records. The middle ground is characterized by mothers working part-time, and mainly dependent for day care on the school system. Such women are typically only minor contributors of earnings to the family budget. The least prosperous mothers, and those least satisfied with their lives, are out of employment, living with an unemployed man or no partner at all.

The economic benefits of the increased female employment and output are largely felt in the secondary earnings of two-earner families. For a minority, recently, it has also involved gains in more equally matched dual-full-time-earner couples. There are also positive impacts on female self-esteem, and perhaps improved health, access to workplace companionship, economic autonomy, and the social status of women. Such gains are moderate for most but considerable for a minority. The impact on the distribution of income of these trends is complex, in the long term it depends on the solidarity and permanence of conjugal partnerships.

There may be a negative effect on unpaid output, e.g. quality of child care, that may have been sacrificed to the increased labour supplied to the market, but there is little evidence on relevant variables such as trends in leisure, productivity of home time, or the 'quality' of children by mother's employment. New opportunities on the labour market may also have affected the number and timing of births. Gains in either material or qualitative terms have not been evenly spread.

Though opportunities for women may have improved over the long run, they remain inferior to those facing men. The latter feature tends to perpetuate the traditional division of domestic labour, the former may reinforce trends towards greater marital instability. One woman's independence gained is another's security lost. The gendered constraints of reproductive responsibilities still offer women a different set of choices to those facing men. Beside the question whether women or men, modern or traditional, are happier with their life-styles, the terms upon which men and women love and work remain unequal.

REFERENCES

Brannen, J., Meszaros, G., Moss, P., and Poland, G. (1994), *Employment and Family Life: A Review of Research in the UK (1990–1994)*, Research Series 41. London: Employment Department.

Coote, A., and Campbell, B. (1982), *Sweet Freedom.* London: Pan Books.

Corti, L. (1994), 'For Better or Worse? Annual Change in Smoking, Self-Assessed Health and Subjective Well-Being', in N. Buck, J. Gershuny, D. Rose, and J. Scott (eds.), *Changing Households: The British Household Panel Survey 1990–1992*. Colchester: ESRC Centre for Micro-Social Change.

Cramer, J. C. (1980), 'Fertility and Female Employment: Problems of Causal Direction', *American Sociological Review*, 45.

Dale, A., and Egerton, M. (1995), 'Highly Educated Women: Evidence from the National Child Development Study'. Report to the Employment Department. Manchester: Census Micro-data Unit, University of Manchester.

Davies, H., and Joshi, H. (1994*a*), 'Gender and Inequality in the UK 1968–1990: The Feminization of Earning or Poverty?' Typescript, London: Birkbeck College.

—— —— (1994*b*), 'Sex, Sharing and the Distribution of Income', *Journal of Social Policy*, 26.

—— —— (1995), 'Social and Family Security in the Redress of Unequal Opportunities', in J. Humphries and J. Rubery (eds.), *The Economics of Equal Opportunity*. Manchester: Equal Opportunities Commission.

DAVIS, K. (1984), 'Wives and Work: Consequences of the Sex Role Revolution', *Population and Development Review*, 10/3.

DEX, S. (1984), 'Women's Work Histories: An Analysis of the Women and Employment Survey', *Research paper No. 46*. London: Department of Employment.

—— (1987), *Women's Occupational Mobility: A Lifetime Perspective*. Basingstoke: Macmillan Press.

——, and SHAW, L. (1986), *British and American Women at Work*. London, Macmillan.

——, WALTERS, P., and ALDEN, D. M. (1993), *French and British Mothers at Work*. Basingstoke: Macmillan.

ELIAS, P. (1993), *ACCNCDS: Software for Access to the Life and Work History Information Collected in the Fifth Sweep of the National Child Development Study*. Coventry: Institute for Employment Research, University of Warwick.

ERMISCH, J. F. (1990), 'European Women's Employment and Fertility Again', *Journal of Population Economics*, 3.

FERRI, E. (ed.) (1993), *Life at 33: The Fifth Follow-up of the National Child Development Study*. London: National Children's Bureau.

FOLBRE, N. (1994), *Who Pays for the Kids? Gender and the Structures of Constraint*. London: Routledge.

FUCHS, V. R. (1988), *Women's Quest for Economic Equality*. Cambridge, Mass.: Harvard University Press.

GIEVE, K. (ed.) (1989), *Balancing Acts: On Being a Mother*. London: Virago.

GOLDIN, C. (1990), *Understanding the Gender Gap: An Economic History of American Women*. New York: Oxford University Press.

GRAHAM, H. (1993), *Hardship and Health in Women's Lives*. Hemel Hempstead: Harvester Wheatsheaf.

GREGG, P., and WADSWORTH, J. (1994), 'More Work in Fewer Households?' Discussion Paper 72. London: National Institute of Economic and Social Research.

GUSTAFSSON, S. (1994), 'Childcare and Types of Welfare States', in Sainsbury D. (ed.), *Gendering Welfare States*. London: Sage.

——, and STAFFORD, F. (1994), 'Three Regimes of Childcare', in R. Blank (ed.), *Social Protection versus Economic Flexibility: Is There a Trade-Off?* Chicago: Chicago University Press for National Bureau of Economic Research.

HARKNESS, S., MACHIN, S., and WALDFOGEL, J. (1995), 'Evaluating the Pin Money Hypothesis'. Discussion Paper 108, STICERD, London: London School of Economics.

HEITLINGER, A. (1993), *Women's Equality, Demography and Public Policy*. New York: St Martin's Press.

HEWLETT, S. A. (1986), *A Lesser Life: The Myth of Women's Liberation in America*. New York: William Morrow.

JENKINS, S. P. (1991), 'Poverty Measurement and the Within-Household Distribution: Agenda for Action', *Journal of Social Policy*, 23.

——, and O'LEARY, N. C. (1994), 'The Incomes of UK Women: Limited Progress Towards Equality with Men?' Discussion Paper 94-10, Swansea: Department of Economics, University of Wales.

JOSHI, H. (1990*a*), 'Changing Roles of Women in the British Labour Market and the Family', in P. Deane, (ed.), *Frontiers of Economic Research. Proceedings of Section F (Economics) of the British Association for the Advancement of Science, Oxford, 1988*. Basingstoke: Macmillan.

—— (1990*b*), 'The Cash Opportunity Cost of Childbearing: An Approach to Estimation Using British Evidence', *Population Studies*, 44.

——, DALE, A., WARD, C., and DAVIES, H. (1995), '*Dependence and Independence in the Finances of Women at age 33*'. London: Family Policy Studies Centre.

——, and DAVIES, H. (1992), 'Daycare in Europe and Mothers' Foregone Earnings', *International Labour Review*, 131.

—— —— (1996), 'Financial Dependency on Men: Have Women Born in 1958 Broken Free?', *Policy Studies*, 17/1.

——, and HINDE, P. R. A. (1993), 'Employment after Childbearing in Post-War Britain: Cohort Study Evidence on Contrasts within and across Generations', *European Sociological Review*, 9.

——, and NEWELL, M.-L. (1987), 'Job Downgrading after Childbearing', in M. Uncles (ed.), *London Papers in Regional Science 18. Longitudinal Data Analysis: Methods and Applications*. London: Pion.

——, and OWEN, S. J. (1988), 'Demographic Predictors of Women's Work Participation in Post-war Britain', *Research in Population Economics*, 6: 401–47.

KEMPENEERS, M., and LELIEVRE, E. (1991), *Employment and Family within the Twelve* (Eurobarometer 34). Brussels: Commission of the European Communities.

MACRAE, S. (1991), *Maternity rights in Britain*. London: Policy Studies Institute.

—— (1993), 'Returning to Work after Childbirth: Opportunites and Inequalities', *European Sociological Review*, 9.

MACRAN, S. (1993), 'Role Enhancement or Role Overload? A Review of Research on the Health Consequences of Women's Domestic and Paid Work'. CPS Research Paper No. 93–1, London: Centre for Population Studies, London School of Hygiene and Tropical Medicine.

——, CLARKE, L., and JOSHI, H. (1996), 'Women's Health: Dimensions and Differentials', *Social Science and Medicine*, 10.

——, JOSHI, H., and DEX, S. (1996), 'Employment after Childbearing: A Survival Analysis', *Work, Employment and Society*.

MARTIN, J., and ROBERTS, C. (1984), *Women and Employment: A Lifetime Perspective*. London: HMSO.

NI BHROLCHAIN, M., and TIMAEUS, I. M. (1985), 'A General Approach to the Machine Handling of Event-History Data', *Social Science Information*, 24.

OECD (1988), *Employment Outlook, 1988*, Paris: OECD.

PACI, P., and JOSHI, H. (1996), *Wage Differentials between Men and Women: Evidence from Cohort Studies*. London: Department for Education and Employment, Research Report 71.

STOCKMAN, N., BONNEY, N., and XUEWEN, S. (1995), *Women's Work in East and West: The Dual Burden of Employment and Family Life*. London: UCL Press.

THOMAS, M., GODDARD, E., HICKMAN, M., and HUNTER, P. (1994), *General Household Survey, 1992*, Series GHS no. 23, London: OPCS Social Survey Division.

WADSWORTH, M. E. J. (1991), *The Imprint of Time: Childhood, History and Adult Life*. Oxford: Clarendon Press.

WALDFOGEL, J. (1993), 'Women Working for Less: A Longitudinal Analysis of the Family Penalty', Welfare State Programme Discussion Paper WSP/93, STICERD, London: London School of Economics.

WARD, C., DALE, A., and JOSHI, H. (1996), 'Combining Employment with Childcare: An Escape from Dependence?' *Journal of Social Policy*, 25.

WEATHERALL, R., JOSHI, H., and MACRAN, S. (1994), 'Double Burden and Double Blessing? Employment Motherhood and Mortality in the Longitudinal Study of England and Wales', *Social Science and Medicine,* 38.

WIGGINS, R. D., and BYNNER, J. (1993), 'Social Attitudes', in Ferri (1993).

WILLIS, R. J. (1973), 'Economic Theory and Fertility Behaviour', in T. W. Schulz (ed.), *Economics of the Family: Marriage, Children and Human Capital*. Chicago and London: University of Chicago Press for National Bureau of Economic Research.

6

Responsibilities and the Quality of Relationships in Families

JANET FINCH

INTRODUCTION

This chapter is concerned with the concept of *quality of relationships* in families, focusing on relationships between adults rather than those which involve young children. By 'families' I do not mean simply people who share the same household, but families in the wider sense of a kin network. This covers relationships across and within generations, with parents, grandparents, grandchildren, sisters, brothers, aunts, and uncles, indeed with anyone whom an individual defines as part of his or her own family.

What is meant by the term 'quality' of relationships in this context? Briefly, I am using it to refer to the phenomenon—found commonly within families—that people feel more identified with some members than with others. In everyday language people talk about 'feeling closer' to one of your adult children than you do to the others, or 'getting on better' with one brother among several. In developing this discussion I shall link these patterns of 'feeling closer' or 'getting on better' with the topic of *obligations and responsibilities* within kin groups—responsibilities to give practical help (of minor and major kinds) when it is needed, to give or lend money, to offer emotional support or personal care when a relative needs assistance. I shall draw on empirical data from a project which has examined these questions in the context of contemporary English kinship, the details of which are explained below.

Thus the questions posed in this chapter revolve around two concepts—responsibilities, on the one hand and quality of relationships on the other—and the links between the two. The central questions posed are:

(i) How far are the responsibilities associated with family relationships predictable simply from genealogical position; or, do they vary with individual relationships?
(ii) If the latter, is the varying quality of relationships an important factor in understanding the different responsibilities which people acknowledge in families?

The point may be put rather less formally: if I lend money to my sister, or look after her children whilst she is in hospital, or take her to live with me after she has had a stroke, am I doing this just because she is my sister? Or because we have always been close? And would I be equally likely to do any of these things for another sister to whom I am less close? The distinction between offering help because of the nature of the relationship between two individuals, and offering it simply because of the genealogical link, forms a central theme of my discussion. Though clearly the two are difficult to disentangle I believe that it is possible, given the right kind of data. And if we can distinguish between the two, we have the basis for understanding something of the significance of the quality of relationships in people lives.

Though this chapter focuses on the quality of relationships, it also bears on more general questions about quality of life, in that it helps us to understand the importance of family and kin relationships in lived experience.

FAMILIES, KIN, AND RELATIONSHIPS

Though the specific questions which I am posing in this chapter have not been addressed by other researchers, more general issues about the quality of family life have been a significant preoccupation both for social scientists and—even more so—for commentators in public debate. These more general issues are implicit in my discussion, and therefore I shall begin with a brief overview of existing sociological and anthropological literature on family and kinship in Britain, in so far as that literature addresses the quality of relationships.

The major focus for discussion of the quality of relationships in families, and especially wider kin relationships beyond the conjugal household, has been a persistent anxiety that the quality of family life has deteriorated especially during recent decades. As Graham Allan wrote in his review of sociological writing on family life, published in 1985, the modern family is regularly portrayed as being in quite a serious state of decline. Unlike times past when family members could rely on each other to meet the contingencies of everyday life, we are told that contemporary families are incapable of providing the collective support and sustenance that used to be their hallmark. Not only has family life become privatized and isolating, with each household living out its existence trapped in its own little box but, perhaps more importantly, family relationships are less stable and apparently less caring.[1]

There are of course questions to be asked about whether the image of the past, implicit in this comparison with the present, itself is an accurate reflection of the experience of previous generations. Is the image of the large, warm, supportive kin group supported by historical evidence, say of the past two hundred years? I have argued elsewhere that it is not, partly because one necessarily is not comparing like with like.[2] However, my point in this chapter is not so much to question the accuracy of the imagery of strong family life in past generations, as to focus upon the present and the very recent past, and to explore the evidence for claims that—whatever was the reality in the past—kin relationships now have relatively little significance in people's lives.

Within discussion of these issues, one finds two features of family life inextricably intertwined, namely practical support and personal attachment. The assumption is that family life is now of minimal significance in both senses: it does not provide a basic support structure for individuals who are unable fully to support themselves (either practically or financially), nor is it the source of significant personal and emotional attachments, save for the co-residing couple and for relationships between parents and children especially whilst the children are young. Beyond those relationships it is assumed that affective ties are minimal and that practical support structures do not operate except unusually, resulting, as Allan puts it, in a quality of family life which is 'privatised and isolating'.

This linking of practical support and personal attachment as key indicators of the quality of family relationships can be found in the earliest studies of family and kinship in the post-war period, most influentially in those undertaken by the Institute of Community Studies in Bethnal Green.[3] Kin relationships were seen to be the basis of a close-knit and supportive community life in stable and working-class Bethnal Green. They provided the foundations of both everyday sociability and of mutual

[1] Allan (1985). [2] Finch (1989).
[3] Young and Willmott (1957), Townsend (1957), Willmott and Young (1960).

assistance in all the eventualities of family life for which, of course, it was largely women who took responsibility. However, the maintenance of relationships of this quality and character depended crucially, in Young and Willmott's analysis, upon geographical proximity. They documented, with a sense of despair and anger which come through clearly in their writing, the breakup of both the physical communities and of the relationships which they fostered, when many residents of Bethnal Green were rehoused in Greenleigh. This was a newly built housing estate at some distance from the East End which stands in a sense symbolically for all such rehousing schemes, in which people who had made the move ended up quite bereft in many cases, feeling keenly the loss of relationships which could no longer be sustained at a distance. When later Young and Willmott conducted a parallel study in the socially more mixed suburb of Woodford, they were not entirely surprised to find that the pattern was a little different, in that they were able to document how middle-class people, never having been exposed to the close, warm ties of the working-class community, were able to deploy their social skills to create, in a form satisfying to themselves, ties of community and friendship unrelated to their kin, though for the most part not of the same character and quality as had been found in Bethnal Green.

The studies undertaken by the Institute of Community Studies are of particular importance because they were aimed at and reached a wide audience, and were quite explicitly intended as an intervention in the politics of housing and urban redevelopment. They were responsible in quite a large measure for fixing the public imagery of the loss of community in the post-war period and—more importantly for the present argument—of symbolizing the presumed disintegration of the kin group or 'extended' family. Subsequent studies, undertaken during the 1960s, which explored similar themes in different settings enabled a much more subtle cumulative picture to be developed.[4] However much that was acknowledged amongst professional social scientists, it seems not to have influenced the public imagery, which remained focused upon the presumed progressive disintegration of family life. The fact that this imagery, and the assumptions behind it, have lasted for so long, may be due at least in part to the fact that sociological studies of family and kinship went out of fashion in the late 1960s and for the next twenty years very little empirical work was undertaken. Indeed the empirical

[4] e.g. Bell (1968), Rosser and Harris (1968), Firth, Hubert, and Forge (1970).

study on which I draw later in this chapter was undertaken as one contribution to redressing that balance. However, the theme that family life, including importantly wider kin relationships, has been greatly impoverished through social and economic forces at work in the second half of the twentieth century, remains central to contemporary understanding. The decline of both practical assistance and personal attachment is integral to that belief, the two acting as twin signals that families no longer 'matter' to us in a way that they did to our grandparents.

Studies of family life undertaken more recently do not straightforwardly support this image of progressive disintegration, though most of them have tackled it obliquely in the course of empirical work with a different focus, rather than addressing it directly. Probably the most influential work of the 1980s was Pahl's study of the Isle of Sheppey, a major piece of empirical work designed principally to explore how people managed to sustain daily life in circumstances where there was a high level of unemployment. In the course of this work, Pahl and his associates were able to demonstrate that, under certain conditions, extended family networks can continue to provide both practical help for their members and the basis for very close personal ties.[5] But neither of these is an inevitable consequence even when one has a large family geographically close, and the ties—whilst perhaps very close—can be characterized by ambivalence and sometimes hostility as well as by genuine warmth and affection. Whether any of this is very different from several generations past—or even from Bethnal Green in the 1950s—is very difficult to say without data which could enable direct comparison of experience. What is clear from Pahl's work is that family and kinship remain significant, at least for some of us, some of the time.

That conclusion would certainly be supported by other empirical studies, perhaps most obviously a whole series concerned with documenting the nursing and practical care provided for elderly people by members of their own families.[6] By contrast, but demonstrating also the continuing importance of kinship in certain circumstances, Grieco's study of the English new town of Corby demonstrates clearly the use of kin networks to secure employment over long distances, where migrants typically had been drawn from Scotland.[7] Although this situation is unusual in respect of internal migration in the twentieth century, Grieco's

[5] Pahl (1984), Wilson and Pahl (1988).

[6] e.g. Wenger (1984), Ungerson (1987), Parker and Lawton (1944).

[7] Grieco (1987).

work also serves to remind us that kin networks have been important in providing practical and personal support to the many migrants who have settled in the UK from other parts of the world in the post-war period, as I concluded in an earlier review of evidence about kin support networks.[8]

In general therefore the relatively limited empirical data on the significance of family in Britain, and particularly of kinship, over the last fifteen years points to a pattern which at minimum is more mixed than the imagery of progressive disintegration would suggest. Looked at more positively, it raises some intriguing questions about the circumstances under which significant kin relationships do flourish in the circumstances of the late twentieth century. *Inter alia* the evidence suggests that both practical help for and personal attachment to kin may be the experience of at least some of our fellow citizens, giving kinship a significance in their lives which may add something—perhaps a good deal—in qualitative terms. Yet at the same time the pattern seems to be very variable, with certainly evidence emerging of people who do have relatively little 'family life' outside the immediate household, and for whom the wider kin relationships do indeed appear to have rather little significance. It is this variability which provides a range of sociologically challenging questions, including the one on which I am focusing in this chapter, that is whether the particular character of relationships between two individuals matters as much as or more than their genealogical tie. If it does, it could certainly account for some of the variability in the significance of kin relationships to which existing research seems to point.

RELATIONSHIPS AND RESPONSIBILITIES IN FAMILIES: SOME BASIC PARAMETERS

It was with these questions in mind that I designed my own study of Family Obligations, on which the rest of the chapter will be based. Initially I shall consider briefly the 'background' questions which I have been discussing in the previous section, namely whether kinship has continuing significance, which itself tells us something about the qualitative importance of these relationships in people's lives. I shall then move on to consider the more specific questions which I introduced

[8] Finch (1989).

at the beginning of this chapter, namely whether the practical acknowledgement of responsibilities, where it occurs, is a product of the specific character and quality of particular relationships, rather than simply of the genealogical link.

I shall make two basic points on the background issue. First, kin *relationships remain important*, at some level, to most people. Second, the pattern of responsibilities associated with kin relationships is *highly variable.* These are both empirical claims and the evidence which supports them comes from the study to which I referred earlier. I will introduce this study briefly and present to some of the data which support these claims. The study from which my data are taken was the Family Obligations project, the data for which were gathered between 1986 and 1989, primarily but not exclusively in the north-west of England.[9] The project comprised two linked empirical studies. The first was a survey of respondents sampled randomly from the electoral register in forty wards in the Greater Manchester region. The achieved number was 978, representing a 72 per cent response rate. The purpose of the survey was to collect normative data about expressed beliefs and values concerning family obligations and responsibilities. The main aim was to answer the question: is there a consensus amongst a random sample of the population on the nature of obligations and responsibilities towards one's kin? This is a question about *normative* issues in the *public* domain. The kinds of questions which we asked (some examples are given below) were designed to distance the respondents themselves from the question as far as possible, and to invite them to offer judgements of a generalizable rather than a personal kind.[10] In so doing, we made no assumptions about whether such judgements would translate to the basis of action in respondents' own lives. Rather our aim was to tap any public consensus which might exist about family morality in this area of responsibilities and obligations.

Thus the survey—unlike many others which collect normative data—was *not* designed to explore what responsibilities people acknowledge in practice. Data on what people do in practice were collected in the second part of the study, which comprised a set of qualitative interviews with eighty-eight individuals, some of whom had been survey respondents and the rest of whom were drawn from their relatives. Where possible we built up sets of interviews with members of the same family,

[9] I am grateful to the Economic and Social Research Council who funded the Family Obligations study, 1985–89 (Grant number GOO 23197).

[10] The basis of this is discussed in Finch (1987).

to enable us to explore people's experience of family responsibilities from different angles. The qualitative interview sample was not randomly selected, but was constructed in such a way as to encompass a wide range of ages, socio-economic backgrounds and experiences.[11]

I can now return to the two claims which I made at the beginning of this section and ask: how far do the data from the Family Obligations study support these claims? My first claim was that kin relationships remain important, at some level, to most people. This emerged as a strong theme in our qualitative interview data, which comes from a group of people living in widely varying circumstances, and aged from 18 to over 80. Though the starting-point for our interviews was a set of survey respondents who were living at that time in the north-west of England, by no means all of them had been born and brought up in this region; and some of their relatives who were also included in the study lived in other parts of the country at the time we conducted the interviews. So we have no reason to believe that we were picking up a pattern which is distinctive to one part of Britain.

What do I mean when I say that kin relationships remain important? This appears to be true in two senses. First, people value a sense that they 'belong' to a family which 'works'. Amongst our eighty-eight interviewees there were widely different experiences of family life in this broader sense. Some had many relatives, others had few. Some lived geographically close to their relatives, for others the kin group was widely scattered. Some people belonged to kin groups who had regular 'family gatherings' on ritual and other occasions, whilst others seldom met certain kin. The actual shape of who counted as kin, and the texture of family life was as varied in our study as earlier work on British kinship has shown it to be.[12]

The striking feature is that, despite these variations, almost all interviewees were at pains to emphasize that they do belong to a wider family group which has a meaning in their lives well beyond a list of names on a Christmas card list. A very common theme was that this wider family group, whilst perhaps relatively dormant for much of the time is meaningful because it 'works' for its members when they need it. The classic example of this 'working' seems to be rallying round in a crisis. We were offered numerous examples of such events—involving sudden illness, traumatic marriage breakdown, various types of unex-

[11] Discussion of the sampling strategy, and the logic which underpins it, can be found in Finch and Mason (1990*a*).

[12] See e.g. Rosser and Harris (1968), Firth, Hubert, and Forge (1970), Allan (1979).

pected misfortune—in which kin were mobilized to provide support. Often what people were giving was moral support as much as practical help but the point remains the same: your family are people whom you can turn to if you need them. This broad generalization applies as much to men as to women, though it is certainly true that it is women who are the more likely to be involved with kin in more extensive ways.[13]

The point which I want to draw from this is not so much that people do actually use their kin in this way. Of greater significance is the fact that almost all our interviewees wanted to project themselves as coming from a family which has these characteristics. My point therefore is that high *value* is placed on 'belonging to a family which works', even if that never gets tested, and perhaps even if it is tested and found wanting.

Nonetheless our data do also demonstrate that, for most people, kin relationships are a significant source of assistance (practical and/or financial) at some point in their lives. This is the second sense in which kin relationships remain important for most people. We found no one who, in adult life, had never been involved in the exchange of mutual aid within their kin group.[14] Amongst our interviewees almost everyone had given or received financial help (though frequently the amounts of money involved were quite small). About half the women—and only slightly fewer of the men—said that they had helped to look after a relative who was ill or incapacitated. About half had had experience of living in a household where there was also a relative outside the immediate nuclear family, usually someone who was being given shelter on a temporary basis. So for all these categories—financial help, help with housing, practical assistance—our data show that the experience of being on either the giving or the receiving end (and frequently both) is quite widespread amongst the population. In this sense the kin group remains a significant source of mutual aid, though simply aggregating people's experiences in this way masks large variations in the amount of aid given and the level of commitment which this entails.

This brings me to the second claim which I made at the beginning of this section: that the pattern of responsibilities associated with kin relationships is highly variable. Perhaps the best way of illustrating this is to take two contrasting examples from the experiences of our interviewees: the cases of Maureen Vickers and Sally Brown. Maureen

[13] For more details of the data referred to here, see Finch and Mason (1993).

[14] See Finch and Mason (1993).

Vickers's experience falls at one extreme end of the spectrum in that she was our interviewee for whom kin relationships were the least significant. She was aged 65 when we interviewed her, recently retired from her job as the manager of a GP practice and health centre. She lived with her never-married son and clearly a good deal of assistance passed between the two of them. But apart from this relationship she told us initially that she had 'no family', though it transpired that she did have a sister, nieces, and nephews in the south of England with whom she resolutely resisted contact. She said that she could think of no examples of assistance passing within this wider kin group. Though clearly with a positive view of mutual aid within parent–child relationships, Maureen otherwise firmly conveyed the message that the kin group was of no importance as a support network, in her experience.

A more common situation is represented by Sally Brown. I have chosen this example as someone who, though having a kin network which is small relative to some others, has been involved in extensive exchanges of support, of various types, over her adult lifetime. When we interviewed Sally she was in her late thirties, with two small children from her second marriage. At various times in her life she had given and received help in ways which are set out in Box 6.1. I shall return to discuss this case in more detail later in this chapter. For the moment, the main point to note is the overall pattern of exchanges in which Sally has been involved over her adult lifetime, many of them with her parents but also including her sister and a cousin. Sally has both given and received help on many different occasions.

The contrast between Sally Brown and Maureen Vickers is an illustration of the wide variation in the kind of support given and received within families. It suggests that individuals have considerable scope for negotiating their own relationships with members of their family or—to put the same point another way—that there is no very clear set of 'rules' about family responsibilities in operation. If there were clear rules about who should do what for whom, in what circumstances, then we might expect to find greater consistency of experience.

The fact that there is no clear consensus about 'rules of family obligation' is confirmed by our survey data, which was designed specifically to address this question at the level of public norms. We probed the question of whether there is any level of agreement on these issues by asking our survey respondents to consider a series of hypothetical situations concerning fictional characters. Respondents were asked to say what the characters in the story 'should' do (*not* what they themselves

Box 6.1. *Sally Brown: experiences of giving and receiving help (Family Obligations Interview Study)*

Sally was aged 39 at the time of her interview. She trained as a primary school teacher and worked until she had her first child (at which point she was a deputy head). She was currently living with her second husband and their two young children. Sally's father, who was widowed, spent much of his time in Sally's household, though he still retained his own home. It was anticipated that eventually he would move in permanently.

(i) Sally and her parents: giving and receiving help

1966 Sally left school and went to college. Her parents helped her financially during her training.

1969 Qualified and got married.

1970 Husband died after less than one year of marriage. Sally moved back to live with her parents.

1970–6 Lived with her parents, apart from periods of foreign travel. Relied heavily on their emotional support.

1976 Bought her own house, with financial assistance from her parents.

1979 (May) Married for a second time.

1979 (August) Mother had a stroke and died several months later. Sally was heavily involved in caring for her mother during her terminal illness.

From this time onwards, Sally gave her father a great deal of emotional support, including having him to live in her home on a temporary basis several times.

1981/1986 Sally's children born. Father acted as regular baby-sitter.

(ii) Sally and other relatives

1980 onwards. Sally gave practical help, from time to time, to a cousin who was caring for her own infirm mother on a long-term basis.

1984 onwards. Helped her sister in various practical ways to establish a small business (as a repairer of children's toys).

'would' do). Some of these situations were explained very briefly, others were constructed as much longer vignettes, with several stages, and respondents were asked to make a judgement at each stage.[15]

A typical example of the shorter vignettes is given in Box 6.2, along with the pattern of responses. In fact both of these are examples of what we call 'split consensus', that is, there is no clear agreement amongst our survey population about what is the right thing to do in this situation.[16] A pattern of split consensus was very common in our survey;

[15] For further discussion see Finch (1987).

[16] The concepts of 'consensus' and 'split consensus' were developed in the context of the Family Obligations study. Since the main purpose of the study was to assess whether there were any normative issues on which there is a general agreement amongst our survey population, we had to address the problem: what are we to count as 'agreement'? This problem is essentially a sociological rather than a statistical one. Clearly

Box 6.2. *Examples of shorter vignettes (Family Obligations Survey, N = 978)*

If a student runs up debts of four hundred pounds whilst at college, do you think that parents should pay off the debts, even if it means financial hardship for them?

Yes	239	24%
No	638	65%
DK/Depends	101	11%

A couple with children aged 9 and 14 have been evicted because they cannot afford to pay their rent. They cannot get a council flat and they cannot afford a private one. Should relatives offer to give them a house for the next six months or so?

Yes	639	65%
No	216	22%
DK/Depends	123	13%

indeed there were very few issues on which we found high levels of normative agreement. Further, the patterns of split consensus were not clearly or consistently linked to socio-economic characteristics of respondents; so they cannot be explained as patterns of varying 'consensus' between different age groups, different social classes, or between men and women.[17]

Quite simply our survey shows that there is *no* significant consensus, at this level of public norms, about rules of obligation within families. This is a conclusion of considerable importance to the issue of the quality of relationships, and their impact on responsibilities. If people are not constrained by public norms about obligations, at least not to any significant degree, a much more open situation is created within families in practice. Given the lack of clear rules about family obligations in Britain, it becomes at least possible that people can negotiate sets of responsibilities on the basis of 'feeling closer' to some kin than to others.

anything less than 50 per cent (on a simple yes/no question) could not count, but 100 per cent agreement is inherently unlikely on any issue. We therefore developed a rule of thumb that any pattern of answers in which there was at least half as much again as could have occurred by chance (i.e. 75%) on a yes/no question would count as a significant level of agreement. We accorded this rule of thumb no greater status than as a starting-point and an aid to interpretation. For more detailed discussion see Finch and Mason (1993).

[17] See Finch and Mason (1991).

RESPONSIBILITIES AND THE QUALITY OF RELATIONSHIPS

I have now reached the point where I can address directly the question: how important is the 'quality' of relationships to understanding the variations in responsibilities which people acknowledge for members of their own families?

In doing so, I perhaps need to make clearer how we can tap the 'quality' of relationships in this context and, in particular, what the data which I am using allow us to say about it. Essentially I am relying on the accounts which people give of their own family relationships, elicited through in-depth interviewing. In those accounts our informants commonly emphasized variation and differences in their family relationships, without necessarily implying that some were 'bad'. Taking my cue from my informants, my analysis focuses on the idea that each of us is involved in sets of *qualitatively different* relationships, with different members of our kin networks.

The next step in the analysis is to make the connection with responsibilities. Is it possible to trace the links between qualitatively different relationships and the types of responsibilities which people are prepared to accept? Are people prepared to do more for a relative to whom they 'feel close' than one with whom they have a more distant, possibly a more difficult, relationship? Does closeness carry with it clearer expectations about providing support?

These questions postulate that responsibilities acknowledged may depend on the quality of particular relationships. An alternative hypothesis would be that genealogical position determines the type of responsibility which people acknowledge; that is, that certain responsibilities are attached to being a son, a grandmother, and so on. If this were so, the question of whether you feel close to the person concerned would be irrelevant.

From the data which I have already presented, it should be clear that our findings do not support the view that responsibilities are linked with genealogical positions, certainly not in any straightforward way. This applies both at the normative level, and also to what happens in practice. At the level of publicly expressed norms, our survey data show that people do not see particular responsibilities flowing straightforwardly from a given genealogical relationship. Relationships between parents and children come closest to linking responsibilities to genealogy, as earlier studies of English kinship have noted.[18] But even here people want to allow considerable room for variation in practice. This is evident in the survey data. It is also reflected in what happens in families in practice, according to the experiences reported by our interviewees. Neither at the normative level, nor in practice, do people treat genealogical links as the simple basis for determining what responsibilities are appropriate.[19]

It does make sense therefore to explore the question of whether it is the varying quality of relationships which explains the wide variations in the types of responsibility which people acknowledge in families. By using the survey data, we can explore this question at the normative level (do people generally think that the quality of a particular relationship *ought* to affect the responsibilities acknowledged?), and the interview data enable us to examine whether quality *does* seem to have a relevance in practice.

Looking first at the survey data, our data suggest that, where respondents are given information about the quality of the relationship between the people in our hypothetical situations, this does influence their judgements about the level of responsibilities which it is appropriate to acknowledge. To illustrate this point I shall draw on some questions which postulated situations in which an elderly man needs practical help and care. These questions enable us to make a comparison between situations where respondents were told that the elderly man and the potential carer 'do not get on' with each other, with other situations in which no information was given about the quality of relationship.

Box 6.3 sets out the core survey question where we were able to test these issues, along with the pattern of responses. The question concerns whether a person has the responsibility to pay daily visits to an infirm father with whom he or she has never got on well; the second part of the question repeats the situation but substitutes uncle for father.

What do the responses to this question tell us about the importance which people attach to 'not getting on' when they are making their judgements about public normative issues? Clearly there is a contrast between the way this factor applies to judgements about responsibilities to a father and responsibilities to an uncle. Almost two-thirds say that it is *not* a relevant factor in responsibilities to help father; but only

[18] See Morgan (1975).

[19] Detailed discussion of data on this issue can be found in Finch and Mason (1993).

BOX 6.3. *Responsibilities and poor-quality relationships (Family Obligation Survey, N = 978)*

a. Should a person be prepared to make daily visits to look after his or her elderly *father*, even if they have never got along well together?

Yes	704	72%
No	220	22.5%
DK/Depends	54	5.5%

b. And should a person be prepared to make daily visits to look after his or her elderly *uncle*, even if they have never got on well together?

Yes	390	40%
No	486	50%
DK/Depends	102	10%

40 per cent are prepared to say that in the case of an uncle. This pattern of responses does not seem to be shaped significantly by the characteristics of respondents. Marginally more women than men are likely to give weight to the factor of 'getting on'. The same is true of younger survey respondents. But neither pattern is very marked, and in general throughout the survey women and younger people do not give a consistently distinctive pattern of answers.

What we cannot tell from this question alone is how far it is the 'not getting on' factor which has influenced the judgements elicited, or whether they were focusing on the other aspects of the question. In order to explore this further I shall focus on the respondents who said 'no': 50 per cent in the case of uncle, and 22.5 per cent in the case of father. It may be that these respondents were focusing on other aspects of the question (for example, the genealogical relationship, or the level of commitment involved) and were not influenced particularly strongly by the 'not getting on' factor. In order to explore this, we need to make comparison with other survey questions where the factor of getting on was not an issue. There were a number of questions which involved the prospect of taking care of an elderly person. Though none of these situations is a precise parallel with the question above, they give some clues about how significant the 'getting on' factor may have been in influencing respondents' answers.

In one question—the first part of a much longer vignette—we postulated a situation in which a middle-aged couple have to take a decision about what level of responsibility they should take for the husband's elderly parents, who had both been injured in a car accident. No mention was made of the quality of the relationship between the parties. We offered various ways in which the children might take some level of responsibility and also included the option 'Let the parents make their own arrangements'.[20] This particular response—the 'not responsible' option—which is important for the present purpose. Only 9 per cent of respondents preferred this option, compared with the 22.5 per cent who (in the question discussed above) said that there was no responsibility to make daily visits to a father with whom you do not get on. This suggests that being given information that the relationship between father and child was of poor quality did influence some people's judgements about whether there is a responsibility to offer help.

Does the same hold true in the case of an uncle? Here we can make comparison with a different question, where we asked about whether a niece or nephew should offer to help an elderly person (we did not specify whether aunt or uncle) who has no children. Again, no information was given about the quality of the relationship between aunt/uncle and niece/nephew.[21] In response to this question, 21 per cent said that 'somebody else' should take responsibility. This compares with the 50 per cent who went for the 'no responsibility for an uncle' option in the question discussed above. So as with the case of a father, so with an uncle—being told that the parties do not get on with each other does appear to influence the judgement of some people. In both cases more than twice as many people took the 'not responsible' option when told that the relationship is poor as did so when no information was given about the quality of the relationship between the parties. On the other hand this clearly is not the sole factor, particularly in the case of parent–child relationships, where almost three-quarters of the sample say that a child should have some responsibility towards an elderly father, even if the relationship is poor.

In trying to judge the effect of information about the quality of

[20] The question read as follows (with percentage responses): Jim and Margaret Robertson are a married couple in their early foirtes. Jim's parents, who live several hundred miles away, have had a serious car accident and they need long-term daily care and help. Jim is their only son. He and his wife both work for the Electricity Board and they could both get transfers so that they could work near his parents. What should Jim and Margaret do? Move to live near Jim's parents: 33 per cent; have Jim's parents live with them: 23.5 per cent; give Jim's parents money to help them pay for daily care: 25 per cent; let Jim's parents make their own arrangements: 9 per cent; dont't know: 1.5 per cent.

[21] The question read as follows (with percentage responses): Suppose an elderly person needs help with shopping and a little help in the house. The elderly person has an adult niece and nephew and no other relatives. Should the niece and nephew take over responsibility for the tasks or should someone else? Yes—niece/nephew: 68 per cent; somebody else: 21 per cent; DK/depends: 10 per cent.

BOX 6.4. *Responsibilities and good-quality relationships (Family Obligation Survey, N = 978)*

a. Jane Hill is a young woman with children aged 3 and 5. She was recently divorced. She wants to go back to work and she needs the money. But if she has a job she must find someone to mind the children after school. Her own family live far away and her former mother-in-law, Anne Hill, who is at home all day lives nearby. Jane has always got on well with her former mother-in-law. Should Anne offer to look after Jane's children?

Yes	847	87%
No	71	7%
DK/Depends	60	6%

b. Anne does offer to help so Jane goes back to work. Some years later Anne has a stroke and needs regular care and help in the home. Should Jane offer to give up her job and look after her mother-in-law?

Yes	420	43%
No	396	40.5%
DK/Depends	162	16.5%

c. Jane does give up her job. A year later Jane remarries. Now that Jane has remarried, should she go on helping her former mother-in-law?

Yes	755	77%
No	106	11%
Depends	117	12%

d. Why do you think that Jane should go on helping/should stop helping? (Open coding).

relationship of people's normative responses, I have concentrated so far on questions which indicate a poor quality of relationship. But what about where it is particularly good? If respondents are told that there is an especially close relationship between the relevant parties, does this alter the judgements that they make about the level of responsibility which is appropriate? The particular question which I shall use here was constructed in such a way as to draw a careful distinction between personal and genealogical closeness. The main characters are genealogically fairly distant but personally on very good terms. It concerns the relationship between a young divorced woman and her former mother-in-law. Box 6.4 sets out the details of this question, which was one of our longer vignettes.

This vignette is interesting for various reasons, but I want to pull out in particular some points about time. We constructed the story so that the relationship between the two women had these features:

- It had built up over a long period of time
- It had a history of reciprocal assistance over practical matters

- Along with the exchange of mutual aid had grown personal closeness and liking

Our survey population seems to have seen these features as creating a relationship of a particular kind, which ought to lead to a continuing acknowledgement of responsibilities between the two women. This was so despite the fracture of the formal, genealogical link through divorce and its further weakening by Jane's remarriage. This pattern of responses offers some interesting insights into normative judgements about the consequences of divorce which we have explored elsewhere.[22] But the main point in the context of this chapter is that it indicates that people do place a premium on good quality relationships and that they see these properly linked to a continuing commitment to mutual aid.

This response at the normative level is mirrored in interesting ways in our interview data. A major finding from our study is that there are processes at work over time in families, through which certain people develop commitments to certain other people; these commitments clearly have a particular rather than a general character. We have used the concept of *developing commitments* to describe this process because it allows us to see that responsibilities are *created* over time between individuals, rather than flowing straightforwardly from genealogical ties.[23] Over a period of time, for example, two siblings out of a larger sibling group will build up a pattern of mutual aid and interdependence which means that each would feel that they have a responsibility to help the other, in ways which go beyond any responsibilities which they may feel to their other siblings.

To explore this further I use the example of Sally Brown whose circumstances I introduced earlier (see Box 6.1). This case is typical of our interviewees in one sense, but not in another. Sally Brown is not typical in the sense that the commitments that she has built up with her father are very extensive and go somewhat beyond most other parent–child commitments which we encountered. However, the *process* by which those commitments were arrived at is very typical of the processes which we observed in other families which we studied.

It is evident that reciprocal aid within the family, and especially between herself and her parents, has been an important factor in shaping Sally's adult life. That aid has encompassed financial assistance (her parents helped her with significant sums of money at two separate

[22] See Finch and Mason (1990*b*). [23] See Finch and Mason (1993).

stages), temporary housing (Sally moved back to live with her parents when she was widowed, and her father moved in with her in the same circumstances), emotional support in both directions in situations of bereavement, practical help in the form of baby-sitting, and nursing care (where Sally has already supported her mother and expects ultimately to do the same for her father).

This reciprocal aid forms a pattern which has built up over time, locking Sally into a close and highly committed relationship with her parents. Though based apparently on a good relationship through childhood and adolescence, the fact Sally's relationship with her parents has developed in this particular way appears to depend on contingent factors to a significant degree. Things happened in Sally's life which were entirely unpredictable (most dramatically, her early widowhood) and the availability of her parents' support in these circumstances set the relationship on a path in which it may not have developed to the same degree without such an event. Similarly, the fact that Sally had two children very soon after her mother's death meant that—on Sally's own analysis—her father coped with his bereavement by developing a deep affection for his grandchildren, thus binding him ever closer to Sally.

This analysis, of the importance of contingent factors in understanding how specific individuals develop a strong sense of commitment to each other, is reinforced by contrasting Sally's situation with her sister's. We did not interview the sister, but according to Sally, she was on good terms with the rest of the family. However, she had always been less closely involved with her parents, and was taking a far smaller part in supporting their father. Sally showed no resentment at this; rather she accepted it as a consequence of their lives simply having been different. Box 6.5 gives an extract from Sally's interview, where she discusses this issue.

The striking thing about Sally's reflections on the differences between her sister's relationship with their parents and her own is the emphasis which she herself puts on contingent factors. The observation 'I think it's just been circumstances' neatly encapsulates this. The series of events which, in her own life, has locked her into a highly committed relationship with her parents simply has not been mirrored for her sister. As a consequence she is both less close and less committed. The genealogical relationship to their parents is the same, but the different histories of these two parallel relationships have led to quite different levels of responsibility being acknowledged.

Box 6.5. *Sally Brown and her sister (extract from Family Obligations interview)*

Interviewer	Is your sister as close, has she always been as close, to your parents as you are?
Sally	Em – No, she's not really. She would like to be but – I don't know. Maybe it's because she was the first to leave home, and I was at home seemingly that much longer. And I was single when my mum died.
Interviewer	Yes.
Sally	So I was able to help my father. No – I'd been married a couple of months, this second time. But my father – having experienced bereavement myself I knew what he was going through. . . . She's very tied up with her own, her sons. Of course her family is spread over so many years as well. And she has a little business. And she's very tied physically to (the place where she lives). And of course when my first husband died I went back home. I am close, I do know that. I think it's just been circumstances.

CONCLUSION

To return to the questions which I posed at the beginning, about the link between responsibilities to kin and the quality of relationships, the evidence suggests that the two are profoundly interlinked. The alternative hypothesis—that responsibilities flow simply from expectations based on particular genealogical relationships—is not supported either by normative data or by evidence of what happens in practice.

In reality the quality of relationships is linked to responsibilities because both build up over time through a common set of processes. What happens is that commitments grow as the relationship grows; and one of the factors which helps the relationship to grow is reciprocal assistance given and received over time. Such relationships grow between particular individuals, but not with others, for reasons which may often rest on chance factors. And what happens in reality is supported at the level of publicly expressed norms—people recognize and approve of the link between obligations and good quality relationships. Conversely they are less ready to link responsibilities to relationships where people do not get on well, though such judgements are tempered to an extent by genealogical factors especially in the case of parent–child relationships.

The existence of good, close relationships with certain members of one's family, where these do exist, undoubtedly enriches the quality of people's lives. In our study relationships were always portrayed as highly valued. They do, however, carry with them a growing commitment to provide mutual aid which can, depending how circumstances develop, shape the lives of the participants in highly significant ways.

REFERENCES

ALLAN, G. (1979), *A Sociology of Kinship and Friendship*. London: Allen and Unwin.

—— (1985), *Family Life*. Oxford: Blackwell.

BELL, C. (1968), *Middle Class Families*. London: Routledge and Kegan Paul.

FINCH, J. (1987), 'The Vignette Technique in Survey Research', *Sociology,* 211: 105–14.

—— (1989), *Family Obligations and Social Change*. Cambridge: Polity.

——, and MASON, J. (1990*a*), 'Decision-Making in the Fieldwork Process', in R. G. Burgess (ed.), *Studies in Qualitative Methodology*. London: JAI Press.

—— —— (1990*b*), 'Divorce, Remarriage and Family Obligations', *Sociological Review*, 38/2: 219–46.

—— —— (1991), 'Obligations of Kinship in Contemporary Britain: Is There Normative Agreement?' *British Journal of Sociology*, 42/3: 345–67.

—— —— (1993), *Negotiating Family Responsibilities*. London: Routledge.

FIRTH, R., HUBERT, A., and FORGE, J. (1970), *Families and Their Relatives*. London: Routledge and Kegan Paul.

GRIECO, M. (1987), *Keeping It in the Family*. London: Tavistock.

MORGAN, D. (1975), *Social Theory and the Family*. London: Routledge and Kegan Paul.

PAHL, R. (1984), *Division of Labour*. Oxford: Blackwell.

PARKER, G., and LAWTON, D. (1994), *Different Types of Care, Different Types of Cover*. London: HMSO.

ROSSER, C., and HARRIS, C. (1968), *The Family and Social Change*. London: Routledge and Kegan Paul.

TOWNSEND, P. (1957), *The Family Life of Old People*. London: Routledge and Kegan Paul.

UNGERSON, C. (1987), *Policy is Personal*. London: Tavistock.

WENGER, G. C. (1984), *The Supportive Network*. London: Allen & Unwin.

WILLMOTT, P., and YOUNG, M. (1960), *Family and Class in a London Suburb*. London: Routledge and Kegan Paul.

WILSON, P., and PAHL, R. (1988), 'The Changing Sociological Construction of the Family', *Sociological Review,* 362: 233–66.

YOUNG, M., and WILLMOTT, P. (1957), *Family and Kinship in East London*. London: Routledge and Kegan Paul.

7

Alternative Approaches to the Assessment of Health-Related Quality of Life

RAY FITZPATRICK

INTRODUCTION

Quality of life is a widely used concept in health care research. This is most clearly indicated by the explosion of publications including the term in either the title or abstract, with about 200 articles using the term in a three-year period (1978–80) to some 1,400 for a two-year period 1988–9.[1] Other more recent searches suggest that the publication rate has increased since 1989 and if one includes terms widely considered closely related to quality of life in the health field such as 'health status' and 'outcome assessment', it may well be over 1,000 articles per annum that now address the concept in some way.[2] The scope for further expansion is enormous. Most authoritative reviews agree on at least one thing—that medical and health care research is not using the concept of quality of life as fully as it could or should. The majority of studies omit to use quality of life measures when they would be appropriate.[3] Recommendations from professional élites as well as external pressures from government and other regulating bodies to incorporate patient-based measures will certainly produce a further expansion in application of the term.

The plan of this chapter is, first, briefly to review various limitations in the conceptualization of quality of life. Problems in clarifying a subset of *health-related* quality of life are then discussed. The main objective of the paper is to draw attention to important differences of emphasis found in two approaches to quality of life in health, those based on patients actually experiencing particular health problems and those based on subjects' views imagining various health states. Neither approach has examined fully the experience and value of *change over*

[1] Schumacher *et al.* (1991). [2] Jenkins (1992), O'Boyle (1992).
[3] Aaronson 1989, Guyatt *et al.* (1989*a*); Schumacher *et al.* (1991).

time in quality of life and a broad and tentative case is made for the value of such a focus in future studies.

CONCEPTUAL PROBLEMS IN QUALITY OF LIFE

Health care research is highly pragmatic and formal conceptual definition of the term quality of life has not been a major preoccupation. Overviews of the field agree on the poor quality of conceptualization and measurement in many studies.[4] Quality of life in medical research can include almost anything from severity of angina to frequency of bowel-movements.[5] There have nevertheless been some attempts to produce a coherent and comprehensive definition of quality of life that would be relevant to health care. However, they are, unsurprisingly, notable mainly for their heterogeneity. Definitions variously emphasize: the capacity of the individual to realize his or her life plans; the ability of the patient to manage life as he or she evaluates it; the difference between reality and expectations; the sum of the individual's health, subjective well-being, and welfare; a composite of ability to perform everyday activities, satisfaction with functioning and with control of disease.[6]

The diversity of concepts and definitions is as nothing compared with the plethora of measuring instruments that have been developed. Discussions of quality of life in health normally move rapidly from the concept to its measurement without concern for intervening stages. One therefore learns far more about how the concept is used in health care by sampling the content of the many hundreds of questionnaire- and interview-based instruments in the field. One review of quality of life measures in health care argues that most instruments contain items that can be placed under one or more of the following dimensions: emotional well-being, spirituality, sexuality, social functioning, family life, occupational functioning, communication, eating, functional ability, physical status, treatment satisfaction, future orientation, and global ratings of health or life satisfaction.[7] The list might have been extended to include: mastery or control over health, self-esteem, stigma, body image, and sense of predictability of symptoms. In reality, most instruments would include only a small subset of such items: emotional status, physical

[4] Najman and Levine (1981); Aaronson (1989); Guyatt *et al.* (1989*a*); Schumacher *et al.* (1991).

[5] Schumacher *et al.* (1991); Hunt and McKenna (1992).

[6] Fowlie and Berkeley (1987); Dimenas *et al.* (1990); Gotay and Moore (1992).

[7] Cella and Tulsky (1990).

function, social functioning, and symptoms. What is clear from most instruments is that quality of life is considered multi-dimensional.

HEALTH-RELATED QUALITY OF LIFE

In many ways there should be no distinct issue or field of enquiry about quality of life in health because patients are human beings and the same general social scientific literature regarding the nature and determinants of quality of life in general populations should apply just as well to groups of people who happen to have health problems. Indeed many general issues and observations from the broader field of quality of life do indeed equally apply. For example, the same challenges in the broader field as in the field of health care arise out of consistent evidence of individuals reporting favourable subjective responses to objective circumstances that might generally be considered unfavourable.[8]

However, a glance at a range of typical quality of life instruments used in medicine would confirm that there are distinctive emphases in the specific field of health. The most common dimension included in such instruments is physical function, followed by symptom-related problems. This distinctive focus is often recognized by more precise discussions of this field which tend to refer to 'health-related quality of life' rather than simply 'quality of life'.[9] Terminology in this area—'quality of life', 'health-related quality of life', 'health status', 'functional status', 'patient-based outcome measures'—is often used interchangeably However, for some, the clear emphasis on 'health-related quality of life' is seen as an important specification and clarification. Medicine and health care are not generally and in practice concerned with aspects of quality of life such as satisfaction with environment, housing, or income. The concern is with those aspects of quality of life that are related to having a health problem and receiving treatment.[10] Of course there are some who are unhappy with the demarcation of matters that are and are not of concern to health care. They argue against a narrow medical model of health care that ignores social and economic determinants of health and would also object to the narrowing of focus involved in quality of life instruments.[11]

The apparent specification and narrowing of focus to those aspects

[8] Olson and Schober (1993).

[9] Guyatt *et al.* (1989a); Jenkins (1992); Rosser *et al.* (1992).

[10] Hopkins (1992). [11] Harwood and Ebrahim (1992).

of quality of life related to health is not as straightforward as the term implies. There would appear to be two distinct ways of identifying components of quality of life related to health. Neither is entirely satisfactory. The first method is correlational. Either in static or longitudinal data on patients, one can examine dimensions of quality of life that are associated with disease or illness. Items that correlate to some extent with disease (in the predicted direction of poorer quality of life) being associated with more severe disease may be considered components of 'health-related quality of life'; items that do not are components of a broader and more global quality of life. The former is of greater concern to health care. There are several problems with this solution. Almost any variable may correlate with disease: income, housing, social support, life satisfaction, self-esteem, mastery, psychological well-being. It is not clear to what extent items should correlate with disease to be included as a component of health-related quality of life. Thus items that correlate too closely may be components of disease rather than quality of life; for example breathlessness in chronic lung disease. If this approach of identifying *health-related* quality of life by correlations with disease seems unconvincing, it is worth emphasizing that it is one of the standard methods of 'validating' a quality of life instrument. Overall this approach is constrained by the consistent evidence, discussed below, that objective features of disease and subjective experience of quality of life are often not highly associated.

A second solution to identifying what is specifically *health-related* quality of life is to leave it to patients to decide which aspects of quality of life they attribute to their health problem. This would appear to be consistent with the inherently personal and subjective nature of the phenomenon. Indeed some approaches to quality of life measurement take this approach to its logical extreme by completely individualizing instruments so that each individual in a trial nominates his or her own personally identified quality of life concerns.[12] However, this approach has not generally found favour. One major problem concerns individuals' attributions; individuals vary enormously in how they perceive and interpret health, illness, and bodily symptoms. In particular many experiences are not related to disease in the way that a physician would, but are normalized. Individuals adapt to symptoms particularly of a chronic nature to such an extent as either not to notice them or disregard them as aspects of ageing or 'wear and tear'. Thus patients cannot always be

[12] Tugwell *et al.* (1987); McGee *et al.* (1991).

relied on to give accurate and consistent accounts of aspects of their quality of life that they attribute to their health problems. Most frequently identification of health-related quality of life is more pragmatic than the two more formal approaches just discussed and dimensions include various intuitively identified subjective experiences of morbidity. Researchers often determine key dimensions of health-related quality of life, by drawing on items contained in previous instruments.

CONTRASTING APPROACHES

In the broader field of quality of life research beyond health care, a contrast is frequently made between objective and subjective approaches to the quality of life construct.[13] This distinction is also used in the health field, where, however, it often appears to have only an epistemological reference; that is that objective measures are those which are more easily verifiable.[14] A purely methodological contrast between measures of quality of life in terms of whether they are 'hard' or 'soft' is increasingly hard to make and not particularly fruitful.[15] However, there is another point to the contrast between approaches. Subjective approaches refer to individuals' subjective feelings about particular states of being, while objective approaches rely on external and normative criteria. In social philosophy a contrast can be made between concepts of well-being based on subjective satisfaction compared with concepts derived from more 'impersonal standards'.[16] There are certainly two quite distinct approaches to quality of life in health that differ in terms of a non epistemological contrast between personal and experiential feelings about actual experience that contrast with normative external judgements of those states. The distinction between experiential and normative approaches also, to some extent, resembles and draws on another useful distinction made in the broader quality of life field, in experimental psychological studies, between 'judgement' and 'choice' approaches to well-being.[17] When asked to assess states of well-being, individuals produce different solutions depending on whether the task involves judgement of the pleasure or pain associated with actual experience rather than decisions or choice about the overall value or attractiveness of options. As will be made clear, in the health field what I have termed experiential approaches to

[13] Campbell (1981); Schwarz and Strack (1991). [14] Ware *et al.* (1981).
[15] Feinstein (1977). [16] Elster and Roemer (1991).
[17] Tversky and Griffin (1991).

quality of life focus on judgements of experiences; normative approaches refer to choices and preferences between states. These two traditions will be considered in turn.

THE EXPERIENTIAL APPROACH TO HEALTH-RELATED QUALITY OF LIFE

The experiential approach focuses on the reports patients with various illnesses give about how they feel. These reports can be used to address a number of issues regarding quality of life. Patients have been asked what they regard as most important dimensions of quality of life. In several of the studies family relationships are cited as either most important or amongst the most important components of quality of life.[18] There is no clear and consistent pattern of other components across studies except that health itself appears to be lower in priority to family relations as a contributor to patients' quality of life. A study compared patients with cancer and two other groups, one receiving orthopaedic surgery for purely temporary health problems and a third, healthy group.[19] This study found that health played a less salient role in determining quality of life in patients with cancer. They speculate that health is only related to quality of life for individuals for whom attainment of health is a realistic goal. In patients with various gastric disorders and in a group of patients about to receive orthopaedic surgery, health and social and leisure activities competed for second place.[20] Amongst patients with breast cancer, after the family, contributions to quality of life were from broader aspects of health such as self-care and mobility rather than more specific health problems such as pain, nausea, and side-effects of treatment.[21]

Whilst some groups of patients appear to downplay the direct effects of health status on quality of life this was not the case in a study of elderly patients with various chronic diseases. Although in response to open-ended questions they also cited family and social relations as important contributors to quality of life, in structured questions health problems were ranked as the most important factor and health experiences were most often cited as factors that had improved or decreased their quality of life over the previous year.[22]

[18] Sutherland *et al.* (1990); McGee *et al.* (1991); O'Boyle *et al.* (1992).
[19] Kreitler *et al.* (1993).
[20] McGee *et al.* (1991); O'Boyle *et al.* (1992).
[21] Sutherland *et al.* (1990).
[22] Pearlman and Uhlmann (1988).

THE IMPACT OF ILLNESS ON QUALITY OF LIFE

An important and fundamental question is whether illness actually influences individuals' quality of life. There are few studies that use clear and convincing measures of quality of life in studies including patients with clearly defined disease characteristics and well-matched healthy control groups. One of the largest studies to date has been the Medical Outcomes Study in which a large number of patients with a number of different chronic health problems completed a QOL instrument in relation to a visit to their doctor. Patients with a prior heart attack, or with congestive heart failure, diabetes, arthritis, gastrointestinal or chronic lung problems had poorer scores than a healthy comparison group especially for physical and role function.[23] Patients with chronic physical health problems also experienced significantly poorer scores for emotional well-being compared with the healthy controls but the differences were not nearly so great as for more physical dimensions. A study in the UK, using the same research instrument based on the general population rather than patients consulting their doctor, also found that patients with chronic physical health problems differed from other respondents most in terms of role limitations, physical function, and pain and least in terms of psychological well-being.[24] Thus people with chronic illnesses most obviously differ from healthy individuals in subjective components of morbidity that reflect the more direct impact of disease.

Patients with arthritis, diabetes, cancer, renal disease, or a dermatological problem were compared to well individuals on various standardized psychological well-being instruments. No differences were found in comparisons with well individuals.[25] This result is unusual in finding no difference in psychological well-being between chronically sick populations and the healthy. However, the overall pattern from a number of studies is clear. Effects of chronic illness are less apparent with regard to psychological well-being than for more physical aspects of QOL. None of the above studies directly invited patients to assess their overall quality of life. One of the few studies to compare various patient groups with chronic health problems using a very detailed QOL assessment obtained interesting results.[26] Patients with severe osteoarthritis and peptic ulcer rated quality of life the same as a healthy sample, patients with irritable bowel syndrome experienced poorer QOL. How-

[23] Stewart *et al.* (1989).
[24] Brazier *et al.* (1992).
[25] Cassileth *et al.* (1984).
[26] McGee *et al.* (1991); O'Boyle *et al.* (1992).

ever, the similarities are more striking than the differences. In another comparative study of three groups—patients with head and neck cancer, patients with a temporary injury requiring orthopaedic surgery, and healthy controls—no overall differences in QOL between groups could be detected.[27]

Illnesses differ from each other in the precise ways in which they impact upon quality of life. Again systematic analysis is difficult because of heterogeneity of samples and methods. The Medical Outcomes Study shows particularly poor scores in physical function for patients with congestive heart failure and myocardial infarction compared with those patients with hypertension, diabetes, gastrointestinal, or back problems.[28] Congestive heart failure and heart disease are also associated with somewhat poorer scores in terms of maintaining normal social activities. By contrast differences between patient groups for psychological well-being are considerably smaller. This pattern of differences has also been obtained for a Swedish study with quite different samples and measures; individuals with congestive heart failure and myocardial infarction scored worse than patients with diabetes or hypertension for physical function measures whereas differences in terms of psychological mood were minimal and in terms of social function were not present at all.[29] Differences between patients with arthritis and controls in terms of psychological well-being are far smaller than differences for pain and mobility.[30] Other comparative studies with varying designs and recruitment criteria consistently indicate fewer differences between chronically sick patient groups for psychological mood than for other dimensions.[31] Where chronically sick patients are asked to provide summary statements of their quality of life, although patients with heart disease and cancer are slightly less favourable in their ratings compared with patients with lung disease, diabetes, and arthritis, differences are not significant and patients tend to give reasonably positive ratings of QOL.[32] In summary illnesses differ in the specific physical challenges and problems they pose individuals but the more that comparisons are made in terms of personal well-being (whether in terms of self-rated quality of life, life satisfaction, or standardized measures of psychological well-being) results are more striking for the similarities than the differences between the sick and the well.

[27] Kreitler *et al.* (1993). [28] Stewart *et al.* (1989).
[29] Tibblin *et al.* (1990). [30] Mason *et al.* (1983); Stewart *et al.* (1989).
[31] Cassileth *et al.* (1984); Rudick *et al.* (1992).
[32] Pearlman and Uhlmann (1988).

Differences in QOL between illnesses may be less marked because underlying disease processes vary in severity, both between individuals and over time. Indeed it has been noted that the majority of variance in QOL is unexplained by means of disease-category.[33] Measures of disease severity are not unproblematic and involve many of the methodological and conceptual issues involved in QOL. Several studies have suggested that increased disease severity is associated with poorer QOL. Thus physiological and clinical measures are associated with QOL in cystic fibrosis,[34] lung cancer,[35] and rheumatoid arthritis.[36] Other studies have found associations between degree of neurological disability and dysfunction and QOL scores in multiple sclerosis[37] seizure frequency and QOL in epilepsy[38] and deteriorating scores for QOL between patients with HIV infection and full ARC and AIDS.[39]

In the majority of studies it is striking that correlations are greater between disease severity and more physical aspects of QOL measures, and weaker or non-significant with dimensions such as psychological well-being. This is the case in studies using a variety of different multidimensional measures of QOL in rheumatoid arthritis,[40] lung cancer,[41] and multiple sclerosis.[42]

Equally striking is the fact that the correlation between disease severity and QOL variables tends to be quite modest, particularly with regard to components such as psychological well-being. In the majority of the studies cited and in other studies of diverse conditions such as stroke[43] multiple sclerosis,[44] and heart disease,[45] very little of the variance in QOL is explained by disease.

THE JUDGEMENTS OF OBSERVERS

One of the main practical reasons for the development of patient-based measures of QOL is that patients and health professionals differ substantially in their judgements of the matter. This body of evidence is considered under the heading of experiential rather than normative approaches, because in the main such studies consider health professionals' views of the quality of life of a particular individual with a

[33] Stewart *et al*, (1989). [34] Kaplan *et al.* (1989). [35] Regan *et al.* (1991).
[36] Deyo *et al.* (1982); Fitzpatrick *et al.* (1992*a*). [37] Rudick *et al.* (1992).
[38] Vickrey *et al.* (1992). [39] Kaplan *et al.* (1989); Wu *et al.* (1991).
[40] Deyo *et al.* (1982); Bulsma *et al.* (1991); Fitzpatrick *et al.* (1992*a*).
[41] Regan *et al.* (1991). [42] Rudick *et al.* (1992). [43] Anderson (1988).
[44] Robinson (1988). [45] Badura and Waltz (1984).

particular health problem and relative and imagined views regarding differing health states are not elicited and not of concern to such research. Doctors' ratings of patients' quality of life and related constructs such as psychological well-being agree only moderately with those of the patients whom they assess.[46] Most commonly a major source of the discrepancies is that health professionals' judgements are more negative than those of their patients.[47] The differences are greater for more subjective aspects of quality of life compared with dimensions that may be more visible such as functional status.[48] The one dimension in which health professionals make more positive assumptions than their patients is pain severity.[49] Other lay persons involved with sick individuals may not make more accurate judgements.[50]

Although the data are patchy, it is possible therefore to summarize the experiential data regarding health-related quality of life in terms of a number of trends:

1. Overall the majority of patients with significant illness report their quality of life (and related constructs) in positive terms.
2. Patients with significant illness emphasize more psychological and social dimensions of quality of life rather than assessing quality of life mainly in terms of physical function.
3. Patients with significant illness differ from healthy individuals only modestly in overall psychological well-being and less with regard to psychological and social dimensions of quality of life than in terms of physical function.
4. Patients with different illnesses differ from each other less in relation to psychological and social dimensions of quality of life than in terms of physical function.
5. Disease severity, whether measured within or between diseases, is weakly related to quality of life and correlations with disease severity are weaker for psychological and social dimensions of quality of life than for physical function.
6. Observers (particularly health professionals) of patients with significant illness agree only modestly with patients' own ratings of quality of life. They agree with patients less with regard to social and psychological dimensions of quality of life than in relation to physical function.

[46] Pearlman and Uhlmann (1988); Slevin *et al.* (1988).
[47] Sprangers and Aaronson (1992).
[48] Uhlmann and Pearlman (1991); Sprangers and Aaronson (1992).
[49] Teske *et al.* (1983) [50] Sprangers and Aaronson (1992).

THE NORMATIVE APPROACH TO HEALTH-RELATED QUALITY OF LIFE

The second and quite distinct tradition of research regarding health-related quality of life, instead of examining the perceptions and evaluations of ill individuals, elicits from panels of experimental subjects evaluations of the desirability, severity, or utility attached to different health states. Although much of the pioneering work in this field did not set out explicitly to assess 'health-related quality of life' *per se*, referring instead to 'valuations'[51] or 'utilities'[52] of health states, the work has rapidly been disseminated into medical and health policy discussions as being concerned with quality of life.

A variety of experimental methods have now been developed to obtain respondents' judgements of the severity or desirability of varying states of ill-health. Six methods are most commonly used: standard gamble, time trade-off, category scaling, magnitude estimation, equivalence and willingness to pay. Many of these methods have origins in other fields such as decision theory and psychometrics. The application of these methods to valuations of health states has generated a substantial and complex body of evidence that it is beyond the scope of this chapter to review. However, it is worth pointing out that as well as obvious differences of approach between these very different methods, there are a number of more subtle issues that all approaches face in eliciting respondents' preferences. There are a number of issues regarding the identification and description of health states to be judged.[53] There are also numerous framing effects that influence judgements; whether for example outcomes of treatment are described in terms of chances of survival or chances of death; or, another influence, whether health states are given a diagnostic label or not.[54]

Recent overviews of the field disagree in the overall extent of convergence of results between methods, while agreeing that methods clearly diverge in relation to specific health states.[55] Some of the methods have predictable biases. Individuals tend to be somewhat risk averse so that in standard gamble exercises they prefer states of ill-health to risks associated with the possibility of complete recovery.[56] The consequence is

[51] Rosser and Kind (1976). [52] Sackett and Torrance (1978).
[53] Froberg and Kane (1989*a*).
[54] Froberg and Kane (1989*b*); Hall *et al.* (1992).
[55] Froberg and Kane (1989*b*); Buxton, (1992); Nord (1992). [56] Nord (1992).

that various states of ill-health are portrayed by this approach as relatively attractive.

Discussions of this field have been more heated than in relation to the experiential data, largely because the normative approach to QOL is more directly tied to policy issues, particularly resource allocation. Frequently, discussions of methodology have been conflated with the many moral and ethical issues arising from the application of normative data to resource allocation.[57] This impassioned debate has served to highlight more dramatically than with parallel experiential studies (prone to similar problems) the shortcomings of results in terms of inconsistencies between methods, impact of framing effects, evidence of lack of consensus in panels, and problems of sampling and sample sizes of studies.[58] Social scientists in particular have emphasized the scope for social and cultural disagreement over health utilities.[59] However, a more balanced appraisal of work regarding social and cultural differences might be more struck by the degree of consensus in this field.[60] On reflection is it so surprising that individuals of different social backgrounds prefer the absence rather than presence of broken legs, confinement to bed, pain, or depression?

The only evidence of any degree of systematic social difference between individuals' reponses to such tasks relates to two variables: age and experience of illness. In some studies[61] but not others[62] older respondents rate some health states more favourably than younger individuals. Again, in some studies[63] but not others[64] those who have a significant health problem rate various health states more favourably than those who are well. Such evidence has given rise to an interesting philosophical debate about whose values should predominate in resource allocation exercises, those of the patients who have health problems and receive health care or those of society more generally who ultimately fund the care.[65] It has even been suggested that the more favourable ratings of health status reported by sick patients in utility judgement studies represent political behaviour to gain resources.[66]

The results of what I have described as normative studies of quality

57 Smith (1987). 58 Mulkay *et al.* (1987); Carr-Hill (1989).
59 Schroeder (1983); Mulkay *et al.* (1987).
60 Patrick *et al.* (1985); Froberg and Kane (1989*c*).
61 Sackett and Torrance (1978); Ebrahim *et al.* (1991).
62 Rosser and Kind (1976).
63 Rosser and Kind (1976); Sackett and Torrance (1978).
64 McNeil *et al.* (1982). 65 Menzel (1990); Potts (1992).
66 Sackett and Torrance (1978).

of life in health are clearly distinctive and different from those obtained by experiential studies. Again one may do an injustice to nuances of difference between studies but the following are tendencies identifiable in a number of studies obtained from samples from diverse Western societies.[67]

1. Overall individuals imagine different health states to vary very considerably in terms of quality of life.
2. Individuals regard physical, social, and psychological function to be equally important to quality of life.

It is clear that there is a quite distinct difference in the judgements about quality of life associated with illness as imagined by experimental panels and as reported by individuals experiencing such states. Before considering the implications arising from such contrasting results of the experiential and normative approaches to health-related quality of life, an important additional issue needs to be considered, the importance of change over time in quality of life.

CHANGE IN QUALITY OF LIFE OVER TIME

Most applications of quality of life measures in health care particularly in clinical trials, evaluation, and resource allocation studies require quantitative assessment of the degree of improvement or deterioration in quality of life due to health care. This is usually obtained by measuring quality of life scores in patients before and after the treatment of concern usually with similar measures obtained from a placebo or control group. There are numerous technical problems associated with the detection and interpretation of such changes over time, many of which turn on the question of what will count as a significant improvement or deterioration. The quantitative expression of the size of change scores in terms of units of a quality of life instrument do not provide intuitively accessible evidence of the importance of the change.[68] Similarly, conventional tests of statistical significance may not provide a clear indication of the personal or clinical significance of change. A number of discussions have considered methods of deriving expressions of what constitutes a significant change over time in quality of life. One method to estimate significance compares quality of life changes

[67] Kaplan and Anderson (1988); Nord (1991); Williams and Kind (1992).
[68] Hopkins (1992).

to health professionals' judgements of change.[69] However, this approach is limited because of extensive evidence of well-established limitations in health professionals' judgements to which reference has already been made. A second method is to examine change scores for quality of life instruments in patients receiving treatments already established to be efficacious.[70] This can be an informative technique but requires knowledge of treatments' efficacy when that is usually the very uncertainty motivating the development of instruments in the first place. The most appropriate method of defining what constitutes a significant improvement or deterioration is to resort to the patient as arbiter. Most commonly this involves examining quality of life change scores of subgroups of patients who independently define themselves either as having experienced a significant change in quality of life or not over the relevant time period.[71]

Thus whilst in relative terms we know a very great deal about how various *states of health* are valued either from the point of view of sufferers or the imagined values of others, we know far less from either perspective about how *change* in health-related quality of life should be measured. There are two issues: how to measure changes in health-related quality of life and how such changes are valued. As with static measures, in relation to the second question there is an important question as to whether direct judgements (via experiential methods) produce similar results to those obtained by normative values.

Studies of change over time in quality of life are too few and arguments at this point are somewhat speculative. A study of patients with rheumatoid arthritis can be used to illustrate some of the problems of measuring change in health status and quality of life.[72] Patients were asked to complete four widely used instruments each time they attended an outpatient clinic. They did so every three months as well as being assessed by means of standard clinical and laboratory measures of disease severity. Change scores were produced by calculating differences for instruments between visits. None of the four instruments consistently produced more sensitive measures of change over time when measured against other criteria such as patients' or doctor's global judgements or changes in disease severity. Moreover patients reported considerable changes in their health status in response to transition questions (directly rating their health status as better than, the same as, or worse

[69] Chambers *et al.* (1987). [70] Bombardier *et al.* (1991).
[71] Guyatt *et al.* (1989*b*); Deyo *et al.* (1991).
[72] Fitzpatrick *et al.* (1992*b*); Fitzpatrick *et al.* (1993).

than at a previous time). Patients had experienced various substantial changes that had not been detected by comparing the differences of scores between visits for any of the static measures. Some evidence for the validity of these direct transition judgements was found when transition judgements were found consistently to correlate more strongly with changes in underlying disease than did the change scores calculated from static measures.[73]

One should not infer too much from one study. However, the overall inference from this study of transition judgements is that patients may detect significant and important changes in health-related quality of life that are not picked up by even the most established of health status measures. Other studies have also begun to explore the value of such direct transition judgements. In direct comparisons with change scores for conventional static measures they may be as sensitive or more sensitive to changes occurring to the patient.[74] In clinical trials they have provided better evidence of the advantages of active drug over placebo than have conventional static measures.[75]

At a more speculative level such data raise the issue of the values attached to such changes. Studies of change over time in quality of life that use values derived from utility studies require the assumption that the value of a change from state *x* to state *y* is the same as the difference between the static values assigned to the two values. Whilst a simple assumption, it may not be accurate. Values attached to health as to other states of well-being may be influenced by prior experience and contrasts.[76] Moreover, according to prospect theory, values attach to changes in well-being and welfare, rather than final states and human perception, is more attuned to evaluating transition and change.[77] Gains and losses to health that to someone in full health seem minimal may have greater significance to someone who has experienced more severe health problems. This is one very plausible way of explaining the results of a study in which patients three years after a cancer operation were found to be happier than a control group.[78] Similarly patients with severe osteoarthritis who underwent total joint surgery were found after detailed assessment of self-assessed quality of life to have more favourable scores six months and two years after surgery compared with healthy controls.[79]

[73] Ziebland *et al.* (1992). [74] Mackenzie *et al.* (1986); Tugwell *et al.* (1987).
[75] Bombardier *et al.* (1991). [76] Tversky and Griffin (1991).
[77] Kahneman and Tversky (1979). [78] Irwin *et al.* (1982).
[79] O'Boyle *et al.* (1992).

DISCUSSION AND CONCLUSIONS

There are two distinct approaches that have been developed to assess the quality of life associated with different health states. Overall they produce different results. The approach that has largely drawn on the experiential judgements of patients who are actually in various health states may be summarized as emphasizing that typically such patients make positive adjustments to the various difficulties posed by their ill-health, so that the majority of individuals experiencing significant ill-health report positive well-being. By contrast the analyses provided by normative studies in which individuals imagine various states of ill-health emphasize instead the marked variation in quality of life associated with different health states, with a wide range of values from positive to very negative levels of overall quality of life.

Differences between the two approaches are not at all difficult to explain. There is now a reasonably substantial literature, particularly in psychology to explain why individuals are not good judges of the actual rather than imagined desirability of different states, so that, in the current case, they make erroneous judgements of the quality of life of the ill.[80] Individuals appear to have very little insight into how to predict or pursue future feelings and preferences. They have little insight into the pervasive effects of habituation to the widest range of perceptual stimuli, not just health states. Moreover, they are unaware of the contextual, comparative, and relative nature of well-being. Kahneman and Varey argue that judgements about other states, such as being paraplegic or seriously ill are more influenced by intuitions about the transition into that state from one's current position than by understanding of the experience of being in that different state: 'powerful intuitions are likely to lead us astray when we compare the utilities of different individuals.'[81]

The recruitment of patients into normative studies of utilities may not address the problem. Broadly, normative studies reveal that unwell patients have much the same preferences as the healthy except in some exceptional states. In the hypothetical judgements required of utility studies the sick reveal the same universal preferences to be well rather than sick. The sick are not much better placed than any one to judge the quality of life of those with various kinds of other illnesses. The clearest evidence is that their estimates of health status utilities do not

[80] Kahneman and Varey (1991).

[81] Kahneman and Varey (1991), 144.

correspond to any of the evidence of quality of life reported by patients with different health problems. Thus it is unlikely to make a very substantial difference to normative studies to alter the constituencies of panels involved in assigning values to health states to include more patients.

It is important to recognize that the two approaches, which have been termed respectively 'subjectivist' and 'normative' correspond to two equally legitimate and apparently irreconcilable positions in welfare philosophy and social choice theory.[82] Arguments of anti-paternalists require respect for personal preferences—such as the claims of most chronically ill individuals that they have a good quality of life. By contrast the normative approach to welfare permits decisions that may be defended as being in the long-term interests of the blind or the foolish who entertain misguided preferences. Most discussions of the more abstract issues appear to conclude with a need to reconcile 'subjectivist' and 'normative' approaches to welfare. I would merely note that the utilities approach clearly errs on the side of the normative and the paternalist.

I have presented the two approaches—studies in which the ill report their own quality of life and studies in which individuals estimate the desirability of various imagined health states—as perhaps more starkly different than is fair and also as if they both seek to achieve precisely the same objective. By most epistemological standards the first approach, for all its definitional and measurement problems, must be relatively closer to accurate description of the quality of life of patients experiencing illness. However, that conclusion is to be unfair in one very important way to the second, normative-approach to health-related quality of life. Those who adopt this approach might reasonably argue that their objective is not primarily to describe the subjective experiences of those who are ill. The objective of most utility studies is to achieve various pragmatic goals, particularly the most appropriate allocation of scarce health care resources. For that purpose the social consensus of the desirability of various imagined health states is a better basis for decision-making than the reported quality of life of the sick. To be simplistic the sick would be their own worst enemies in such an approach, given their tendencies to view severe health states favourably.[83] It is a reasonable defence of normative approaches that society in general's preferences for various health states is a more sensible basis for resource allocation, not least because it may have more beneficial resource allocation consequences for the sick than reliance on the latters' own judgements.

[82] Gibbard (1986). [83] Menzel (1990).

On the surface it is plausible that normative data are more likely to be sensitive to gains in quality of life associated with particular treatments because of the greater variability of scores *associated with health states* found in normative compared with experiential studies. However, a more meaningful comparison would be to examine by the two contrasting approaches the perceived value of changes over time in quality of life arising from health care interventions. It is even less clear that individuals can make the appropriate imaginary leap to assess transitions that would be required. In which case it would be more appropriate to derive our quality of life values directly from patients experiencing changes in relation to treatment. Patients would assign values to the changes in health status experienced in the course of treatment for their problems. It may be argued that such an approach would be hopelessly difficult to manage across diverse dimensions of quality of life transitions for diverse patients for diverse therapies. However, current estimates of Quality-adjusted Life Years (QALYs) for diverse treatments also have to be grounded in complex and time-consuming studies to be plausible. The proposed modification to such studies may merely involve that patients in such studies directly express the value attached to changes over time. Problems may inhere more in deriving standardized scores from such evaluations to permit comparisons across studies. However, such difficulties are no greater than existing methodological challenges in deriving scores for static states from hypothetical exercises. The merit of the proposed amendment to current methods is the greater legitimacy of values derived from those experiencing transitions.

As experimental evidence accumulates of individuals' lack of insight into their future utilities[84] it will be increasingly difficult to defend health policies derived from panels' judgements about hypothetical states and resource allocation will need to be more closely grounded in evidence of experienced benefits of health care.

REFERENCES

Aaronson, N. (1989), 'Quality of Life Assessment in Clinical Trials: Methodological Issues', *Controlled Clinical Trials*, 10.

Anderson, R. (1988), 'The Quality of Life of Stroke Patients and their Carers',

[84] Kahneman (1994).

in R. Anderson and M. Bury (eds.), *Living with Chronic Illness*. London: Unwin Hyman.

BADURA, B., and WALTZ, M. (1984), 'Social Support and Quality of Life Following Myocardial Infarction', *Social Indicators Research*, 14.

BOMBARDIER, C., *et al.* (1991), 'A Comparison of Health-Related Quality of Life Measures for Rheumatoid Arthritis Research', *Controlled Clinical Trials*, 12.

BRAZIER, J., *et al.* (1992), 'Validating the SF-36 Health Survey Questionnaire: New Outcome Measure for Primary Care', *British Medical Journal*, 305.

BULSMA, J., *et al.* (1991), 'Relation between Patients' own Health Assessment and Clinical and Laboratory Findings in Rheumatoid Arthritis', *Journal of Rheumatology*, 18.

BUXTON, M. (1992), 'Are we Satisfied with QALYs? What are the Conceptual and Empirical Uncertainties?', in A. Hopkins (ed.), *Measures of Quality of Life*. London: Royal College of Physicians.

CAMPBELL, A. (1981), *The Sense of Well-Being in America*. New York: McGraw-Hill.

CARR-HILL, R. (1989), 'Assumptions of the QALY Procedure', *Social Science and Medicine*, 29.

CASSILETH, B., *et al.* (1984), 'Psychosocial Status in Chronic Illness: A Comparative Analysis of Six Diagnostic Groups', *New England Journal of Medicine*, 311.

CELLA, D., and TULSKY, D. (1990), 'Measuring Quality of Life Today: Methodological Aspects', *Oncology*, 4.

CHAMBERS, L. *et al.* (1987), 'Sensitivity to Change and the Effect of Mode of Administration on Health Status Measurement', *Medical Care*, 25.

DEYO, R., *et al.* (1982), 'Physical and Psychosocial Function in Rheumatoid Arthritis', *Archives of Internal Medicine*, 142.

——, DIEHR, P., and PATRICK, D. (1991), 'Reproducibility and Responsiveness of Health Status Measures', *Controlled Clinical Trials*, 12.

DIMENAS, E., *et al.* (1990), 'Defining Quality of Life in Medicine', *Scandinavian Journal of Health Care*, Suppl. 1.

EBRAHIM, S., BRITTIS, S., and WU, A. (1991), 'The Valuation of States of Ill-Health: The Impact of Age and Disability', *Age and Ageing*, 20.

ELSTER, J., and ROEMER, J. (1991), 'Introduction', in J. Elster and J. Roemer (eds.), *Interpersonal Comparisons of Well-Being*. Cambridge: Cambridge University Press.

FEINSTEIN, A. (1977), 'Clinical Biostatistics XLI. Hard Science, Soft Data and the Challenge of Choosing Clinical Variables in Research', *Clinical and Pharmacological Therapeutics*, 22.

FITZPATRICK, R., *et al.* (1992*a*), 'A Generic Health Status Instrument in the Assessment of Rheumatoid Arthritis', *British Journal of Rheumatology*, 31.

——, *et al.* (1992*b*), 'Importance of Sensitivity to Change as a Criterion for Selecting Health Status Measures', *Quality in Health Care*, 1.

——, *et al.* (1993), 'Transition Questions to Assess Outcomes in Rheumatoid Arthritis', *British Journal of Rheumatology*, 32.

FOWLIE, M., and BERKELEY, J. (1987), 'Quality of Life: A Review of the Literature', *Family Practice*, 4.

FROBERG, D., and KANE, R. (1989*a*), 'Methodology for Measuring Health-State Preferences—I: Measurement Strategies', *Journal of Clinical Epidemiology*, 42.

—— (1989*b*), 'Methodology for Measuring Health State Preferences—II: Scaling Methods', *Journal of Clinical Epidemiology*, 42.

—— (1989*c*), 'Methodology for Measuring Health State Preferences—III: Population and Context Effects', *Journal of Clinical Epidemiology*, 42.

GIBBARD, A. (1986), 'Interpersonal Comparisons: Preference, Good and the Intrinsic Reward of a Life', in J. Elster and A. Hylland (eds.), *Foundations of Social Choice Theory*. Cambridge: Cambridge University Press.

GOTAY, C., and MOORE, T. (1992), 'Assessing Quality of Life in Head and Neck Cancer', *Quality of Life Research*, 1.

GUYATT, G., *et al.* (1989*a*), 'Measuring Quality of Life in Clinical Trials: A Taxonomy and Review', *Canadian Medical Association Journal*, 140.

——, *et al.* (1989*b*), 'Responsiveness and Validity in Health Status Measurement: A Clarification', *Journal of Clinical Epidemiology*, 42.

HALL, J., *et al.* (1992), 'A Cost Utility Analysis of Mammography Screening in Australia', *Social Science and Medicine*, 34.

HARWOOD, R., and EBRAHIM, S. (1992), 'Quality of Life', *Lancet*, 338.

HOPKINS, A. (1992), 'How Might Measures of Quality of Life be Useful to Me as a Clinician?', in A. Hopkins (ed.), *Measures of the Quality of Life*. London: Royal College of Physicians.

HUNT, S., and MCKENNA, S. (1992), 'Do We Need Measures other than QALYs?', in A. Hopkins (ed.), *Measures of the Quality of Life*. London: Royal College Physicians.

IRWIN, P., *et al.* (1982), 'Quality of Life after Radiation Therapy: A Study of 309 Cancer Survivors', *Social Indicators Research*, 10.

JENKINS, C. (1992), 'Assessment of Outcomes of Health Intervention', *Social Science and Medicine*, 35.

KAHNEMAN, D. (1994), 'New Challenges to the Rationality Assumption', *Journal of Institutional and Theoretical Economics*, 150/1.

——, and TVERSKY, A. (1979), 'Prospect Theory: An Analysis of Decision under Risk', *Econometrica*, 47.

——, and VAREY, C. (1991), 'Notes on the Psychology of Utility', in J. Elster and J. Roemer (eds.), *Interpersonal Comparisons of Well-being*. Cambridge: Cambridge University Press.

KAPLAN, R., and ANDERSON, J. (1988), 'The Quality of Well-Being Scale: Rationale for a Single Quality of Life Index', in S. Walker and R. Rosser (eds.), *Quality of Life: Assessment and Application*. Leicester: MTP Press.

KAPLAN, R., and ANDERSON, J. *et al.* (1989), 'The Quality of Well-Being Scale: Applications in AIDS, Cystic Fibrosis and Arthritis', *Medical Care*, 27.

KREITLER, S., *et al.* (1993), 'Life Satisfaction and Health in Cancer Patients, Orthopedic Patients and Healthy Individuals', *Social Science and Medicine*, 36.

MACKENZIE, R., *et al.* (1986), 'A Patient-Specific Measure of Change in Maximal Function', *Archives of Internal Medicine*, 146.

MASON, J., *et al.* (1983), 'Health Status in Chronic Disease: A Comparative Study of Rheumatoid Arthritis', *Journal of Rheumatology*, 10.

MCGEE, H., *et al.* (1991), 'Assessing the Quality of Life of the Individual', *Psychological Medicine*, 21.

MCNEIL, B., *et al.* (1982), 'On the Elicitation of Preferences for Alternative Therapies', *New England Journal of Medicine*, 306.

MENZEL, P., (1990), *Strong Medicine*: *The Ethical Rationing of Health Care*. Oxford: Oxford University Press.

MULKAY, M., ASHMORE, M., PINCH, T. (1987), 'Measuring the Quality of Life: A Sociological Invention Concerning the Application of Economics to Health Care', *Sociology*, 21.

NAJMAN, J., and LEVINE, S. (1981), 'Evaluating the Impact of Medical Care and Technologies on the Quality of Life: A Review and Critique', *Social Science and Medicine*, 15F.

NORD, E. (1991), 'EuroQol: Health Related Quality of Life Measurement: Valuations of Health States by the General Public in Norway', *Health Policy*, 18.

—— (1992), 'Methods for Quality Adjustment of Life Years', *Social Science and Medicine*, 34.

O'BOYLE, C. (1992), 'Assessment of Quality of Life in Surgery', *British Journal of Surgery*, 79.

——, *et al.* (1992), 'Individual Quality of Life in Patients Undergoing Hip Replacement', *Lancet*, 339.

OLSON, G., and SCHOBER, B. (1993), 'The Satisfied Poor: Development of an Intervention-Oriented Theoretical Framework to Explain Satisfaction with a Life in Poverty', *Social Indicators Research*, 28.

PATRICK, D., *et al.* (1985), 'A Cross-Cultural Comparison of Health Status values', *American Journal of Public Health*, 75.

PEARLMAN, R., and UHLMANN, R. (1988), 'Quality of Life in Chronic Diseases: Perceptions of Elderly Patients', *Journal of Gerontology*, 43.

POTTS, S. (1992), 'The QALY and Why It Should be Resisted', in E. Mathews and M. Menlowe (eds.), *Philosophy and Health Care*. Aldershot: Avebury.

REGAN, J., *et al.* (1991), 'Palliation and Life Quality in Lung Cancer: How Good are Clinicians at Judging Treatment Outcome?', *British Journal of Cancer*, 64.

ROBINSON, I. (1988), *Multiple Sclerosis*. London: Routledge.

ROSSER, R., and KIND, P. (1976), 'A Scale of Valuations of States of Illness: Is There a Social Consensus? *International Journal of Epidemiology*, 7.

——, *et al.* (1992), 'Index of Health-Related Quality of Life', in A. Hopkins (ed.), *Measures of the Quality of Life*. London: Royal College of Physicians.

RUDICK, R., *et al.* (1992), 'Quality of Life in Multiple Sclerosis: Comparison with Inflammatory Bowel Disease and Rheumatoid Arthritis', *Archives of Neurology*, 49.

SACKETT, D., and TORRANCE, G. (1978), 'The Utility of Different Health States as Perceived by the General Public', *Journal of Chronic Diseases*, 31.

SCHROEDER, E. (1983), 'Concepts of Health and Illness', in A. Culyer (ed.), *Health Indicators*. Oxford: Martin Robertson.

SCHUMACHER, M., OLSCHEWSKI, M., and SCHULGEN, G., (1991), 'Assessment of Quality of Life in Clinical Trials', *Statistics in Medicine*, 10.

SCHWARZ, N., and STRACK, F. (1991), 'Evaluating One's Life: A Judgement Model of Subjective Well-Being', in F. Strack, M. Argyle, N. Schwarz (eds.), *Subjective Well-Being*. Oxford: Pergamon Press.

SLEVIN M., *et al.* (1988), 'Who Should Measure Quality of Life, the Doctor or the Patient?', *British Journal of Cancer*, 57.

SMITH, A. (1987), 'Qualms about QALYs', *Lancet,* 1.

SPITZER, W., *et al.* (1981), 'Measuring the Quality of Life of Cancer Patients', *Journal of Chronic Diseases*, 34.

SPRANGERS, M., and AARONSON, N. (1992), 'The Role of Health Care Providers and Significant Others in Evaluating the Quality of Life of Patients with Chronic Disease: A Review', *Journal of Clinical Epidemiology*, 45.

STEWART, A., *et al.* (1989), 'Functional Status and Well-Being of Patients with Chronic Conditions', *Journal of American Medical Association*, 262.

SUTHERLAND, H., LOCKWOD, G., and BOYD, N. (1990), 'Ratings of the Importance of Quality of Life Variables: Therapeutic Implications for Patients with Metastatic Breast Cancer', *Journal of Clinical Epidemiology*, 43.

TESKE, K., DAUT, R., and CLEELAND, C. (1983), 'Relationships between Nurses' Observations and Patients' Self Reports of Pain', *Pain*, 16.

TIBBLIN, G., CATO, K., and SVA-RDSUDD, K. (1990), 'Goteburg Quality of Life Study of Men Born in 1913 and 1923—Age, Sex, Job Satisfaction and Cardiovascular Diseases', *Scandinavian Journal of Primary Health Care* Supplement, 1.

TUGWELL, P., *et al.* (1987), 'The MACTAR Patient Preference Disability Questionnaire', *Journal of Rheumatology*, 14.

TVERSKY, A., and GRIFFIN, D. (1991), 'Endowment and Contrast in Judgements of Well-Being', in F. Strack, M. Argyle, N. Schwarz (eds.), *Subjective Well-Being*. Oxford: Pergamon Press.

UHLMANN, R. and PEARLMAN, R. (1991), 'Perceived Quality of Life and Preferences \for Life-Sustaining Treatment in Older Adults', *Archives of Internal Medicine*, 151.

Vickrey, B., *et al.* (1992), 'Reliability and Validity of the Katz Adjustment Scales in an Epilepsy Sample', *Quality of Life Research*, 1.

Ware, J., *et al.* (1981), 'Choosing Measures of Health Status for Individuals in General Populations', *American Journal of Public Health*, 71.

Williams, A., and Kind, P. (1992), 'The Present State of Play about QALYs', in A. Hopkins (ed.), *Measures of the Quality of Life*. London: Royal College of Physicians.

Wu, A., *et al.* (1991), 'A Health Status Questionnaire Using 30 Items from the Medical Outcomes Study: Preliminary Validation in Persons with Early HIV infection', *Medical Care*, 29.

Ziebland, S. *et al.* (1992), 'Comparison of Two Approaches to Measuring Change in Health Status in Rheumatoid Arthritis', *Annals of Rheumatic Diseases*, 51.

8

The Quality of Employment: Perspectives and Problems

DUNCAN GALLIE

While one can detect the emergence of a distinct 'quality of employment' movement from the 1960s, the central issues it raised can be seen as a continuation of a much older concern within industrial sociology with the impact of employment conditions both on the subjective well-being of employees and on their ability to realize their potential. In particular, it built upon two broad research traditions. The first consisted of researchers working within a neo-Marxian perspective, seeking to sharpen their critique of capitalist society by exposing the alienating qualities of the division of labour. It focused on the way in which work tasks and employment relations curbed the potential for human creativity and development. The second comprised researchers primarily concerned with subjective well-being, sometimes influenced by a belief in its importance for productivity. I shall start by outlining the assumptions and conclusions of these two contrasting perspectives, and then examine some of the problems that arise in trying to assess the quality of work life and the way it is changing over time.

THE OBJECTIVE QUALITY OF WORK LIFE: THE NEO-MARXIAN APPROACH

Georges Friedmann: mechanisation and the despiritualization of work

The defining characteristic of the Marxian approach is its assumption that human beings develop their powers through material practices and, most centrally, through their practices in work. The pre-eminent sociologist who developed this into a major perspective in social research was Georges Friedmann, whose work had a pervasive influence over French industrial sociology for more than a decade.[1] The most influential statement of his views was *Problemes humains du machinisme industriel*, originally published in France in 1946 and translated into English as *Industrial Society* in 1955. For Friedmann, the critical determinant of the capacity for self-development was the extent to which the work task entailed the integration of both conception and execution in the work process. The underlying model of the ideal work setting was that of the nineteenth-century craftsman, who had individual responsibility for both designing and producing the product. The principal criteria for assessing change in the quality of work were the extent to which it integrated or separated the intellectual and non-intellectual components of the work process and the extent to which it gave the worker direct individual control over the process of production.

Friedmann focused on the way in which changes in managerial practices and in technology were transforming the nature of the work task in a way that was destroying the very possibility for human creativity and self-development. His starting-point was the transformation of managerial philosophies of worker productivity, in the wake of the growing influence of the ideas of Frederick Winslow Taylor, commonly referred to as 'scientific management'. For Taylor, the independent craftsman was a major obstacle to increased industrial efficiency. To overcome this, it was necessary for management itself to take over responsibility for the conceptual part of the work process, thereby giving it the power to organize employees in a way that would maximize the efficiency of production. This would be ensured by scientific assessment, through time and motion study, of the ways of minimizing wasted effort and movement in work. The innovation in Taylor's method was to move beyond the measurement of the time taken for the whole task, to focus on the time taken in carrying out the constituent components of tasks. Waste time, he argued, could be eliminated by breaking down tasks into very simple components, requiring employees to use only very easy, repetitive gestures.

The central focus of Friedmann's critique of the Taylorist work system was that it was morally corrosive because of its systematic tendency to deskill employees and to increase the separation between manual and intellectual labour. While accepting that the processes of change in work could generate new skills for the creation and maintenance of new

[1] For a good account of Friedmann's influence both through his seminar and, less directly, through the work of the *Institut des Sciences Sociales du Travail*, see Rose (1979).

types of equipment, Friedmann's view was that the principal trend of change was towards the deskilling of work. As he put it, 'The steady trend of "scientific management" is to cause semi-skilled workers to perform all operations which can be performed, without calling on the worker's intelligence and personality'.[2]

It was above all through these consequences for skill that the evolution of industry was undermining the quality of people's experience of work. It destroyed the vital functions of work for the stability and development of the personality. 'Though Taylor tried to defend himself against this charge,' he wrote, 'it is incontestable that Scientific Management and its variants actually destroy all individual initiative in many workers.' The destruction of the intellectual content of the work led to what Friedmann called the 'despiritualization of work'.[3]

Naville: the implications of automation

Friedmann's fundamental concern was with the processes of mechanization and division of labour that had culminated in the assembly line. It was soon evident, however, that in a number of industries the nature of the technology of work was undergoing a profound transformation with the introduction of advanced automation. The central question, then, was whether Friedmann's analysis of the direction of change in work was simply relevant to a transitional historical era, characterized by a particular type of mass technology production, or whether the trends he had detected would continue even with the extension of automation.

The most substantial research programme on automation conducted within a neo-Marxian perspective was directed by Pierre Naville. Its conclusions were reported in two principal publications—*L'automation et le travail humain* (1961), which provided the detailed research results of a number of case-studies of automation and, *Vers l'automatisme social?* in (1963), in which Naville speculated on the implications of the research for the more general theory of the evolution of work.

For Naville, automation represented more than a simple extension of the types of processes that had been central to Friedmann's analyses. It introduced a qualitatively new phase in the work process. The essential feature of automation was that it was a form of technology in which the machinery was to a considerable degree self-regulating, due to the introduction of a complex system of feedback mechanisms. The worker no longer dealt directly with the product (or indeed with any particular

[2] Friedmann (1955: 214). [3] Ibid. 210, 212, 390.

piece of machinery), but was responsible for the surveillance or control of a complex integrated unit. Hence automation produced the final rupture between the producer and the product and it eliminated any personalized relationship between the worker and the machine. It meant an effective end to the technically determined division of labour, since the organization of work was now no longer strongly constrained by the nature of the machinery. A system based on the allocation of individuals to specific work posts was replaced by the relatively fluid distribution of work between individuals working together as part of a team.

While automation could be seen as leading to certain improvements in work (in particular, through freeing the worker from the rhythm of the machine, by decreasing the harshness of physical effort and by leading to a much cleaner work environment), it at the same time had a sharp negative impact in terms of increased mental strain. But most notably it accentuated the decline of skill and the possibility of finding interest and meaning through the work task itself. Naville believed that the relationship between automation and skill change was a complex one, involving to some degree a polarization of the skill structure. But while one of its effects was to produce a highly specialized technical élite, this was far outweighed numerically by its effects in undercutting the skills of the majority of the work-force. Moreover, the emphasis on team work, flexibility, and polyvalence fundamentally undermined traditional occupational identities.

Whereas, in his more optimistic moments, Friedmann could still speculate about the possibility of reconstituting meaningful and enriching work tasks, Naville believed that automation had swept this off the historical agenda.[4] Alienation in capitalist society, he believed, could not now be overcome through an improvement in the quality of work. Rather, it would require trying to use the greater freedom from the constraints of work provided by automation to change the wider structures of ownership and control.

Braverman: the extension of the analysis to the middle class

While this general approach to the analysis of employment was being developed in France from the mid-1940s, it only became influential in

[4] The difference between Naville and Friedmann on this issue underlay a somewhat obscure debate between the two. For Friedmann's reply to the 'accusations', see Friedmann (1962: 395–8).

Britain and the United States some three decades later with the publication in 1974 of Harry Braverman's *Labor and Monopoly Capital*, resonantly subtitled 'The Degradation of Work in the Twentieth Century'. The similarity between the central structure of Friedmann's and Braverman's argument is so striking that the lack of more than a passing reference to Friedmann in Braverman's book is more than a little puzzling.

But Braverman's work was important in elaborating the basic argument. The occupational structure had changed a good deal since Friedmann had been writing and Braverman extended the analysis to include white-collar and service sector work. A central objection that could be made to Friedmann and his followers was that they had concentrated overwhelmingly on changes in the nature of manufacturing work. However, a major trend in the development of industrial societies was arguably the expansion of the middle classes, whose work was based in the office rather than in the factory. Whatever the accuracy of Friedmann's analysis of the fate of the manual worker in manufacturing industry, it might only apply to a category of the work-force that was rapidly diminishing and losing its significance for understanding the wider dynamics of employment relations.

Braverman directly challenged the view that the expansion of non-manual work was undercutting the relevance of traditional analyses of alienation in work. He argued that precisely the same processes of scientific management were being applied to the expanding sectors of clerical and service sector work. In the early part of the century, clerical work could be likened to a 'craft'. But with the expansion of the office and the growing centrality of clerical work for the overall work process, it too became subject to management's concern to secure a high level of control through greater technical division of labour and mechanization.[5]

'Just as in manufacturing processes', he wrote, 'in fact even more easily than in manufacturing processes—the work of the office is analysed and parcelled out among a great many detail workers, who now lose all comprehension of the process as a whole and the policies which underlie it'... 'The functions of thought and planning become concentrated in an ever smaller group within the office, and for the mass of those employed there the office became just as much a site of manual labour as the factory floor'.[6]

[5] Braverman (1974: 312). [6] See ibid. 314–16.

Braverman's version of the thesis was to provide the central theme of British industrial sociology for nearly a decade from the mid-1970s, leading to a wide array of highly discrepant case-study accounts of the nature of the labour process in different industries and occupations.

Some problems with the 'Neo-Marxist' thesis

A central problem with this tradition of research was its rather limited underlying conception of skill. The fundamental image of the type of work that provided a high quality of working life, in the sense of realizing the individual's potential, was that of craft or artisanal work, with its very direct individual control over the production process.[7] However, the case that other types of work could not be equally skilled and equally enriching for the individual is merely assumed rather than argued.

For instance, there is little consideration of the possibility that forms of co-operative or team responsibility could enable people to participate significantly in decision-making with respect to more complex production processes. With more advanced technologies, it is improbable (as Naville cogently argued) that a craft work pattern, where an individual worker has total responsibility for a single product, is a remotely viable pattern of work organization. But if the underlying concern is with the extent to which work combines conceptual and execution skills, or with the opportunities it provides for learning and self-development, then it is difficult to see any inherent reason why such characteristics should not be called upon and developed in a collective production process.

Second, this approach never really escapes from the assumption that most work is of an essentially manufacturing type. Even Braverman's analysis of non-manual work focuses on those types of activities which are concerned with the production of material outputs, albeit in paper or electronic form. It has to be admitted that this is problem that infects a great deal of the literature on work. For instance, one of the most widely read introductions to the social-psychological literature on work

[7] Naville is less dogmatic about this and raises the possibility that other types of work process might have compensatory advantages (Naville 1963: 221). But his overall pessimism about the possibilities of recreating work tasks that would be, in themselves, sources of self-development and fulfilment leads him, in practice, to much the same position with respect to the issue of skill.

TABLE 8.1. *Principal types of work*

Principal type of work (50% or more of time)	Men	Women	All employees
Caring	6	31	18
Dealing with clients	21	35	28
Organizing people	15	10	13
Production with machines	12	6	9
Maintenance of machines/vehicles	10	0	6
Assembly-line production	4	3	3
Monitoring equipment	3	0	2
Analysing information	21	14	18
Driving	9	1	5
N	1,424	1,316	2,740

Source: Employment in Britain Survey (see n. 9).

informs us that work 'consists of doing things to raw materials in order to change them into a more finished product'.[8]

But is this really an adequate characterization of work at the close of the twentieth century? One of the striking characteristics of the distribution of work in our society is how much of it is concerned not with material production, but rather with organizing, servicing, and caring for people. A recent national survey reveals that approximately half of employees spend the majority of their time in what might be termed people work (see Table 8.1).[9] Such types of work involve forms of skill for which analysis in terms of craft categories is simply misplaced. However, given such discontinuities in the underlying notion of skill, the problem arises of how the researcher is to make an assessment of whether skill levels are increasing or decreasing.

One approach might be to take the level of educational qualifications currently required for the job as a more generally applicable measure of skill levels, reflecting the general cognitive complexity of the work. The adoption of such a criteria, however, indicates that, far from the main trend being one of deskilling, there has been a marked tendency

[8] Argyle (1989: 29).

[9] The data are drawn from a representative national survey, carried out in 1992, of British employees aged 20–60. This survey was directed by Duncan Gallie and Michael White (of the Policy Studies Institute, London). For details and first results of the survey see Gallie and White (1993).

TABLE 8.2. *Change in task characteristics over previous five years by class*

Class	Increase in skill	Increase in responsibility	Increase in variety
Professional/managerial	74	79	74
Lower non-manual	70	66	68
Technician/supervisor	73	78	77
Skilled manual	64	62	70
Non-skilled manual	45	50	54
N	3,369	3,377	3,369

Source: Employment in Britain Survey (see n. 9).

for skill levels to increase in the working population.[10] A more direct approach is to rely on people's own reports about whether the skills required in their work have increased or decreased in recent years. But, data from the nationally representative Employment in Britain survey suggests that these also show that the major trend has been one of upskilling rather than deskilling (Table 8.2).

A majority of employees (63 per cent) reported that the skill they used in their job had increased over the previous five years, whereas only 9 per cent reported that the skills they used had decreased. Indeed, with the exception of semi- and non-skilled manual workers, a majority of employees at all job levels reported an increase in their skills. Very similar patterns emerge with respect to people's accounts of the ways in which the responsibility and variety of their jobs has increased. Moreover, these changes of skill level were regarded by most people as substantial. Of those that had experienced an increase in their skills, 85 per cent said that they had increased either a great deal or quite a lot. This, together with the fact that a majority of employees have also experienced an increase in the responsibility involved in their work and in the variety of the work, suggests that there has been, at least over the last decade, a significant enrichment of aspects of the work task.

In short, whether one takes the level of general educational qualifications required or people's own report of the way in which their work is changing a rather similar picture emerges. The general direction of change would appear to be towards more skilled work, rather towards the type of generalized deskilling so heavily emphasized by researchers in this tradition.

[10] Gallie and White (1993).

SUBJECTIVE WELL-BEING

In contrast to the development of the literature in France, the main concern of British and American studies in the first two post-war decades was with the factors that affected employees' sense of *subjective well-being* in work. Interestingly, the point of departure for this tradition of research was, in one respect, rather similar to that of Friedmann. It developed as a critique of the assumptions of Taylorism. Taylorism, it was argued, was self-defeating, since its particular prescription for maximizing efficiency generated a work environment which destroyed satisfaction in work and thereby undercut motivation to work well.

The most frequent operationalization of subjective well-being was employee's own reports about their satisfaction in work. It can scarcely be said that job satisfaction was a well-defined notion, but it was generally used to designate a positive cognitive and affective appreciation of the work task, the work environment and the employing organization. In exploring the issue of the quality of work life, there was a considerable interplay between the work of economic sociologists and of social psychologists. While social psychologists have extended the conception of subjective well-being to include measures of psychological strain, there are a number of interesting points of convergence with respect to the explanatory variables that are emphasized in the two research literatures.

Very broadly, it is possible to distinguish three principal theoretical approaches to the determinants of subjective well-being in work, although each has a wide range of variants. The first locates the key to worker satisfaction in the social supportiveness of the work environment, embracing both relations between colleagues and between individuals and their superiors. The second underlines the importance of the work task, in particular the extent to which it avoided fragmented, repetitive work and provided employees with scope to use their initiative. (This tradition was influenced by the neo-Marxian perspective discussed earlier, but it shifted the focus to subjective well-being). The third was concerned with the implications of the degree of participation in work, the extent to which employees were involved in the decisions that affected their everyday working lives.

Social support in the work environment

The theory that might be termed, in its most general form, the theory of social support, lay at the very foundation of industrial sociology as a subject. It came to prominence with the pioneering research project, carried out between 1927 and 1932, at the Hawthorne plant of the Western Electric Company in Chicago (Roethlisberger and Dickson 1939). The Hawthorne Works, which manufactured telephone equipment, could be seen as a pointer to the future of industrial organization due to its sheer scale (employing some 40,000 workers) and to its widespread utilization of the most advanced technology of its time. The research itself was on a remarkable scale, combining experimental methods, observation techiques, and interviews with some 10,000 employees. The detailed report of the research was provided by F. J. Roethlisberger and W. J. Dickson in 1939. But much of its influence was due to its popularization by the Harvard social scientist Elton Mayo as part of his more general speculations about the ills of industrial society. Particularly influential among Mayo's writings were the *Human Problems of an Industrial Civilisation*[11] and *The Social Problems of an Industrial Civilisation.*[12]

The central conclusion that was drawn from the research was that people, even in their work behaviour, were ultimately 'social' not 'economic' actors. Their most fundamental need was to belong to a relatively cohesive micro-community, and their status within this community was more important in determining their behaviour than any type of economic incentive. In particular, the critical factor for worker satisfaction was the degree of social integration into a workplace community. Mayo interpreted this in the light of the changing nature of the wider society. As the society became increasingly individualized and isolating, as a result of the breakdown of traditional community life, the experience of social relations within the workplace were becoming ever more crucial to people's identity and life satisfaction.

With respect to the future development of research, the 'Hawthorne experiments' focused attention on two characteristics of the work environment: the importance of the social cohesiveness of the work group and the significance of the role of first-line supervision. Subsequent research certainly confirmed the importance of the quality of social relationships for employee's experiences and behaviour. The central importance of cohesive work group organization for satisfaction was one of the major conclusions of the research of the British socio-technical school in the 1940s and 1950s.[13] The significance of social support has also been well documented through the work of J. S. House.[14]

[11] Mayo (1932). [12] Mayo (1949). [13] For instance Trist *et al.* (1963).
[14] House (1981).

What was more contentious, however, was whether membership of cohesive work groups led to social integration in the sense of greater commitment to the employing organization. The Hawthorne experiments themselves had shown that attachment to such groups might lead to the establishment of informal worker controls over production which might undermine management's efforts to exercise control, and this was confirmed by later anthropological studies of workplace behaviour.[15]

How was it possible to ensure both the satisfaction of employees as a member of a work group and their commitment to the wider employing organization? It was the attempt to answer this question that led to the emphasis given to the role of first-line supervision. As well as directly providing social support to employees and fostering cohesive work groups, supervision was seen as the key bridge between the work group and the wider organization. The effectiveness of supervisors, it was argued, depended on their 'human relations' skills, their ability to communicate well the purposes of the organization, to demonstrate its caring character, and to construct a sense of community.

However, experimental training programmes to provide supervisors with the necessary skills soon revealed that there were serious limits to an approach that assumed a relatively high degree of autonomy of supervisory action. While supervisors might be able to adopt democratic supervisory styles in temporary experimental situations, they found it difficult to sustain them on an ongoing basis in the real life situations of organizations that were still essentially run on hierarchical lines. As researchers worked through the implications of theories that primarily emphasized the importance of social support for subjective well-being at work, they increasingly confronted the fact that work group cohesiveness provided no guarantee of social integration into the wider organization without taking account of the problem of participation.

The characteristics of the job task

The second approach to subjective well-being at work focused on the characteristics of the job task. In common with Friedmann, its initial concern was with the deeply negative consequences of assembly-line work. Studies such as Walker and Guest's *The Man on the Assembly Line*[16] and Ely Chinoy's *Automobile Workers and the American Dream*,[17] provided powerful accounts of the way in which the repetitive and fragmented work, and especially the low level of personal control associated with assembly-line production, generated high levels of dissatisfaction.

[15] e.g. Lupton (1963). [16] Walker and Guest (1952). [17] Chinoy (1955).

Later research saw an attempt to break down in finer detail the particular characteristics of jobs that generated satisfaction or dissatisfaction. Whereas the French tradition had focused on how similar or different particular types of work were to the ideal of the craft, 'job characteristics' research sought to separate out a number of different task dimensions that might be present to a greater or lesser extent in a wide range of jobs. This led to the development of standardized schemes for the assessment of jobs such as the Job Diagnostic Survey[18] and the Job Characteristics Inventory.[19] It was then possible to explore the relationship between jobs classified in terms of such criteria and different measures of job satisfaction or work stress.[20]

Several of these job characteristics were consistently found to be associated with levels of satisfaction: for instance, variety, pace, opportunities for use of initiative, autonomy, availability of feedback, and whether the job was a recognizable whole/a clear and identifiable piece of work.[21] A significant advantage of this approach was that it allowed for the possibility that types of job task that were quite different in character from traditional craft work might still provide high levels of satisfaction. It was to lead to a strong practical emphasis on the possibilities for job redesign and task enrichment, and it was the most important influence on the Quality of Working Life Movement that emerged in the 1960s and 1970s.

One task characteristic that has become increasingly central to research on subjective well-being is the degree of discretion or control allowed to the individual. Control over pace of work had been highlighted in the earlier assembly-line studies. Subsequent studies were repeatedly to emphasize the importance of control over methods of work. For instance in a major study into the relationship between job characteristics and work motivation, Martin Patchen concluded that: 'What is particularly impressive and noteworthy . . . is that, when the effects of a large number of factors affecting job motivation are compared (each controlled for the effect of other factors), control over work methods emerges as the one factor that has sizeable associations with all indicators of job motivation'.[22]

Task discretion was also an important focus for social psychologists of work. For instance, in their major study *Work and Personality*, Kohn and Schooler argued for the central importance of 'occupational

[18] Hackman and Oldham (1975, 1980). [19] Sims *et al.* (1976).
[20] Caplan *et al.* (1975). [21] Warr (1987). [22] Patchen (1970: 234).

self-direction' or the 'use of initiative, thought and independent judgement at work'. Indeed, their longitudinal data indicated that occupational self-direction had major implications not only for people's immediate attitudes to their jobs, but for their wider values and social orientations. It affected for instance their basic orientations to authority and non-conformity, their attitudes to rule systems, their trustfulness towards other human beings, their receptiveness to innovation and change, and their flexibility of thinking. They concluded that: 'occupational self-direction has the most potent and widespread psychological effects of all the occupational conditions we have examined'.[23]

Self-direction in the work task has been found to be a key variable not only for job satisfaction but also for accounting for vulnerability to psychological distress.[24] Karasek and Theorell[25] have developed the argument further suggesting that 'decision latitude' is an important factor in mediating the effects of work demands on psychological health. It is not a high degree of pressure at work *per se* that is the key risk factor, but rather the combination of demanding work and low decision latitude. While there is still an ongoing debate about definitions of control and whether effects are additive or interactive, there is a reasonably strong consensus emerging from the research literature that job control has a significant association with mental health.

Participation in decision-making at work

The third broad approach to the subjective quality of working life has focused not on the immediate work task but on the extent to which the employing organization permits employee participation in decision-making. The interest in participation has come from a number of directions. One was from personality theorists that have postulated the growing importance of aspirations for self-realization. A culturally contingent version of this argument was presented by Chris Argyris (1957), who suggested that, at least in Western societies, individuals were socialized into a basic pattern of personality growth in which maturation was associated with a person becoming increasingly independent from others and able to control their own behaviour. These generalized expectations for self-control could only lead to frustration and

[23] Kohn and Schooler (1983: 81).
[24] Wall and Clegg (1981), Karasek and Theorell (1990), Parkes (1982).
[25] Karasek and Theorell (1990).

withdrawal in the sphere of work unless organizations were designed in a way that allowed people to participate meaningfully in decisions.

An alternative sociological perspective suggested that there was a pressure towards increased participation deriving from the inconsistency between general citizenship norms, with their assumption of equality, and the persistence of relations based on subordination at work. The classic presentation of this argument was by T. H. Marshall (1964).[26] For Marshall the institutionalization of legal and political citizenship generated a conception of equality and equal social worth that led naturally to a challenge to the legitimacy of economic inequalities and forms of organization based on traditional hierarchical principles. The principle of citizenship is likely to prove contagious. Marshall saw this affecting work life primarily through the extension of the role of trade unions. 'Thus the acceptance of collective bargaining', he wrote, 'represented the transfer of an important process from the political to the civil sphere of citizenship . . . Trade unionism has, therefore, created a secondary system of industrial citizenship parallel with and supplementary to the system of political citizenship'.[27]

Whatever the precise theoretical grounds for believing that participation is likely to be important, the research evidence certainly seems to suggest that it does have significant consequences for the subjective quality of work experience. There is a striking consistency between the results of studies using quite different research methods: laboratory experiments on small groups, field experiments in which organizational change is introduced in different ways among different groups of employees and large-scale cross-sectional surveys.

White and Lippitt, in *Autocracy and Democracy* (1960), provided laboratory-based experimental evidence suggesting that 'democratic forms of decision-making' led to much stronger forms of work motivation than autocratic modes. A number of field experiments in diverse types of organizations, where change was introduced to increase employee participation in decisions, also showed a favourable outcome for employee satisfaction (although rather less consistently for productivity). Particularly influential were Coch and French (1948), and Morse and Reimer's 1956 study of experimental change among non-manual insurance workers. A larger non-experimental study by Martin Patchen of the Tennessee Valley Authority, involving the collection of questionnaire data from 834 employees, found that the level of participation

[26] Marshall (1964). [27] Ibid. 103–4.

in decision-making was strongly associated both with identification with the organization and with the acceptance of technical and organizational change.[28]

DIRECTIONS OF CHANGE IN SUBJECTIVE WELL-BEING?

The neo-Marxian theorists discussed earlier had a very clear view about the general direction of change in the objective quality of working life: the key process was towards a deterioration in (or degradation of) the quality of work. Those who have worked on subjective well-being generally have been more cautious about formulating theories of change. There was, however, one particularly ambitious attempt to develop a longer-term scenario of the future—that of Robert Blauner in *Alienation and Freedom* (1964).

Blauner accepted the evidence that the development of mass production technologies undermined work satisfaction by fragmenting the work task, reducing the level of individual control in the work task, and destroying any meaningful sense of workplace community. But he disagreed with the view that the extension of automation through industry would accentuate the deterioration of work conditions. Rather automation, he argued, led to a reversal of the tendency for an ever greater division of labour; it encouraged the upskilling of work tasks, and a new emphasis on work groups with responsibilities for decision-making. Interestingly this theory drew on each of the three theoretical traditions outlined above. Automation was held to enhance subjective well-being by increasing the sense of social integration in a cohesive work community, improving the quality of the job and providing greater participation in collective decision-making through the emergence of autonomous work groups.

Blauner's argument effectively stood the neo-Marxian analysis of the evolution of the objective quality of work on its head and at the same time provided a highly optimistic scenario of the long-term trends for subjective well-being. Yet, while it welded earlier research findings together in an imaginative way, its empirical basis was weak. In particular, it relied for its crucial analysis of automation on little more than a relatively small-scale study of one chemical plant. However,

[28] Patchen (1970: 244).

subsequent research has put us in a much better position to assess the strengths and weaknesses of his argument.

In general, research has supported Blauner's view about the implications of automation for satisfaction with the work task. This appeared to be primarily due to improvements in the job task. Those in workplaces using advanced automation found their work more interesting and more varied, and felt that their jobs had higher levels of responsibility.[29] In contrast, there is no consensus about the implications of automation for work group cohesiveness, for participation or for the degree of social integration of employees into their organizations.[30]

While there are grounds for accepting some aspects of Blauner's analysis of the direction of change in industrial work, his attempt to generalize from this to work in general was misconceived. For Blauner was as much at fault as the neo-Marxists in assuming that trends in the experience of manufacturing work were equivalent to trends in the experience of employment. Given the high proportion of work tasks for which automation will be at best of only peripheral importance, there is no way that his theory could predict overall trends in job satisfaction. In particular, he provides no analysis of the nature of work in the strongest area of employment growth, namely work primarily involving organizing, servicing, and caring for people.

THE DECLINING SUBJECTIVE IMPORTANCE OF EMPLOYMENT?

The most threatening challenge to the major theories of the subjective quality of work came from research adopting a social action perspective. This contested the view that work conditions had any *necessary* consequences for employees' experiences and instead placed the emphasis upon peoples' broader life values and their consequences for expectations about employment. The most notable contribution to this critique was the *Affluent Worker* study, directed by John Goldthorpe and David Lockwood in 1968. Indeed, these researchers went further and suggested that the major long-term trend was for a shift away from work-centred values towards a preoccupation with family and leisure life. As a result workers would increasingly see their employment in instrumental terms,

[29] Mann and Hoffman (1960), Chadwick Jones (1969), Wedderburn and Crompton (1972).

[30] Gallie (1978).

as primarily a means of financing their non-work interests. It followed that the quality of employment was likely to become of declining importance for subjective well-being, as people consciously traded interesting work for higher income.

There are, however, grounds for doubting whether there has been any such long-term shift to greater instrumentalism. It is of interest, for instance, to examine the available measures of non-financial employment commitment, for which we have representative national data at more than one point in time. The pioneer study of non-financial employment commitment was carried out by Peter Warr, using a national survey conducted in 1981.[31] The measure it used was a question asking people whether or not they would wish to work even if they had enough money to live as comfortably as they would like for the rest of their lives. A decade later, in 1992, the same measure was included in the Employment in Britain survey. A comparison of the data across time shows no overall tendency for non-financial employment commitment to decline. In 1981, 69 per cent of employed men said that they would wish to continue in paid employment even if there was no financial necessity to do so, whereas in 1992, the figure was 68 per cent.[32] The really significant change is among women. The proportion highly committed to employment has risen from 60 per cent in 1981 to 67 per cent in 1992. The difference in the significance of employment to men's and women's lives would appear to have largely evaporated.

A very similar conclusion can be drawn from a slightly differently worded measure used in the British Social Attitudes Surveys.[33] This asks people whether they would prefer to have a paid job even if they had 'a reasonable income' without working. Far from showing a decline in employment commitment, this data shows a tendency for employment commitment to have risen over time. Whereas 69 per cent of employees still preferred to have a paid job in 1984, the proportion had risen to 74 per cent in 1993. Again, it is the sharp rise in employment commitment among women that stands out. While in the early 1980s, women showed markedly lower levels of commitment than men, by 1993 they appeared to have even stronger commitment.

In short, employment remains central to people's values and identities and, indeed, for women is probably becoming of increasing relevance. Moreover, that commitment is not purely of a financial type but is rooted in the intrinsic benefits that people feel that they can gain from

[31] Warr (1982). [32] Gallie and White (1993: 18). [33] Hedges (1994: 41).

working. The quality of work experience is likely to be as fundamental as ever for people's subjective well-being. The key question, then, is not whether the study of the quality of employment is becoming redundant due to changing values, but what needs to be done to improve our understanding of the nature of and trends in people's work experiences.

PROBLEMS IN THE STUDY OF THE QUALITY OF WORKING LIFE

How far have we progressed then in setting the foundations for a programme of research that would provide a clear picture of the trends in the quality of working life and its determinants? As has been described, there is a rich body of research, diverse in both the procedures used and the work settings studied, that has provided some very plausible suggestions about the factors that may account for the subjective quality of working life. However, much of this has been highly fragmented in type, leaving us with little overall picture of the direction of change. Further, the development of a more coherent programme of research would need to take on board a number of key difficulties that have to date received relatively little attention.

THE LACK OF A REPRESENTATIVE PICTURE

A first point to note is that, although there is now a wealth of small-scale studies, there is no way of aggregating these into an overall picture of the changing experience of employment. Attempts such as those of Blauner to use case-study evidence representing different stages of technological development fail both to cover the complexity of work situations and to deal with criticisms about the potential historical variability of employees' aspirations. Moreover, attempts to infer trends over time from one-off cross-sectional studies, even when they include questions about experience of change, confront unresolvable problems in trying to disentangle changes that relate to life-cycle processes from changes that reflect historical shifts in work structures or attitudes to work.

The meaningful study of trends requires properly representative data, taken at different time periods. The best way of achieving this would be repeated, nationally representative, surveys, comparable to the path-setting studies carried out in the United States in 1969, 1972, and 1977.[34] The main alternative would be a nationally representative panel. But while a panel provides greater strength with respect to causal interpretation, there are significant disadvantages in terms of panel attrition and the absence of information about new entrants to the labour market as the panel progresses across time.

VARIATIONS IN JOB PREFERENCES

While there is no evidence that employment is becoming less important to people's life interests, the claim by social action theorists that there may be significant variations between employees and groups of employees in terms of the aspects of work that are most critical to them does seem plausible. A concern to explore the mediating effects of employment aspirations has been markedly absent, however, from the majority of sociological studies into the quality of work. In contrast, this is an issue that social psychologists have taken much more seriously. For instance, J. R. P. French *et al.*[35] explicitly adopted a Person-Environment Fit perspective as their general explanatory approach.

The central sociological issue is whether there are variations in work preferences not only between individuals but between significant subgroups of the population, leading to a tendency to assess similar work conditions in very different ways. For instance, it is frequently suggested that there are important differences in job preferences between male and female employees, with women placing greater emphasis on the function of work in providing social relationships. If this is the case, there may be no simple answer to the question of the types of work conditions that provide a high level of subjective well-being. The conception of 'good employment' might prove to be relative to the subgroup in question. By extension, it might also change over time with shifts in cultural preferences.

CONCEPTS AND MEASUREMENT

Despite the apparent consistency in research findings about the determinants of subjective well-being, when one comes to look more closely at the studies, there is an alarming degree of difference in the definition of key concepts and the way they are measured. For instance, a number of

[34] Quinn and Staines (1979). [35] French *et al.* (1982).

studies have revealed that the degree of job control is a factor of major importance. But, on closer inspection, the same concept seems to be being used in rather different ways. For instance, the emphasis in some cases tends to be mainly on the degree of autonomy of the employee, whereas in others the term is used to refer to an amalgam of the degree of discretion over decision-making and the substantive complexity of work. Even when the term is being used in broadly similar ways, it is rare to find two studies that have measured job control in precisely the same way. Moreover, there is usually little attempt to justify particular ways of measuring control against others. It is almost perplexing that a notion that has been operationalized in such different ways should provide such consistent leverage on subjective well-being.

This rather *ad hoc* approach to measurement is not limited to the explanatory variables. Another area of varying procedure is the measurement of the key dependent variable of job satisfaction. The most common method, doubtless in part because it is so economical, is simply to get people to indicate on a scale their level of job satisfaction—ranging from highly satisfied at one end to highly dissatisfied at the other. But, it could be argued that people are being asked to do something rather unusual (and, indeed, highly artificial) in providing an *overview* of their satisfaction with their job, in that their normal way of experiencing their work is likely to be in terms of satisfaction or dissatisfaction with particular components of it.

A second approach designed to take account of these problems uses facet-specific measures: focusing for instance on satisfaction with pay, with their colleagues, with the nature of the work task, etc. The information can then be collected in a way that is more natural to the respondent and summed later by the researcher into a composite scale of job satisfaction. However, the objection to this approach is that even a relatively long list of job facets may miss just the aspect of the work which is the principal source of satisfaction or dissatisfaction to the individual concerned. Yet another procedure for assessing job satisfaction has been to ask questions of a hypothetical behavioural type, for instance whether people would move if they were free to go into any type of job, take the same job again with the information they now have, or recommend their own job to a friend.

Overall, it is clear that there is still little consensus in the literature about what might constitute a single overall measure of job satisfaction; a range of different devices have been used with little knowledge of (and remarkably little concern about) their real properties. There is a long way to go to produce the type of well-tested, clearly validated, measure that is needed for studies of change over time. The issue is not a trivial one. As Quinn and Staines were to find in their analyses of trends in job satisfaction in the United States, different measures can produce rather different results about trends.

Perhaps even more fundamentally, there are grounds for worry about the adequacy of measures of job satisfaction as the key outcome variable in studies of the subjective quality of working life. Job satisfaction measures are not particularly demanding measures of someone's psychological satisfaction with their work. Expressions of satisfaction may reflect the view that the job is adequate or is as good as the person is likely to get given their qualifications or the conditions of the labour market. It may reflect the level of adaptation to a job rather than the degree of joy in work. This has led some to seek to move to measures of involvement or interest in the job or of organizational commitment rather than to rely on weakly specified notions of job satisfaction.

The discussion has centred on the difficulties facing the development of an adequate summary measure of subjective well-being. But the problem of establishing a convincing outcome measure is even greater for those concerned with the 'objective' quality of working life. Researchers in this tradition have often been sceptical about the value of the subjective reports of those directly involved in the work process. This may partly reflect the belief that people lower their aspirations to fit their circumstances, leading to 'adaptive' satisfaction with even rather poor working conditions. It may also derive from a view that it may be inherently difficult for people to be aware of the nature of the conditions that are essential to their own long-term well-being.

For those concerned with the objective quality of work the fundamental criteria for assessing a job are the possibilities it provides for self-development and self-realization. Yet, while these terms certainly have an intuitive appeal, remarkably little effort has been devoted to specifying what precisely they imply and how they are to be assessed. Equally formidable is the task of determining how to provide measures, independent of the subjectivity of the employees themselves, of the extent to which particular types of work structure facilitate or undermine such processes. The technique traditionally used by researchers in this perspective is to send in 'expert' assessors (often the researchers themselves) to describe jobs according to checklists of job characteristics. But while this may have been relatively unproblematic when tasks were predominantly of a fairly simple nature, it poses far greater problems with the highly complex and decreasingly transparent nature of work tasks in the modern economy. As work increasingly becomes conceptual rather than physical, people-orientated rather than object-based, the creation of reliable measures by which the 'developmental' properties of tasks can be compared becomes truly daunting. It is clear that the establishment of this tradition as a rigorous type of research enquiry is still at a very early stage.

CONTRADICTORY TENDENCIES IN THE DEVELOPMENT OF WORK

Finally, the assessment of the direction of change in the quality of work may be difficult not only because of the technical problem of determining suitable outcome measures, but because of the deeper problem that processes of change may be inherently ambivalent in their effects on well-being. The ideal of the quality of work programme would be to have some clear summary measures which would enable us to say whether the general tendency was towards an improvement or a deterioration in work tasks and employment relations. But any such aspiration is likely to come adrift if it turns out to be the case that the same set of changes have highly positive consequences for some aspects of well-being, but very negative consequences for others.

There is some evidence that the changing character of work may have precisely such ambivalent consequences. It was seen earlier that the data from the 1992 Employment in Britain survey show that the majority of employees report an improvement in the skill levels of their job, the variety of their work and the responsibility they are allowed to exercise. It has been well established that each of these factors is associated with higher levels of job satisfaction and, particularly, with higher levels of satisfaction with the intrinsic characteristics of the work task. Yet, at the same time, it should be noted that a majority of employees (54 per cent) reported that the stress involved in their work had increased.

A closer examination shows that it is precisely the conditions that are leading to an improvement in what are generally regarded as the important intrinsic features of work that are at the same time generating increased levels of stress. It was those who reported that the skill level and the variety of their work had increased over the previous five years who were the most likely to report that work stress had increased.

Among those who were in jobs where skill requirements had increased, 67 per cent had experienced an increase in stress, compared with 32 per cent of those in jobs where there had been little change or a decrease in skill requirements. Whereas 66 per cent of those who were in jobs where the variety of work had increased reported higher work stress, the proportion was only 25 per cent among those who had seen decreased variety in their work.

CONCLUSION

Whether one takes the objective or the subjective approach to the quality of employment, it is clear that the research programme that is needed to document the major trends in advanced Western societies is still in its infancy. Research on the objective quality of work life has failed to specify its key concepts of self-development and self-realization, it has generally used a rather narrow definition of skilled work and it has major unresolved problems of measurement. Research on the subjective quality of working life has provided some remarkably consistent evidence about the importance of social support, the nature of the job task, and the degree of participation at work for job satisfaction and psychological well-being. But we still lack any clear picture of trends over time, there is considerable work to be done in clarifying both the explanatory and outcome variables and too little attention has been paid to the possibility that there may be marked variations in cultural preferences about work. Finally, there are problems that apply to the research of both perspectives. First, their preoccupation with the manufacture of objects has led to the neglect of the growing importance of work primarily concerned with the organizing, servicing, and caring of people. Second, any attempt to define trends in the quality of working life may have to confront the possibility that there is no simple pattern: any given set of changes in work characteristics may have highly ambivalent consequences for the quality of employment.

REFERENCES

Argyle, M. (1989), *The Social Psychology of Work*. Harmondsworth: Penguin.
Argyris, C. (1957), *Personality and Organization*. New York: Harper and Row.

BLAUNER, R. (1967), *Alienation and Freedom: The Factory Worker and his Industry*. Chicago: University of Chicago Press.

BRAVERMAN, H. (1974), *Labor and Monopoly Capital: The Degradation of Work in the Twentieth Century*. New York: Monthly Review Press.

CAPLAN, R. D., COBB, S., FRENCH, J. R. P., VAN HARRISON, R., and PINEAU, S. R. (1975), *Job Demands and Worker Health*. Washington: US Department of Health, Education and Welfare.

CHADWICK JONES, J. (1969), *Automation and Behaviour: A Social Psychological Study*. London: Wiley-Interscience.

CHINOY, E. (1955), *Automobile Workers and the American Dream*. Garden City: Doubleday.

COCH, L., and FRENCH, J. (1948), 'Overcoming Resistance to Change', *Human Relations*, 1: 512–32.

FRENCH, J. R. P., CAPLAN R. D., and VAN HARRISON R. (1982), *The Mechanisms of Job Stress and Strain*. New York: Wiley.

FRIEDMANN, G. (1946), *Problèmes humains du machinisme industriel*. Paris: Gallimard; trans. in 1955 as *Industrial Society: The Emergence of the Human Problems of Automation*, Glencoe, Illinois: The Free Press.

—— (1962), 'Proudhonien? Optimiste?', *Sociologie du travail*, 4/4: 395–8.

GALLIE, D. (1978), *In Search of the New Working Class*. Cambridge: Cambridge University Press.

——, and WHITE, M. (1993), *Employee Commitment and the Skills Revolution*. London: Policy Studies Institute.

HACKMAN, J. R., and OLDHAM, G. R. (1975), 'Development of the Job Diagnostic Survey', *Journal of Applied Psychology*, 60: 159–70.

—— —— (1980), *Work Redesign*. Reading, Mass.: Addison-Wesley.

HEDGES, B. (1994), 'Work in a Changing Climate', in R. Jowell, J. Curtice, L. Brook, D. Ahrendt, with W. Park, *British Social Attitudes, the 11th Report*. Aldershot: Dartmouth.

HOUSE, J. S. (1981), *Work Stress and Social Support. Reading*, Mass.: Addison-Wesley.

KARASEK, R., and THEORELL, R. (1990), *Healthy Work: Stress, Productivity and the Reconstruction of Work Life*. New York: Basic Books.

KOHN, M. L., and SCHOOLER, C. (1983), *Work and Personality*. Norwood, NJ: Ablex Publishing Corporation.

LUPTON, T. (1963), *On the Shop Floor*. Oxford: Pergamon.

MANN, F. C., and HOFFMAN, L. R. (1960), *Automation and the Worker*. New York: R. Hall & Co.

MARSHALL, T. H. (1964), 'Citizenship and Social Class', in *Class, Citizenship and Social Development*. Chicago: University of Chicago Press.

MAYO, E. (1932), *Human Problems of an Industrial Civilisation*. New York: Macmillan.

MORSE, N., and REIMER, E. (1956), 'The Experimental Change of a Major

Organizational Variable', *Journal of Abnormal and Social Psychology*, 52: 120–9.

—— (1949), *The Social Problems of an Industrial Civilisation*. London: Routledge and Kegan Paul.

NAVILLE, P. (1963), *Vers l'automatisme social? Problemes du travail et de l'automation*. Paris: Gallimard.

—— with BARRIER, C., GROSSIN, W., LAHALLE, D., LEGOTIEN, H., MOISY, B., PALIERENE, J., and WACKERMAN, G. (1961), *L'Automation et le travail humain*. Paris: CNRS.

PARKES, K. R. (1982), 'Occupational Stress among Student Nurses: A Natural Experiment', *Journal of Applied Psychology*, 67: 784–96.

PATCHEN, M. (1970), *Participation, Achievement and Involvement on the Job*. Englewood Cliffs, NS: Prentice Hall.

QUINN, R. P., and STAINES, G. L. (1979), *The 1977 Quality of Employment Survey*. Ann Arbor, Mich.: Institute for Social Research.

ROETHLISBERGER, F. J., and Dickson, W. J. (1939), *Management and the Worker*. Cambridge, Mass.: Harvard University Press.

ROSE, M. (1979), *Servants of Post-Industrial Power? Sociologie du travail in Modern France*. London: Macmillan.

SIMS, H. P., SZILAGYI, A. D., and KELLER, R. T. (1976), 'The Measurement of Job Characteristics', *Academy of Management Journal*, 19: 195–212.

TRIST, E. L., HIGGIN, G. W., MURRAY, H., and POLLOCK, A. B. (1963), *Organisational Choice*. London: Tavistock.

WALKER, C. R., and GUEST, R. H. (1952), *The Man on the Assembly Line*. Cambridge, Mass.: Harvard University Press.

WALL, T. D., and CLEGG, C. W. (1981), 'A Longitudinal Field Study of Group Work Redesign', *Journal of Occupational Behaviour*, 2: 31–49.

WARR, P. (1982), 'A National Study of Non-Financial Employment Commitment', *Journal of Occupational Psychology*, 55: 297–312.

—— (1987), *Work, Unemployment and Mental Health*. Oxford: Clarendon Press.

WEDDERBURN, D., and CROMPTON, R. (1972), *Workers' Attitudes and Technology*. Cambridge: Cambridge University Press.

WHITE, R. K., and LIPPITT, R. (1960), *Autocracy and Democracy: An Experimental Inquiry*. New York: Harper.

9

Time Use, Quality of Life, and Process Benefits

JONATHAN GERSHUNY AND BRENDAN HALPIN

INTRODUCTION

There are two distinct approaches to the evaluation of time in the measurement of well-being that go beyond the money values of conventional GNP. One is the 'national income extension' approach, of finding ways to place money values on activities that take place outside the money nexus. The other, rather less familiar, is the attempt to evaluate the extent of satisfaction with daily activities (the 'process benefit' approach associated with Dow and Juster).[1] Both of these activities are difficult to implement. This chapter argues nevertheless that the principles underlying both are of great importance, and that the two approaches must be used together in the analysis of the consequences of economic growth.

What follows will consider two distinct notions of the 'quality of life'. The first is a straightforward extension of conventional money-based estimates of national wealth to include various sorts of non-market production in private households and community groups. The other concerns, not so much wealth in the abstract, but rather the extent of enjoyment of the activities of producing and consuming it. Since these two may in principle (and in practice) vary quite independently of each other (as, for example, in an economy getting richer by degrading the quality of its jobs), we should find a consistent means of measuring *both* of them.

First, however, we shall briefly introduce a rather unfamiliar form of time use accounting (Figure 9.1).[2] The horizontal dimension shows how the 1,440 minutes of Britain's 'great day' (i.e. the total time of all the adults in the UK, in 1961 and 1984) was divided among sleep, the satisfaction of basic and of sophisticated wants. The vertical dimension shows the percentage of the total of time devoted by UK adults to each

[1] Dow and Juster (1985). [2] Gershuny (1989).

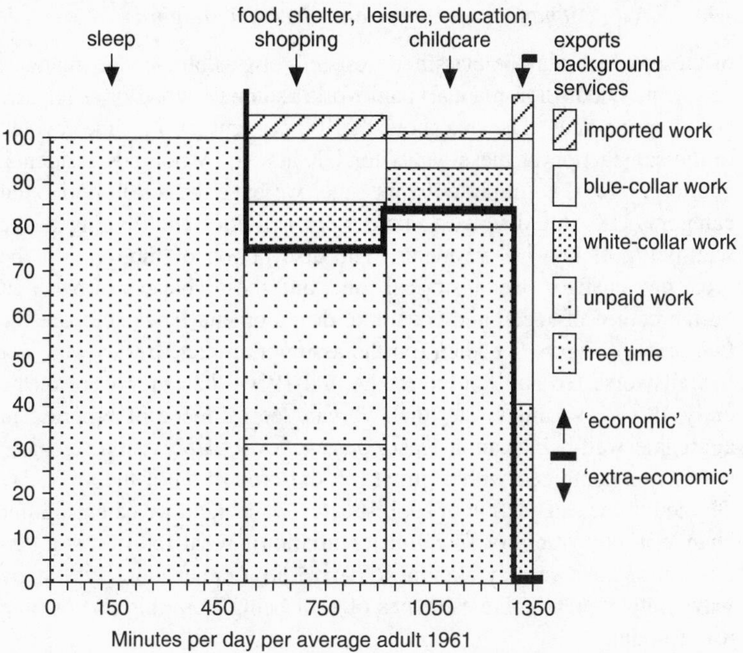

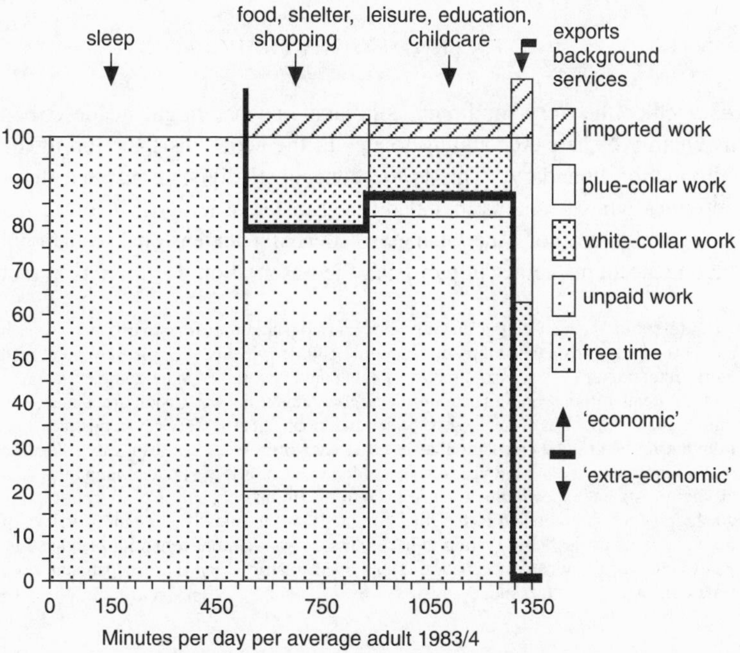

FIGURE 9.1. *The Distribution of Activities*
(*a*) *UK 1961*
(*b*) *UK 1983/4*

of these, which may be classified, respectively, as blue-collar (manual) and white-collar (non-manual) paid work, as unpaid work, or as leisure/consumption time.[3] The area above the 100 per cent level is time devoted to the satisfaction of these wants for UK adults, by non-UK residents; and to pay for this 'imported work time' we have the fourth horizontal category, UK time devoted to paid work activities contributing to the well-being of non-UK residents. The distribution of time within the great day changes over historical time, and these changes throw light on the course of social and economic development. If we compare the two parts of Figure 9.1, then (on the assumption that Britons were not overall worse fed and housed in the mid-1980s than they were in the early 1960s), we might say that we can see evidence of progress in aggregate well-being: an at least constant level of provision for basic wants was combined with a growth in the proportion of the great day devoted to the satisfaction of sophisticated wants (and we can also infer change in the pattern of social differentiation). What follows, is a discussion of how we may attempt to derive, in a rather more systematic way, simple quantitative estimates of well-being from this sort of time use account.

EXTENDED INCOME

Altogether the very minimum approach to what might be described as Quality of Life Accounting relates to the economists' notion of the 'production boundary'. This is the conceptual division between those activities whose value is included in estimates of national income, and those which are not. The business of deriving 'extensions' to national income accounts comes in part from the observation that there is in fact

[3] Refers to Figure 9.1: the unpaid work and consumption time contributed to each class of activity is calculated directly from time budget evidence. The distribution of paid work time among the various purposes is calculated in a rather more complex manner: first, all items of household expenditure and government final provision are allocated to one or other of the 'final wants' (just 'basic' and 'sophisticated' services in this presentation, but in the original calculation, a set of 21 categories of want); then, using standard input-output matrices, all the year's value-added to each of these final commodities, and all the investment expenditure is traced back to the originating industry, so as to capture all the production embodied in the final commodities; and finally, the money values of the various industries' contribution to each class of want are converted into labour time equivalents using industry/occupation employment matrices and the occupational work time evidence from time budgets.

activity that we would certainly want to consider to be production, but which takes place outside the production boundary (for example in private households or in volunteer agencies).

Including this sort of extra-economic economic activity in our national accounts is important for two distinct reasons. First, we get *a misleading view of historical change* if we look just within the boundary of 'the economy' as conventionally considered:

1. Because the production of various sorts of services continuously shifts between the household and the market. For example, transport services, originally provided largely outside the money nexus (i.e. walking), were subsequently dominated by purchased train, tram, and bus services, and more recently by, for the majority of all trips, households using their own domestic capital and materials (i.e. private car and petrol). National accounts lose the value of service production as it shifts from the public market sphere to the private household (they capture merely the price of the car, and not the value of the stream of services accruing when it is combined with the unpaid work of its driver).
2. Because of the growth of costs from 'crowding' or 'pollution' broadly considered (these range from private medical costs, to public environmental engineering). Hospital admissions of road casualties and automobile emissions controls are costly, and are taken to add to the national product, even though they are really what have been called 'defensive expenditures', undertaken only to compensate for negative consequences of other forms of expenditures.

In the main part of this chapter, however, we are mainly concerned with a second sort of argument: that extra-economic economic activity is important for our understanding of social structure and differentiation. Including things outside the production boundary may affect our view of how well-being is distributed across a society. There are two quite different possibilities:

1. Production 'outside the boundary' may *compensate for money-income inequality*. It might be argued that those who have no paid jobs can therefore use their plentiful labour time in the household-based production of services, 'self-servicing'; their time is devoted to the *direct production of use values* where it is not engaged in production for exchange. Or contrarily,

2. Production does not compensate for but *intensifies money-income inequality*. Those that have access to benefits that come from within the formal economy also get the benefits from the informal—because informal production relies on all sorts of human and material capital either derived from the money economy (e.g. DIY tools purchased from money wages) or otherwise relevant to it (e.g. using scarce production skills which can and are also sold in the labour market). In this case, the inclusion of production from outside the production boundary would actually make well-being seem more socially polarized than would be the case from money income.

Whichever of these possibilities is correct, there is certainly an effect of non-money production on the pattern of advantage and disadvantage in a society. This is one of the reasons that underlies the growing interest in a particular sort of 'national income extension', which involves the valuing of household production in a society, and adding this to the society's national income.[4] The procedure is quite straightforward: (*a*) quantify the extent of unpaid production activities beyond the boundary—generally using time budget data; then (*b*) place a money-equivalent value on the unpaid production time.

There are two broad classes of procedure used to put a value on time.

1. A rational individual, so it may be argued, will adjust his or her activity pattern so as to achieve a constant marginal utility across all the activities. Since paid work is also one of the activities, and it has a clear money value, this procedure can be used to impute a money value (the marginal wage rate) for non-market time. Assuming that rational folk will adjust their activity distribution to give constant marginal returns across all the activities, it follows that the marginal wage rate is also the value of the marginal moment in each activity. So we can put the individual's marginal wage rate as a value on time.[5] And, by extension, we can use some kind of 'shadow wage rate' for the non-employed.

2. An alternative line of reasoning, however, is that the point of unpaid work is to produce final services. There are other sources of services: in particular, we can buy them. So it could be argued that the value of time in unpaid work is equivalent to the cost of those purchased services for which the unpaid work is to substitute. Hence, the wages that would be paid to a housekeeper or more specialized service worker (the 'shadow service cost') is an alternative to the 'shadow wage' method of valuing unpaid household work time.

[4] Eisner (1988).

[5] This is a minimum value, since marginal utility diminishes.

UNPAID WORK AND INCOME DISTRIBUTIONS

It is possible to estimate the scale of these two sorts of national income extensions using time budget data from the 1987 ESRC Social Change and Economic Life household survey. We have constructed household data files with information on personal characteristics, economic status, wage rates, the overall household income level and its sources (earned versus unearned, private versus state). We have chosen one or two individuals in each household—either for a central 'spouse pair', or (in households with single working-age adults with or without children) for a 'central adult'. We have excluded multi-adult households which do not include a 'spouse pair', and also, because of limitations in the 1987 time budget data, we have excluded households whose head is 60 years of age or older.

There is only a very weak association between household income levels and unpaid work time. Table 9.1 shows the mean amounts of the various sorts of unpaid work for successive household income deciles ordered from the poorest to the richest (using 'time budget' data, derived from diaries kept by 486 married or cohabiting couples in the UK in 1987).[6]

For women there is no significant association between household income and any of the unpaid work time categories; for men (who anyway do much less unpaid work in total), the two components of the 'narrow unpaid work' category are significantly, but only very weakly, associated (results for men not included in table). We can see that the absolute amounts of each of the various sorts of unpaid work undertaken by the poorer households corresponds really quite closely with those of the richer households.

Table 9.2 shows the effects of the two alternative methods for imputing value for unpaid work on the estimated incomes of the households. The opportunity cost method (taking the individual's average wage as a shadow wage) has really quite dramatic effects on the estimated distribution of welfare. Richer households with higher levels of income contain, in general, higher paid individuals than poorer households do. So the gain in income as a result of the imputation is larger for the richer households than for the poorer.

The service price method (taking here the mean hourly wage of a housekeeper in Britain in 1987 as the value of an hour of unpaid work

[6] Gershuny *et al.* (1994).

TABLE 9.1. *Women's unpaid work time (minutes per average day)*

	Position in household income ranking	Core domestic	Odd jobs	Shopping	Child care
Poorest	0–49	157	50	62	31
	50–99	144	30	57	45
	100–49	175	60	45	49
	150–99	174	64	56	42
	200–49	184	46	69	57
	250–99	180	33	64	48
	300–49	172	35	60	57
	350–99	174	34	63	42
	400–49	161	52	55	35
Richest	450–86	173	40	58	19
Proportion of variation in unpaid work time explained by household income (none sig. at .05 level)		.0554	– .0516	.0191	– .0843

TABLE 9.2. *Absolute change in income from imputation*

	Broad version of extension (core + odd jobs + shopping + child care)			
	Position in household income ranking	Own shadow wage	Housekeeper method	Housekeeper estimated data
Poorest	0–49	68	464	509
	50–99	88	487	488
	100–49	192	616	618
	150–99	265	636	668
	200–49	397	708	688
	250–99	448	675	650
	300–49	435	662	655
	350–99	520	646	648
	400–49	659	636	646
Richest	450–86	763	630	630
Gini[a]	0.32	0.34	0.22	0.22

[a] Inequality measure: lower Gini coefficient indicates lower inequality.

time) has exactly the opposite effect on the estimate of inequality. Since the value of the unpaid work is now a constant across households, and approximately the same amount of housework is done in each household irrespective of income, the effect of this method is to add a substantial constant sum to each household's estimated income. In contrast to the opportunity cost method, more, proportionately speaking, is added to poor households' income than to rich households'.

There are only 486 couples that match our definitions in the time budget data set. Though we were reasonably confident of the finding that income and domestic work time are only weakly correlated, this was a rather thin basis for estimating any sort of income distribution. So our next step was to match the time use information with the much larger UK Family Expenditure Survey (FES) for 1986 (which also provides superior income estimators).

The final column of Table 9.2 again employs the housekeeper method for income imputation, but using the FES data rather than the time budget data. There are some differences between the two data sources for some of the deciles, but the general shape of the relationship is similar. From these and a number of other results with similar correspondences between the real and the estimated time use data, we conclude that the estimated data is usable as a proxy for the actual time use data. Which allows us to use the model to match the time estimates to the more reliably representative income distributions from the FES.

The fact that unpaid work is uncorrelated with household income (and hence constant across households with different income levels) means that the choice between the two imputation methods critically determines the effect on the income distribution. The service price method makes the income distribution more equal, whereas the shadow wage method makes it more unequal. The Gini coefficient is used to indicate the extent of income equality in a society: the lower the Gini index, the more equal the income distribution. Table 9.3 compares the Gini indices for 'extended' UK national income calculated using the two alternative methods, with the Gini index for the distribution of money incomes in the UK. It shows that whether we take the broad or the narrow view of unpaid work, and whether we take the small time budget dataset or the larger 'matched' time and income survey, the choice of imputation procedure determines the outcome.

This dependence of the evaluation of unpaid work on the imputation method need not cast doubt on the project of extending national income. There must be some real, and in principle measurable, effect of unpaid

TABLE 9.3. *Household inequality with alternative definitions of unpaid work and alternative datasets*

Gini indices	Narrow unpaid time budget data	Narrow unpaid Family Expenditure Survey data	Broad unpaid time budget data	Broad unpaid Family Expenditure Survey data
Money only	.32	.32	.32	.32
Opportunity cost	.34	.36	.34	.38
Service price	.24	.24	.22	.22

production within the household, and hence there must be some ascertainable consequence for the actual distribution of well-being. But it does cast doubts on the standard methods for valuing unpaid work that are proposed in the standard research literature. We have two alternative approaches to suggest.

The first of these is to make use of information from the time use diary itself (combined with information contained within ancillary questionnaires) on the intensity of work, and also on capital equipment employed. We know about the diarists' households, so when the diarist writes 'made supper for family' we know how many meals have been produced. Often the diary information is not sufficiently precise—but for a large proportion of domestic tasks (e.g. 'made beds', 'did the wash') quite rudimentary descriptions of the activities provide adequate information. And time budget diaries provide other sorts of clues: they normally register the presence of other individuals (so the household member who cooked the meal may be considered to have provided meals for all those present). Most time budget diaries register multiple simultaneous activities, so the intensity of work could be assessed by the frequency of multiple activities and the nature of the combinations. The questionnaires associated with diaries frequently register the presence of domestic equipment within households, and so it may be possible to allow for the impact of domestic capital equipment in estimating the output of domestic work.

The second approach, more speculatively, turns the question round. The root of the problem is that the unpaid work simply and in principle has no real market value. But conversely, the market goods and services consumed by households do really embody the work time spent by those who produce them. So instead of turning time values to money, we might turn households' money expenditure into time (using the procedures described in the first section of this chapter). Households would be revealed as having at their disposal different amounts and different sorts of time.

Members of low-wage households might have at their disposal less than twenty-four hours (since, at half the average national wage, eight hours of paid work might only buy four hours of work time embodied in goods and services) while members of high wage households would have considerably more than twenty-four hours per day. Households would differ in the skill content of the time they consume—richer households consuming more high-skill labour. And finally households might differ in the purposes to which their time is devoted: so poor households might spend more time meeting more basic sorts of needs, perhaps devoting a large amount of their time to unpaid house cleaning and little to cooking, instead buying the low skill service labour of a fast-food take-away, while a rich household might buy-in housecleaning services, and devote more of its unpaid work time to fancy cooking for a dinner party. This approach promises a much more comprehensive view of the distribution of life-styles and well-being than can be derived from either time or money budget analysis in isolation.

We might alternatively summarize the process of income extension rather more generally than in the previous paragraphs: reading down each column in Figure 9.1, the various sorts of work and consumption time can be considered as factors of production of the satisfaction of wants. We could apply some functional transformation of these different sorts of time to produce a money value for the final services received by the members of the population—rather in the manner that Becker conceptualizes consumption as the process of combining purchased commodities with consumers' time to produce those 'household commodities' (or 'Z-goods' as he calls them), such as 'nutrition', 'shelter', and 'entertainment', which are the ultimate goal of economic activity.[7]

PROCESS BENEFITS

But rather than pursuing the implications of this line of argument, we now turn to another, much less familiar approach, one which, if anything,

[7] Becker (1965).

further complicates the issue. We have so far proceeded on the assumption that there is a unique and ascertainable purpose to each of our activities. Becker's Z-goods approach is in fact a grand but over-reductive conceptualization; we may well do the things we do for a number of concurrent reasons (or indeed for no reason at all). The alternative line of argument, constitutes a modest retreat from this reductionism. Instead of a single class of value (the value of the final service), consider activities as contributing to the joint production of two distinct classes of value: (1) the Becker-type values, in which time is used instrumentally to produce abstract final goods; (2) the immediate *affective* (i.e. emotional) consequence of spending time in particular ways . . . For example, people may enjoy (or alternatively dislike) their paid work. Clearly the instrumental and affective consequences of an hour of work may vary from person to person. These two dimensions of benefit are not limited to work. Every aspect of life, every sort of time use has, in addition to its longer-term outcomes in terms of the satisfaction of abstracted human wants or needs for final outcomes such as food or shelter, also much more immediate consequences. Each of the things we do has at least the potential to evoke immediate pleasurable sensations (or unpleasurable ones). We actual enjoy, or alternatively dislike, doing particular things. Quite apart from the benefits we or others may eventually get from eating the cake slice by slice, we as cooks may like, or dislike, cooking it.

We shall refer to the immediate affective responses to particular activities (following Dow and Juster) as 'process benefits',[8] and to the affect dimension as 'process well-being'.

> people have preferences for every potential activity they engage in, and these preferences . . . should influence both the way in which people allocate their time and the well-being derived from these time allocations.[9]

Dow and Juster propose a straightforward empirical procedure for estimating process well-being. They start with diary-derived estimates of time devoted to various activities; they multiply each of these totals by a questionnaire-derived preference score (a simple 1 to 9 like it/hate it scale), and sum these products (in a more sophisticated version, they also standardize the preference scales to take account of spurious interpersonal differences).

We might still have some doubts about the empirical estimation of

[8] Dow and Juster (1985). [9] Ibid. 400.

the preference scale. Do people really know, in the abstract, what their preferences are? In particular, we are persuaded by the economic psychologists' arguments that there may be some considerable disjunction between the anticipated enjoyment of particular activities and the level of enjoyment actually achieved.[10]

'Process benefits' can be investigated in another time budget dataset collected for market research purposes by a commercial company (Unilever) in the UK in 1986. The survey covers members of couples only. This means that we cannot use the evidence to investigate one of Juster and Dow's most important conclusions, the very substantial positive effect of marriage on process well-being. But in one particular respect the Unilever data collection may be greatly superior to the evidence used by Dow and Juster. The survey includes, in addition to questionnaire items about activity preferences, also diary information. The Unilever survey included a conventional (fixed interval) time use diary, with an additional column in which diarists registered, for each time interval, how much they enjoyed their 'main activity' on a scale of 1 ('very much') to 5 ('not at all'). So, in addition to questionnaire data on how much people enjoy activities, we can calculate 'mean enjoyment scores' for those same activities from the diary evidence. The Unilever dataset allows us to investigate the association between the questionnaire and diary evidence on the enjoyment of activities.

Table 9.4 shows, for various categories of activity, the mean preference scores from the diaries for each respondent, broken down by their questionnaire response about that activity (note that the questionnaire scale moves in the opposite direction to the diary: 1 = dislike, 5 = like). *If people can accurately estimate their enjoyment of particular sorts of activity, the questionnaire answers should be strongly associated with the diary scores.* We can see, in fact, a relatively weak (though certainly non-negligible) association. The eta squared statistic estimates the proportion of variation in the diary-derived enjoyment score that is explained by the answers to the questionnaire enjoyment items. Only in the cases of ironing and sewing is more than 30 per cent of the variation in the diary estimate explained by the questionnaire answers. And for playing with children, DIY, and working on the car, where we might have expected respondents to have strong and well-established views, the proportions of variance explained by the questionnaire instrument (.14, .12 and .11 respectively) are really rather low. This result somewhat

[10] Kahneman and Varey (1991).

TABLE 9.4. *Questionnaire and diary preference scores*

Questionnaire answer	Diary answers How much do you like. . . . ?				
	planning food	buying food	cooking	clearing table	general tidying
1 I dislike doing it	3.42	3.37	2.99	3.50	3.45
2	2.69	3.18	2.85	3.10	2.95
3	2.71	2.74	2.75	2.96	2.88
4	2.81	2.63	2.59	2.68	2.82
5	2.81	2.65	2.38	2.54	2.84
6	1.93	1.96	2.08	2.56	2.36
7 I Like doing it	2.36	2.12	1.92	2.14	2.54
eta squared	0.12	0.21	0.19	0.18	0.14
	cleaning kitchen	cleaning bathroom	other routine cleaning	machine clothes wash	hand clothes wash
1 I dislike doing it	3.49	3.38	3.64	3.26	3.58
2	3.18	3.25	3.33	2.86	2.68
3	3.07	3.04	3.21	2.88	3.17
4	2.84	2.51	2.80	2.75	2.94
5	2.59	2.89	2.54	2.70	2.44
6	2.42	2.91	2.43	2.37	2.40
7 I like doing it	1.77	1.92	2.17	2.08	2.17
eta squared	0.22	0.19	0.27	0.16	0.21
	hanging clothes	put away clothes	ironing	sewing knitting	clothes shopping
1 I dislike doing it	3.67	3.67	4.16	2.75	3.00
2	3.15	3.21	3.62	4.00	3.00
3	3.17	3.08	3.34	2.00	2.33
4	2.90	3.04	3.28	2.69	2.43
5	2.36	2.89	3.08	1.83	1.84
6	2.60	2.50	2.64	2.03	1.98
7 I like doing it	2.19	2.19	1.92	1.30	1.43
eta squared	0.25	0.17	0.39	0.34	0.24

TABLE 9.4. *Cont'd*

Questionnaire answer	Diary answers How much do you like. . . . ?				
	diy decorating	work on car	care/play with baby	put kids to bed	supervise kids
1 I dislike doing it	2.63	2.86	1.75	3.43	2.42
2	2.50	3.20	2.90	3.22	1.00
3	2.56	2.57	2.33	2.83	1.98
4	2.6	3	2.69	2.2	1.97
5	2.35	2.25	2.26	2.39	1.82
6	2.03	2.23	2.02	1.94	1.76
7 I like doing it	1.79	2.05	1.59	1.88	1.44
eta squared	0.12	0.11	0.25	0.21	0.11
	play with kids	cleaning kids	hair care	skin care	dressing self
1 I dislike doing it	1.56	2.53	2.83	1.00	2.31
2	2.00	3.25	2.40	2.50	2.63
3	2.10	2.47	2.36	2.50	2.88
4	1.78	2.38	2.65	2.39	2.58
5	1.51	2.18	2.23	1.80	2.47
6	1.25	1.77	1.74	2.01	2.31
7 I like doing it	1.29	1.74	1.71	1.70	2.14
eta squared	0.14	0.15	0.18	0.14	0.07

undercuts the particular procedure used by Dow and Juster. The questionnaire-derived preference score may be taken to represent anticipated utility, the diary-derived score, the actual: it would appear that the Michigan approach uses preference estimates that are not strongly associated with the actual enjoyment of activities. But nevertheless, the argument suggests a closely analogous procedure, using the diary-derived data rather than questionnaire-based material.

First, let us look at the preference data itself. Figure 9.2 gives a summary of the diary evidence of which activities are liked and which are disliked. Each bar gives (separately for men and women) the aggregate proportion of the total time spent in each activity in each preference state. The activities are ordered according to the proportion of time

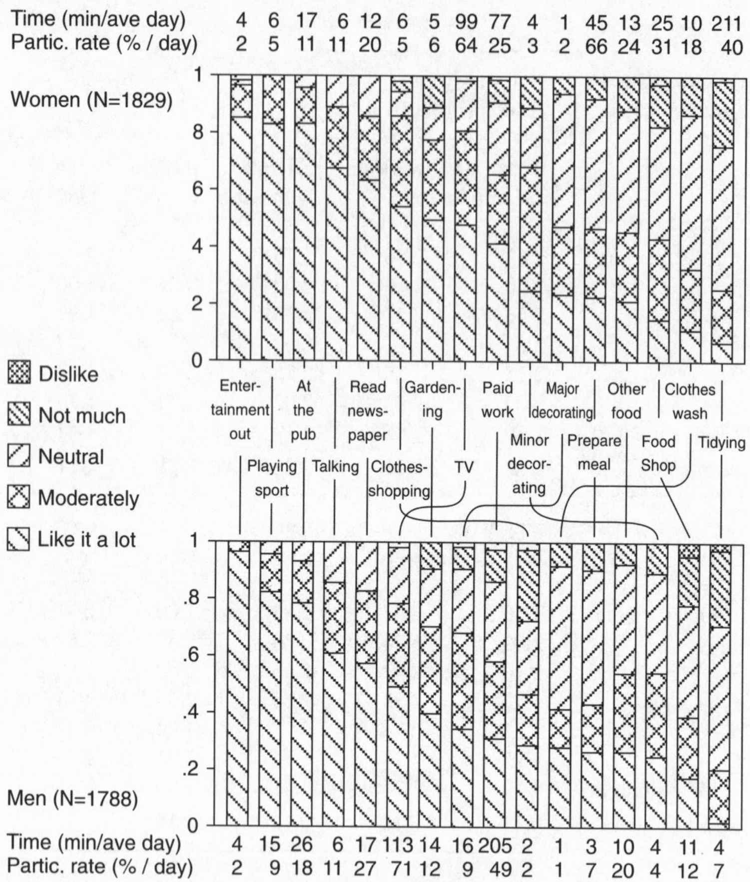

FIGURE 9.2. *How much do you enjoy it?*

spent enjoying the activity 'very much' (though approximately the same ordering emerges if we use the opposite end of the scale). The men's and women's orderings correspond quite closely, with major difference only in the placing of decorating, clothes wash, and clothes shopping. Paid work comes pretty much in the centre of the ordering, close to watching television.

Next, we can calculate an analogy to Dow and Juster's process benefit score (analogous to their 'raw process benefit score'). In our case (since we have a preference ordering for each half-hour of the day) this can be computed simply as the mean diary preference score across the

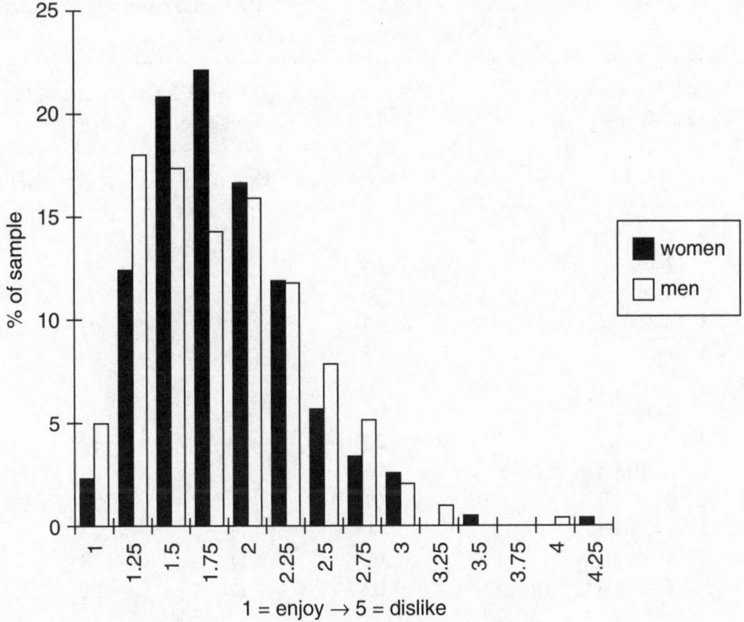

FIGURE 9.3. *Raw process benefits*

full range of activities. We have a version of a process benefit score, simply the diary-keepers' average enjoyment level. Figure 9.3 shows a clear, if somewhat skewed, normalish frequency distribution of process benefits for both men and women; the lower the process benefit score, the happier the respondent.

How do the process benefits differ between different sorts of people? Table 9.5 gives a 'Multiple Classification Analysis' which shows how variation in the process benefit score is associated with various personal characteristics. *The overall average score for the sample as a whole is 1.84*; the first column shows the effect on each sort of characteristic on its own. So those aged 18–24, for example, have a mean process benefit score of 1.79 (i.e. 1.84 – .05). Reading down the column, we see the effects of age, hours of paid work per week, yearly income, employment status, sex, family status, and job satisfaction. Note that those who enjoy their jobs are considerably happier overall than those who do not; the former have a mean process benefit score of 1.71 (i.e. 1.84 – .13), the latter, 2.19 (1.84 + .35).

The second column gives equivalent estimates, but adjusted so that

TABLE 9.5. *Multiple classification analysis of raw welfare process benefits (5-day sample; 755 cases)*

Variable + Category Grand Mean = 1.84	Unadjusted		Adjusted for variates only		variates plus covariate	
	Dev'n	Eta	Dev'n	Beta	Dev'n	Beta
Age						
1 18–24	−.05		−.06		−.06	
2 25–34	.06		.02		.01	
3 35–50	.03		.01		.01	
4 51+	−.08		−.02		−.02	
		.12		.04		.03
Hrs/Week						
0	−.05		.13		.17	
1 40 HRS OR MORE	.05		−.02		−.04	
2 30–39 HRS	.01		−.10		−.12	
3 20–29 HRS	.00		−.11		−.13	
4 10–19 HRS	.03		−.11		−.14	
5 LESS THAN 10 HRS	.02		−.17		−.22	
		.08		.20		.26
Income						
0	−.26		−.20		−.13	
1 3,000 OR LESS	.00		.01		.02	
2 3,001–5,000	−.01		.00		.00	
3 5,001–10,000	.06		.01		−.01	
4 10,001–15,000	−.01		.00		−.01	
5 15,001–20,000	−.04		.00		.02	
6 over 20,000	.05		.04		.06	
		.13		.09		.07
Working						
1 YES	.03		.01		.03	
2 NO	−.06		−.02		−.06	
		.09		.03		.09
Soclass						
0	−.11		−.03		−.01	
1 A	−.11		−.07		.01	
2 B	−.02		.01		.00	
3 C1	−.01		−.03		−.03	
4 C2	.05		.03		.03	
5 D	.11		.05		.03	
		.14		.07		.05

TABLE 9.5. *Cont'd*

Variable + Category Grand Mean = 1.84	Unadjusted		Adjusted for variates only		variates plus covariate	
	Dev'n	Eta	Dev'n	Beta	Dev'n	Beta
Sex						
1 MALE	.00		−.03		−.03	
2 FEMALE	.00		.03		.02	
		.01		.05		.05
Kids						
0 none	−.04		−.01		.00	
1 1 child	−.06		−.04		−.02	
2 2 children	.04		.00		−.01	
3 3+ children	.11		.09		.06	
		.11		.07		.05
Job satisfaction						
0	−.06		−.14		−.15	
1 ENJOY JOB A LOT	−.13		−.08		−.08	
2 ENJOY JOB A LITTLE	.23		.27		.27	
3 ENJOY JOB NOT MUCH	.29		.31		.34	
4 DON'T ENJOY JOB	.35		.39		.45	
		.31		.36		.38
Multiple R Squared				.128		.207
Multiple R				.357		.455

Variates: age, workhours, income, employment class, sex, kids, job satisfaction.
Covariate: spouse's raw welfare process benefits. Reg. coeff. = .289.

each category takes account of the effects of the other characteristics of the diary-keepers. (The 'eta' scores indicate the relation importance of the various characteristics in determining the process benefit score, and the 'beta' does the same for the adjusted effects). We see from Table 9.5 that we can explain a small proportion of the variation in process benefits by age, hours of paid work, employment status, social class, sex, and child status. But much the most important influence is job satisfaction. Even if we enter it last in an hierarchical analysis of variance, it still emerges as a very important factor in explaining the distribution of process benefits.

The Unilever survey instruments were completed by both members of the couples. So we are able to use spouses' process benefit scores as independent variables in predicting respondents process benefit scores. The third column of Table 9.5 adds in the effect of the spouses' process benefit score. There is a strong association between spouses' well-being: each extra unit of an individual's process benefit score is associated with an extra .289 of a unit in his or her spouse—the happier the spouse, the happier the diary respondent.

We should note that the presence of job satisfaction as an independent variable provides a very serious potential for circularity in this analysis. Work is itself a large activity in terms of time, and we have some direct evaluation of work in the dependent variable itself. So perhaps we have here simply a reflection of the association between anticipated and actual measures of work satisfaction. We can remove this potential circularity simply by recalculating the process benefit score excluding all work time. Table 9.6 shows that the overall association of job satisfaction with the revised process benefits score is weaker—but it still remains substantial once the potential for circularity is removed. And the spouse effect is actually stronger in this case. Clearly (and as we know from other contexts), satisfaction with the work situation is positively associated with enjoyment of non-work activity.

Michael Argyle, in his seminar presentation, jokingly summarized the findings of his extensive review of the psychological evidence on the causes of happiness as follows: 'To be happy for a day get drunk. To be happy for a year get married. To be happy for a lifetime get a garden.' The Unilever evidence may be summarized as: if you want to be happy, get a rewarding (though not necessarily well-paid) job, and a happy wife.

PROGRESS IN TWO DIMENSIONS

But we do not by any means intend to stop here. So far, we have discussed what we might consider to be two dimensions of quality of life, the instrumental and the affective. We shall conclude by sketching in a preliminary way how we might begin to pull them together into a general time-based accounting system.

Return to the picture of the society's 'great day' given by Figure 9.1. The horizontal dimension relates to the instrumental category, that looks at the eventual outcomes of the various sorts of activity in terms of the satisfaction of abstract wants: these are what we try to value in terms described by the first part of this paper—we combine the various different sorts of time input in one column according to some formula (call

TABLE 9.6. *Multiple classification analysis of raw welfare process benefits (excluding paid work time) (5-day sample; 755 cases)*

	excluding paid work (reg. coeff. 0.309)				COMPARISON ITEM incl. paid work (reg. coeff. 0.289)	
	Unadjusted		Adjusted for variates plus covariate		Adjusted for variates plus covariate	
Grand Mean =	1.79		1.79		1.84	
Variable + Category	Dev'n	Eta	Dev'n	Beta	Dev'n	Beta
Age						
1 18–24	−.05		−.04		−.06	
2 25–34	.03		−.01		.01	
3 35–50	.04		.02		.01	
4 51+	−.06		−.01		−.02	
		.09		.04		.03
Hrs/week paid work						
0	−.01		.22		.17	
1 40 HRS OR MORE	.01		−.09		−.04	
2 30–39 HRS	−.04		−.15		−.12	
3 20–29 HRS	.05		−.13		−.13	
4 10–19 HRS	.04		−.15		−.14	
5 LESS THAN 10 HRS	.05		−.19		−.22	
		.05		.34		.26
Income						
0	−.25		−.15		−.13	
1 3,000 OR LESS	.03		.03		.02	
2 3,001–5,000	−.01		.00		.00	
3 5,001–10,000	.01		−.01		−.01	
4 10,001–15,000	−.01		−.01		−.01	
5 15,001–20,000	−.05		.00		.02	
6 over 20,000	.13		.13		.06	
		.12		.08		.07
Working						
1 YES	.01		.05		.03	
2 NO	−.02		−.10		−.06	
		.03		.14		.09
Soclass						
0	−.06		.01		−.01	
1 A	−.12		−.01		.01	

TABLE 9.6. *Cont'd*

	excluding paid work (reg. coeff. 0.309)				COMPARISON ITEM incl. paid work (reg. coeff. 0.289)	
	Unadjusted		Adjusted for variates plus covariate		Adjusted for variates plus covariate	
Grand Mean =	1.79		1.79		1.84	
Variable + Category	Dev'n	Eta	Dev'n	Beta	Dev'n	Beta
2 B	.03		.01		.00	
3 C1	−.02		−.04		−.03	
4 C2	.03		.02		.03	
5 D	.06		.00		.03	
		.09		.05		.05
Sex						
1 MALE	−.04		−.05		−.03	
2 FEMALE	.04		.05		.02	
		.08		.10		.05
Kids						
0 none	−.04		−.01		.00	
1 1 child	−.05		−.02		−.02	
2 2 children	.03		.00		−.01	
3 3+ children	.12		.06		.06	
		.11		.05		.05
Job satisfaction						
0	−.02		−.15		−.15	
1 ENJOY JOB A LOT	−.06		.00		−.08	
2 ENJOY JOB A LITTLE	.13		.20		.27	
3 ENJOY JOB NOT MUCH	.03		.11		.34	
4 DON'T ENJOY JOB	.07		.21		.45	
		.15		.26		.38
Multiple R Squared				.154		.207
Multiple R				.392		.455

Variates: age, workhours, income, employment class, sex, kids, job satisfaction.
Covariate: spouse's raw welfare process benefits.

this a 'vertical summation'), to produce a notional money value analogous to (though more inclusive than) a standard money value of output of some branch or sector of industry. The second part of the paper has discussed a quite independent calculation, in which we combine the direct satisfactions generated by each sort of activity (so as to get the society's total of process benefits derived from white-collar paid work, from blue-collar work and so on—we might call this by contrast a 'horizontal summation').

And corresponding to these two sorts of summary of aspects of quality of life, there are two sorts of change over historical time. There is the change in the horizontal dimension, which we see in Figure 9.1, in which resources are transferred from the satisfaction of basic wants to the satisfaction of more sophisticated wants. This is what has always been accepted as 'economic development'. We may not be entirely happy with the particular way we carry out the 'vertical summations' that we use to calculate the value of the production for each category of want. But it is nevertheless indisputable that some such calculation ought to be carried out. There is also change in the vertical dimension; the mix of jobs changes, as do the characteristics of each sort of job. The distributions and characteristics of unpaid work and consumption activities also change. Jobs may get less or more enjoyable, the numbers of enjoyable jobs may increase or decrease; similarly for unpaid work and leisure. We may not be happy about the particular 'horizontal summation' techniques we use to calculate these totals. But calculations are nevertheless of undeniable importance. The levels of problem involved in both sorts of summation are of the same order; the operational difficulties in both detract from the importance of neither of them.

There are interactions between the two sorts of historical change. Consider two opposing poles of socio-economic development; on one hand we might have a technocratically effective society, able to produce quantitative economic growth, but ineffective at producing process benefits (i.e. economic growth produced through long hours of work in unpleasant jobs, with relatively short time for consumption); on the other an economically inefficient but much more relaxed society that is shorter on material benefits and long on process benefits. Anglophone countries are currently concerned that they may well be short on both dimensions. And what we want, of course, are societies that do well in both. Achieving these is what politics ought to be about. And the provision of statistics about both dimensions is a major task, arguably the major task, for social statisticians.

REFERENCES

Becker, G. S. (1965), 'A Theory of the Allocation of Time', *Economic Journal*, 80: 493–517.

Dow, G. K., and Juster, F. T. (1985), 'Goods, Time and Well-Being: The Joint Dependency Problem', in F. T. Juster and F. P. Stafford (eds.), *Time, Goods and Well-Being*. Ann Arbor, Mich.: Institute of Social Research.

Eisner, R. (1988), 'Extended Accounts for National Income and Product', *Journal of Economic Literature*, 26: 1611–84.

Gershuny, J. I. (1989), 'Technical Change and the Work Leisure Balance: A New System of Socio-economic Accounts', in A. Silberston (ed.), *Technology and Economic Progress*. Basingstoke: Macmillan.

Gershuny, J. I., Goodwin, M., and Jones, S. (1994), 'The Domestic Labour Revolution', in M. Anderson, F. Bechhofer, and J. Gershuny (eds.), *The Social and Political Economy of the Household*. Oxford: Oxford University Press.

Kahneman, D., and Varey, C. (1991), 'Notes on the Psychology of Utility', in J. Elster and J. E. Roemer (eds.), *Interpersonal Comparisons of Utility*. Cambridge: Cambridge University Press.

10

The Mask of Intimacy: Advertising and the Quality of Life[1]

AVNER OFFER

As the motor car began to diffuse in Britain in the early 1920s, the petrol companies erected billboards and signs to attract motorists to their pumps. They showed little respect for the rural landscape. A cyclist wrote to *The Times* in 1923, 'I found my anticipations of Tintern Abbey profanely broken in upon by a horrible yellow advertisement of petrol standing in a field by the roadside, quite close to the spot which Wordsworth's poetry has doubly hallowed.' Public outrage was fanned by a Society for Checking the Abuses of Public Advertising (SCAPA). Eventually, succumbing to public pressure, the oil companies withdrew their signs from the countryside voluntarily, not only in Britain, but across most of Europe (though not in the United States).[2]

If billboards in a country meadow can impinge on the quality of the natural environment, the marketing message can have a similar effect on the quality of the interpersonal environment. In Chapter 2 above, Argyle shows that personal relations form the core of subjective well-being. The web of social interactions is a source of intense satisfaction, and thus an important ingredient of the quality of life. The effect of marketing on the interpersonal environment forms the subject of this essay. It indicates why advertising *has* to intrude into the interpersonal domain, how it does so, and with what consequences. Like several other forms of environmental degradation, advertising came under public scrutiny between the 1950s and the 1970s, and the essay concludes with an assessment of the efforts to control, regulate, and restrain the practice of advertising in the United States, Britain, and Europe.

[1] Thanks to Annie Chan, Harriet Jackson, Juliet Dowsett, and Martin Spät for effective research assistance, to David Halpern and Robert Lane for vital data, to Harriet Jackson, Joachim Voth, and seminar participants in Oxford and Canberra for helpful comments, and to the History of Advertising Trust, Duke University Library, the Ford Motor Company, and the Henry Ford Museum in Dearborn, Michigan, for generous access to their archival collections.

[2] Brown (1993). Quotation, p. 348, from *The Times*, 16 Oct. 1923.

It is hard to deny that advertising *enhances* the quality of life in a variety of ways. It engages the senses, stimulates novelty, broadens the range of experience and choice. It makes our townscapes, our newspapers, magazines, and television more lively than they might otherwise be. It diffuses information about products and services. It commits suppliers to consistent standards of quality. It pays for a good part of the media, and underwrites sporting and cultural events. Would we wish to be without advertising? When we waver, the memory of the grey cities of Eastern Europe under communism persuades us that we would miss it.

For purveyors of such benefits, advertisers have been curiously defensive and insecure.[3] There is a widespread sense that advertising is at best a mixed blessing. It has been under continuous attack for most of this century.[4] Critics assail advertisers in two different ways: it promotes the wrong kinds of goods, and is also a bad in itself.

The wrong kind of goods. One distinction is between virtuous goods and vicious ones. Almost everyone agrees that illegal narcotic drugs should not be advertised, and racial and religious abuse is similarly banned, but there is little accord on publicity for alcohol and tobacco. Some critics claim that advertising promotes spurious wants. J. K. Galbraith, for example, used to argue that it diverts outlays from public and communal goods towards private ones.[5]

A bad in itself. Advertising, it is said, creates an artificial differentiation between identical goods, and thus makes them more expensive. In 1992 American food companies launched 11,500 new products, many of them copies of existing brands.[6] Advertising, it is said, undermines rational choice: it conveys seductive but misleading information, thereby undermining our ability to compare quality and prices. If we want novelty and stimulation, some critics argue, let us pay for them directly, rather than in the form of an indirect tax on advertised goods and sporting events. Some economists argue that the need for advertising in order to establish a presence in the market acts to raise barriers

[3] e.g. O'Toole (1981); Bullmore (n.d.).

[4] Extensive (but not exhaustive) survey, Pollay (1986); Cogently in e.g. Whitehead (1973); most recently, Preston (1994); Lears (1995). Some prominent book-length critiques are Chase and Schlink (1927); Schlink and Kallet (1933); Thompson (1943); Packard (1960); Seldin (1963); Baker (1968); Wight (1972); Preston (1975); Ewen (1976); Schudson (1986); Marchand (1986); Leiss *et al.* (1990). A comprehensive bibliography of advertising is in Pollay (1979).

[5] Galbraith (1958: 133–5).

[6] Giles (1993: 8).

of entry. It stifles innovation and entrenches monopoly.[7] Both scholars and lay persons have argued that its preoccupation with sex degrades women.[8] Environmentalists and urbanists sometimes deplore the visual impact of advertising on the environment.[9]

Here, in a paragraph, is an outline of *my* argument. Advertising seeks the attention of a jaded and wary consumer. In order to persuade, it needs to be credible. It needs to establish trust. Credibility, however, is not easy: few products or services are remarkably superior to the competition. So there is a temptation to stray from the literal truth, which makes the achievement of credibility more difficult. Now the more credible advertising becomes overall, the higher its standards of truthfulness, the more tempting it is for individual advertisers to mislead. In formal terms, the dominant strategy for an individual advertiser is to mislead. But if everyone follows this strategy, credibility is seriously undermined. Discourse becomes less truthful than anyone individually would want. Such situations give rise to a form of market failure known as 'the tragedy of the commons': every grazier believes that one additional cow on the common will hardly be noticed. When each of them releases just one more cow, the common is soon trampled into mud. The 'commons' in this case are credibility and trust. We end up with less than we would like. Hence advertising becomes less beneficial than it might be, for the public of course, but also for those who commission it.

It is not impossible that misleading advertising creates spillovers for society as a whole, undermining credibility not only in the discourse of marketing, but also in other interactions: political, social, personal. Trust depends on truthfulness; it is necessary for effective leadership, and it underpins co-ordination and co-operation at every level of economic and social life. In its absence, personal interaction is fraught with uncertainty, and requires costly monitoring and enforcement. Society has recognized these hazards, and has acted historically to counter them in several ways: by means of conceptual analysis, of economic, social and cultural critiques, of which this essay may be taken as an example; it has mobilized voluntary action to resist the contamination of the public

[7] See Borden (1942); Kaldor (1950–1). Other economists dispute this reasoning. A survey of the arguments, from a point of view favourable to advertising, can be found in Bullmore and Waterson (1983: part 5); Ekelund and Saurman (1988); see also Becker and Murphy (1993).

[8] e.g. Haug (1986); Bartos (1989: ch. 20).

[9] e.g. Tunnard and Pushkarev (1963); Brown (1993).

domain, and to demand political action. This has led to legislation and to systems of regulation and control, which differ from one country to another, but are nowhere completely absent. Finally, people change their life-styles and consumption patterns to take account of the contamination of the common, to limit the damage, or to respond to it. This repertoire of repair is the essence of what we mean by 'the pursuit of the quality of life' in the domains of marketing and consumption.

1

In a business or retail exchange, both sides enter the transaction with the expectation of gain. Since both sides stand to benefit, there is scope for dividing the gain in different ways. A market exchange, while capable of benefiting both sides, also has an adversarial undertone. Many people experience it as stressful.[10] Information can narrow down the scope for disagreement: if both sides are well informed about the quality of the good, about its cost, and about each others' preferences, the scope for dispute is smaller. In retail environments, however, it is more typical for information to be distributed asymmetrically. A specialist vendor usually knows more about cost and quality than the casual buyer. This gives the vendor a broad choice of pricing strategies to maximize returns. One device is pricing goods higher than marginal cost in the hope of capturing intra-marginal buyers, and letting others earn their surplus by means of bargaining or search. Hence, list prices tend to be higher than 'street prices'. In the motor industry, list prices are known as the 'vicar's wife' price: the vicar's wife is unlikely to haggle, and has to pay a premium.[11] The buyer might well suspect that a better deal could be obtained, but often lacks the resources to bargain effectively or to investigate the options.

Over and above legitimate price discrimination, fraud and sharp dealing appear to be endemic in retail trading, especially with regard to advertised and actual prices.[12] A common device is the mark-up/markdown gambit. In many lines of commodities it is rare to see prices which are not compared to some recommended retail price. Prices are sometimes marked up for brief periods of time, so that they can then be marked down for a deceptive 'sale'. The 'sale' gambit is universal but reductions in pricing do not always accompany the big ads. Sometimes

[10] Frey (1986). [11] Letter, *The Times*, 10 Jan. 1994.
[12] Blumberg (1989); Shorris (1994); Yang and Stern (1995).

prices are even raised at the time of a 'sale'. Another gambit is 'bait and switch', in which a store has the advertised goods, but attempts to switch the customer to something more expensive. Or the shop may have limited quantities, insufficient to meet demand; sometimes it never actually has the advertised goods at all.[13]

This is acknowledged in advertising itself. There is a genre which acknowledges that opportunism is rampant, but which then claims honesty in its particular case. An ad in a computer magazine announces candidly 'SOME ADVERTISERS WILL SELL YOU ANYTHING: Most computer suppliers sell first and ask questions later'. A mail order catalogue states, 'We price our products fairly and honestly. We do not, have not, and will not participate in the common retailing practice of inflating markups to set up a future phony sale.'[14]

Buyers may be eager, but they are wary as well. The problem for advertisers is to dispel their inhibitions. Several approaches are commonly used. One is a straightforward presentation of product merits, the *value* approach. It was pioneered by David Ogilvy, whose 1950s display advertisements spelt out product attributes in big chunks of small print. Another example is the two-page spread prepared by J. Walter Thompson agency for the launch of the Ford Falcon compact car in 1959, headed with a signed statement by Henry Ford II (the company President), and followed by a long sequence of factual questions and answers, and small informative sketches.[15] Even such factual advertisements rarely contained price information. They are more common in trade periodicals, and tend to be rare in consumer-oriented ones.

On the whole, however, value-oriented advertising is uncommon. Much more popular is *'appetite appeal'*. A famous advertisement for 'Life-savers' shows a colourful array of the tinted, transparent, ring-shaped sweets laid out on a magazine page, over the slogan, 'please do not lick this page!'[16] 'Letters from parents followed the appearance of this ad, informing the client that they had caught their children actually licking the page.'[17] Advertising can make goods appear to be succulently tempting: a single, big, yellow peanut, shining with oil and sprinkled with salt, appears over the following copy: 'Something no one ever ate

[13] Blumberg (1989: 32–40).

[14] *Personal Computer World* (Mar. 1994), following 509; *Land's End Direct Merchants*, Spring 1994, ordering insert.

[15] Ogilvy (1962); 'The first official facts about the new size Ford for 1960', *Life*, 28 Sept. 1959, Ad. no. 4,925, J. Walter Thompson Papers, Duke University Library.

[16] e.g. *Saturday Evening Post*, 30 Jan. 1960, 62 (henceforth *SEP*).

[17] Schofield (1954: 22).

. . . Just one Planters Cocktail Peanut! No one we know of ever stopped after eating only one Planters Cocktail Peanut.'[18] Both ads use verbal and visual cues in order to get the juices flowing, to evoke the visceral attributes of sweetness and saltiness that these goods exude. Food in particular lends itself to this type of sensual appeal, but it is also found in ads for cars and for travel.

A shiny blue Rover Metro Tahiti Special, incongruously parked on a palm-fringed tropical beach, appeals to two sensual appetites at once, those for waxed and polished metal, and those for sun and surf. It also uses another familiar marketing device. The headline says 'JUST £99* PER MONTH'.[19] Psychologists call this device *'anchoring'*, a mental process of rounding-down which brings the perceived price to the next-lower reference point (perhaps in this case £90?) on the mental scale, and certainly below £100, which constitutes a higher threshold.[20] The price is entirely contrived: the asterisk refers to a table of fine print from which it is possible to work out that the monthly payments cover only 20.6 per cent of the full cost of the car. Like the picture, the price is too good to be true.[21] Often the word 'only' precedes the price, to achieve another anchoring effect. In this case, the word used is 'just'. The practice of setting a price a fraction short of the next perceptual step is universal. A letter in *The Times* recently proposed that the next coin to be minted should be for a value of 99 pence.[22] A very common 'anchoring' device, is the separate quotation of price (in large figures) and Value Added Tax (in smaller ones).[23] Like 'appetite appeal', anchoring also bypasses the filter of reason. The tactic is transparent, we understand how it works, and yet it is difficult to resist.

Another method, which also seeks to reach visceral sources of motivation, is *puffery*. 'The Greatest Show on Earth!' (Barnum & Bailey); 'The World's Greatest Newspaper' (Chicago Tribune); 'Nothing acts faster than Anadin'; 'Hands that do dishes can feel soft as your face' (Fairy Liquid)—these are examples of puffery.[24] Many more follow

[18] JWT archives, Duke University, Ad. no. 13,433, for *Life*, 16 Feb. 1962.

[19] From *Radio Times*, 1994 (date uncertain), in possession of the author.

[20] On the psychology of anchoring, see Tversky and Kahneman (1974).

[21] Cash price, £7,553; deposit £2,544; deal covers two years, at 6,000 miles a year; final payment £3,300; credit charge £702; miscellaneous charges £47. The picture is also quite obviously a studio collage.

[22] *The Times*, 10 Jan. 1994.

[23] Office of Fair Trade, 'VAT Exclusive Prices', Reference to the Consumer Protection Advisory Committee by the Director General of Fair Trading (1977), Dossier 17/4; Advertising Association Papers (henceforth AA), History of Advertising Trust (henceforth AA) 11/15/4.

[24] Preston (1975: 18–19); Wight (1972: 68).

further below, taken from American magazines of the 1950s and the 1960s. The legal definition of a puff is a claim that is not capable of substantiation, and one which no reasonable person would believe.[25]

'Puffs' are manifestly untrue, or at least impossible to substantiate, yet the law rules that they are not deceptive, since no reasonable person would believe them. Kool cigarettes, for example, are 'measurably long . . . immeasurably cool'; immeasurably indeed. Sometimes the puff is in the name of the product, e.g. 'Wonder Bread', or, indeed the 'Rover Metro Tahiti Special'; each element in its name conveying exaggerated pretensions for what is no more than an ordinary subcompact car.[26] Puffs are ubiquitous; every newspaper, every television commercial, is full of statements which are not intended to be taken literally. Why then are they used? To the extent that advertising forms a pre-commitment to quality, puffs reinforce that commitment. Maybe it does not 'wash whiter than white', but at least we can rely on mere whiteness. Large numbers of people do regard puffs as literally true. In one test, Alcoa's puff that 'Today, aluminium is something else' was appraised as completely true by 47 per cent, and partly true by 36 per cent of those questioned.[27] Tests of advertising comprehension indicate that typically between 30 and 35 per cent of television viewers and press media readers either understand advertising messages incorrectly, or fail to comprehend them altogether.[28] Most importantly, puffs, like anchoring, affect people even when known to be untrue. What else could account for their widespread use? Hence the legal attitude is misconceived: it applies the test of reason to claims that are designed to bypass the filter of reason.[29] Decisive evidence for the effectiveness of puffs is how ubiquitous they are. Whether effective or not, advertisers cannot afford not to use them, for fear of losing ground to the competition. If truthfulness is a public good, then puffs are an example of the 'tragedy of the commons', in which no competitor feels they can hold back, for fear of losing out.

The more truthful marketing discourse is, the more tempting it is for any individual advertiser to dissimulate or deceive. To avoid this ever-present hazard, misleading advertising is banned or regulated in most countries, though the systems of regulation vary.[30] These constraints are

[25] Preston (1975: 3).
[26] These examples are taken from Preston (1975: 18–19).
[27] Preston (1975: 29).
[28] Jacoby and Hoyer (1982, 1989, 1990).
[29] Preston (1975, 1994).
[30] Boddewyn (1992); Wagner (1971); John C. Braun, 'Unfair Competition and the Regulation Laws in the Common Market Countries' (offprint, 28 June 1972).

quite weak, and tolerate a good deal of puffery. There is also a grey area between puffs and misleading claims, which advertisers can try to exploit. Advertisers claim that regulations have pushed them away from deception and into puffery.[31] As Dorothy Sayers (crimewriter and copywriter) wrote, 'Plain lies are dangerous. The only weapons left are the *suggestio falsi* and the *suppressio veri*'.[32]

In Britain, advertising is constrained by more than eighty statutes, it is regulated by a voluntary body (the Advertising Standards Authority) and is also policed by the media. Nevertheless, the occurrence of misleading claims is quite high. A large sample of ads taken by the government Office of Fair Trading in March 1978 revealed that 13 per cent of advertisements in national newspapers and magazines failed to comply with the ASA code, 17 per cent of display ads that were larger than a quarter-page, 12 per cent of retail ads, and 29 per cent of mail order advertisements.[33] Of 2,993 advertisements sampled, 315 (10.5%) were considered to have breached the code (see Table 10.1).[34]

The information available to buyers and sellers is *asymmetric*. To dispel the wariness of buyers, sellers resort to a repertoire of gambits: value claims, price manipulation, honesty ploys, appetite appeal, anchoring, puffery, dissimulation. The challenge for advertising is to overcome this mistrust, which arises at the adversarial interface of buyer and seller.

2

The efficient solution is to establish trust between buyer and seller. Trust turns adversaries into co-operators. It enables the buyer to accept the seller's claim on good faith. For the buyer, it reduces uncertainty, and the effort of monitoring and enforcement. It helps to overcome the reluctance to buy. Many people find conflict and mistrust stressful, and are willing to pay a premium in order to avoid the experience.

Given that trust can be efficient as well as agreeable, it has attracted a good deal of analytical and empirical attention in recent years, on the part of social scientists.[35] In any single encounter, it pays to take advantage of a trusting protagonist. If the encounters are to be repeated, however, defection will be punished by the withdrawal of trust. As further

[31] Ogilvy (1962: 155); Preston (1975: 259).
[32] Ogilvy (1962: 155); see Borden (1942: 810).
[33] Borrie (1978: ch. 3).
[34] Ibid., table 1, 14–15.
[35] Axelrod (1984); Taylor (1987); Ostrom (1990); Bromley (1991).

TABLE 10.1. *Breaches of Advertising Standards Authority Code, May 1978*

Type of breach	Breaches	
	No.	%
1. Truthful presentation of product or company.	47	15
2. Bargain offer claims or prices.	107	34
3. Use of testimonials.	10	3
4. Use of word 'Guarantee'.	39	12
5. Medical products.	15	5
6. Absence of specified information.	77	24
7. No substantiation provided.	20	6
TOTAL	315	100

encounters take place, the evidence of trustworthiness builds up into a *reputation*, into a stock of goodwill. Repetition and reputation, then, are necessary in order to reap the benefits of co-operation. 'Your . . . dealer counts on your continued business week after week, month after month' says a car battery ad.[36] A 'candid statement on the car owner's problems' [of questionable candour] states that 'the essential industry need today is for increased confidence and trust between serviceman and car owner.'[37] 'The man from Nationwide is on your side.'[38] Any number of books on salesmanship and advertising will testify that the first requirement is to win the client's trust.[39]

Repetition and reputation occur naturally in a *face-to-face relationship*. Indeed, in this respect advertising is a second-best. Research in the 1930s found that although advertising had already reached its current level of about 3 per cent of GDP, for most sectors personal selling costs were 'several times as large' as advertising and promotion costs. A compelling face-to-face interaction with a salesperson is vital for selling.[40]

Each face is unique and individual. Facial expressions are a preverbal form of communication, recognized by babies from the age of a few weeks. A smile, a frown, a scowl, are universal messages, which carry the same meaning in all cultures.[41] The eye's ability to make finely

[36] For Atlas Batteries, *SEP*, 28 Sept. 1957. Not perhaps the most appropriate line for a durable like car batteries.
[37] For Carter Carburetors, *SEP*, 28 Sept. 1957.
[38] Nationwide Insurance, *Life*, 20 May 1966, 126.
[39] Shorris (1994).
[40] Borden (1942: 61–8 (68 cited), and table 106, p. 444).
[41] Ekman (1985), 16; Brown (1991: 112).

graded qualitative distinctions among different facial expressions is exploited in Chernoff faces which statisticians use to represent a large spectrum of information using only the curvature and size of the mouth, the length of the nose, the size of the eyes, and the shape of the face. These reduce well, maintaining legibility even with individual areas of 0.05 square inch.[42] The simple smile is the easiest expression to recognize: it can be seen from further away (up to 300 feet) and with briefer exposure, than any other expression. People enjoy looking at most smiles and will reciprocate them even when seen in a photograph.[43]

Facial expressions convey *attitudes* much better and more concisely than words. They provide an immediate insight into mental states. A smile conveys acceptance, approbation, ease. Non-verbal signals communicate a friendly attitude: proximity, orientation (more direct, side by side for some situations), gaze, facial expression (more smiling), gestures (head nods, lively movements), posture (open with arms stretched towards other rather than arms on hips or folded)—all of these are cues of acceptance. And confidence of acceptance is the basis of trust. Facial expressions and non-verbal communication convey clear evidence of attitudes and emotional states. An intriguing idea is that emotive experience has a functional basis. Strong emotions are expressed in the face and in other non-verbal gestures. Such expressions allow individuals to make a good estimate of the trustworthiness of other individuals. The selection of trustworthy partners for co-operative ventures has a survival value, and is thus likely to have been selected by an evolutionary process. The emotions facilitate the creation of trust. They can do so because facial expressions are difficult to fake.[44] It is interesting, however, that it is only the negative emotions (and non-facial cues) that are difficult to fake. False bonhomie is very easy to simulate. Most people are confident in their ability to detect it, but in fact do not seem to do so at a rate that is better than chance.[45]

Advertising aims to simulate trust. 'Ayer has a way of creating intimacy with its client's customers . . . They believe you need to find a way to touch people.'[46] 'Ads Are Like People' was the title of a presentation at J. Walter Thompson's creative forum in July 1966:

> People feel a kinship, a sympathy, an identity with other people . . . other human beings. They do not feel this for a large, impersonal, bloodless corporation.

[42] Tufte (1983: 96, 142). [43] Ekman (1985: 145).
[44] Frank (1989: chs. 5–6). [45] Ekman (1985: 35, 48, 86).
[46] 'Ayer at 125: "Creating Intimacy with Customers"', *Advertising Age*, 4 Apr. 1994, A-6.

It stands to reason then, that if an ad can have a warm, human personality, if it can share unashamed, genuine emotion with the viewer, it can set up a feeling of understanding and affection that can be a real asset to an advertiser just as it can for a person.[47]

Another presentation makes a similar point: 'Products whose advertising lacks sincerity fail for the same reason insincere people fail. Other people do not trust them.'[48] Advertising simulates the emotional cues of closeness and intimacy, above all, the cues of non-verbal communication; in particular, it projects a great many *faces*. This is what I call 'the mask of intimacy'. A wink, for example, is a concise arrow of intimacy, a one-bit invitation. And there she is, 'The sassy one from Canada Dry', a fetching woman in her twenties, winking at the reader with the puff, 'You'll come up a winner with Wink' (a soft drink).[49] This is probably too brassy, since winks are not in common use, and the soft drink has not survived.

To simulate an interpersonal relationship, the prime device in advertising is the *testimonial*. Often what this means is simply to project a face (Figure 10.1). A statement coming from a friendly face is accorded a friendly acceptance. Testimonials fall into several groups. One is the *expert* testimonial. In a series of classical experiments, the psychologist Stanley Milgram showed that the vast majority of ordinary Americans will cast aside their avowed ethical values in obedience to men in white coats.[50] Hence doctors were often recruited to provide testimonials. 'Doctors Warn You: "Harsh toilet papers are dangerous".' It sounds like a joke, but is taken from a real ad.[51] The classic instance was J. Walter Thompson's campaign which established Fleischmann's Yeast as a health food, making use of a series of medical testimonials. Since the product had no genuine medical benefits, American doctors were barred by professional ethics from participating. The agency evaded this obstacle by recruiting European doctors.[52] Likewise, doctors testified widely to the benefits of particular brands of cigarettes.[53] When testimonies were not available, a white-coated figure in the advertisement

[47] Chip Meads, 'Ads Are Like People', J. Walter Thompson, Creative Forum no. 2, July 1966, fo. 3; Speeches and Writings, Creative Forum Papers, JWT papers, Duke University.

[48] Robert Westerfield, 'Style in Advertising' (29 Dec. 1966), Speeches and Writings, Creative Forum Papers no. 11, JWT papers, Duke University.

[49] Canada Dry, *Life*, 20 May 1966, inside back cover.

[50] Milgram (1974).

[51] Scott Paper Company, *Good Housekeeping*, Apr. 1928, 177. Copy in JWT, Wallace Elton Papers, Oversize 4, Duke University.

[52] Fox (1990: 89).

[53] Pollay (1988: 5); Pollay (1990: 3, 7).

FIGURE 10.1. *'The smile that wins'*

Source: *Better Homes and Gardens* (Sept. 1948), 7.

would suffice.[54] Another type of testimonial is from the *celebrity*. Ed Sullivan, the popular broadcaster, proclaims 'Chesterfield is best for YOU!' For good measure, he also reports 'scientific evidence' from a medical specialist, observing 'no adverse effects . . . from smoking Chesterfield.'[55] David Ogilvy paid the President's widow Eleanor Roosevelt $35,000 to tell television viewers that 'the new Good Luck margarine really tastes *delicious*'.[56] If trust is based on reputation, with celebrity endorsement, the advertiser simply buys a ready-made reputation to associate with his product.

Even more common, and certainly cheaper, is the *ordinary testimonial.*

[54] Viceroy ad, Schofield (1954: 95).
[55] *SEP*, 7 Feb. 1953, back cover.
[56] Ogilvy (1983: 109).

A Sylvania Television ad ('Halolight: The Frame of Light That's Kinder to your Eyes') is framed by eighteen passport-type photos of named 'ordinary' people, from locations all over the country, each providing a rather implausible personal testimonial (e.g. 'Day or night, HALOLIGHT makes the Sylvania picture wonderfully clear and restful to watch').[57] Such 'ordinary' testimonials were often bogus.[58] Others were acquired as entries in competitions offering prizes. Testimonialists were paid a substantial sum, $25 in 1931, rather more than a weekly manual wage.[59] The face of 'Betty Crocker' ('I guarantee a perfect* cake every time you bake'), was invented, her fictional character part of the 'personality' of the brand.[60] Even more common is the *anonymous endorsement,* a nameless face, in colour or black and white, in photograph, painting, or drawing, gazing intently, candidly at the viewer and communicating a friendly message. Sometimes, in radio or television, it is merely a disembodied voice. Often, when the appeal takes some of the other forms, a small face is thrown in as well. Advertisers call this 'touching all bases'.[61]

Faces are ubiquitous in the advertising of the 1940s and the 1950s. A convenience sample of 1,128 ads between 1946 and 1966 indicates that about two-thirds of display ads in general circulation and women's magazines used 'face-appeal' as a basic form of endorsement. This theme of trust runs right through advertising literature. And yet, for all the resources at its command, advertising has little awareness of its own methodology: a speaker at a J. Walter Thompson seminar stated, with no fear of contradiction, 'Communication is not an exact science and advertising is simply communication between people. Mass communication, to be sure. But still, just people talking to people.'[62] A recent (and the first) academic collection on *Non-verbal communication in advertising* managed to overlook entirely the pervasive use of faces as a form of non-verbal endorsement.[63]

Some ads draw the viewer into a richer web of interpersonal interaction. In the 1950s, the decade of domesticity, family themes abounded.

[57] *SEP*, 7 Feb. 1953, 106. 11/17/2

[58] See e.g. paper by F. A. Bell, 'Legal Pitfalls' (11 Oct. 1934), describing two instances indicating routine use of bogus testimonials, JWT Staff Meetings, box 6/4, Duke University.

[59] Letter to Arthur Ritter from J. Walter Thompson, 2 Dec. 1931, JWT Inactive Accounts, box 18, History of Fleischmann Yeast Account, JWT papers, Duke University.

[60] General Mills ad, *Ladies Home Journal*, Feb. 1956, 45. The small print reads '*PERFECT? Yes, we DO mean perfect,' followed by a money-back guarantee.

[61] e.g., One-Dollar Book Club, *Ladies Home Journal*, Feb. 1956, 9; Seldin (1963: 185).

[62] Meads, 'Ads Are Like People', fo. 2.

[63] Hecker and Stewart (1988).

TABLE 10.2. *Faces in magazine display ads, c.1946–1966.*

Periodical	Date	Pages	Ads	Faces	No faces	% faces
Saturday Evening Post	7 Sept. 1946	168	129	90	39	70
McCall's	1 May 1947	176	135	108	27	80
Better Homes & Gardens	1 Sept. 1948	262	232	179	53	77
Saturday Evening Post	7 Feb. 1953	120	68	48	20	71
Ladies' Home Journal	1 Feb. 1956	178	121	73	48	60
Saturday Evening Post	28 Feb. 1957	176	127	96	31	76
Ladies' Home Journal	1 Apr. 1957	134	88	65	23	74
Saturday Evening Post	30 Jan. 1960	96	43	24	19	56
Ladies' Home Journal	1 Mar. 1962	138	66	29	37	44
Saturday Evening Post	15 Jan. 1966	80	27	17	10	63
Life	20 May 1966	130	92	60	32	65
TOTAL		1,658	1,128	789	339	67

Childhood and its *rites de passage* is another abiding theme, much favoured by Kodak, the film company, and by Hamilton, the watch company.[64] The 1960s added youth bonding. 'The Pepsi Generation' campaign, starting in the early 1960s, identified the soft drink with peer approbation and acceptance. One ad shows a colour photograph of two young women in bikinis, big smiles, reclining on a dinghy. Two tanned, muscular young men, cling to the dinghy in the green water. There are two six-packs of Pepsi on the raft. This campaign hit a chord, and helped Pepsi to catch up with the market leader, Coca-Cola.[65] Romance and sexual attraction, the most intimate of emotions, are very common in advertising. They are mocked in a Volkswagen ad, which shows two beauties curled on a car bonnet, and asks, 'Why don't they ever sit on a Volkswagen?'[66] In a car ad of 1956, a tall cowboy is pointing the way to an adoring woman driver over the slogan 'long, lean and packed with punch' (Figure 10.2).[67]

From the 1960s onwards television increasingly took over from magazines as the main advertising medium. As the old static formulas began to jade, advertisers increasingly sought novelty and visual surprise. This was the 'creative revolution', originating in London in the late 1960s, in which an inventive and creative post-modern mix of stimulations and enticements attempted to capture the fragmentation of expectations and values in the 1970s and 1980s.[68] But the theme of interpersonal trust is a hardy perennial, and a random trawl in current advertising shows no lack of effort to simulate the bonds of interpersonal obligation. An infant is shown sucking at a breast, which is also bisected by a spiralling black telephone cord. The copy says, 'when you breastfeed, you create an important bond with your child; when you talk to First Direct [a telephone-based bank], you're treated as a person, not a number.' A highlighted slogan declares, 'humanity in a bank.'[69]

What advertising attempts to do, is to simulate the gift relationship in the market economy.[70] A 'gift' is an exchange in which a transfer is not mediated by price, but is rather reciprocated at the discretion of the receiver. It is driven by the pursuit of 'regard', i.e. the intrinsic benefits

[64] On the family in American advertising, see Belk and Pollay (1985).

[65] e.g. Pepsi-Cola, *Life*, 20 May 1966; Tedlow (1990: 371); the salience of 'person' ads during the 1940s and 1950s, and the subsequent shift to 'life-style' ads is documented in Leiss *et al.* (1990: 274–84).

[66] *Design and Art Direction 71* (1971), 46.

[67] *Better Homes and Gardens*, Nov. 1956, adv. no. 1,712-A, Wallace Elton papers, outsize box 3, Duke University.

[68] Goldman (1992); Whitwell (1989).

[69] First Direct, *The Guardian*, 8 Feb. 1995, 9.

[70] This paragraph based on Offer (1996). See also Schudson (1986: 135–43).

FIGURE 10.2. *'Long, lean and packed with punch!' (Car advertisement, Nov. 1956)*

Source: J. Walter Thompson papers, Wallace Elton collection, box 3, Duke University.

of social and personal interaction. Gifts are used to personalize the exchange, and to authenticate regard. In contrast, a market transaction is *impersonal* and is mediated by a money price. Reciprocal gifting gives rise to obligation; according to Marcel Mauss, gift relations are underpinned by an obligation to give, an obligation to receive, and an obligation to reciprocate.[71] Gift-giving motivates much retail purchasing. Reciprocity abounds at work, it affects management, agriculture, marketing, entrepreneurship, and politics. The gift survives on a surprisingly large scale in interpersonal exchange. It does so *where there are few economies of scale*. The market is not a good provider of authentic regard, but when standard commodities have to be sold, prices are an efficient and parsimonious method of co-ordination and exchange.

[71] Mauss (1954: 10–11).

Face-to-face relationship cannot be mass produced. The role of advertising has been to use the methods of mass reproduction to simulate (to the best of its ability), the cues of regard. Hence the predominance of interpersonal and obligation cues in advertising, and the normal absence of price information in national media advertising. Where price information is included, it is usually misleading, e.g. the marked-up 'list price'. This allows vendors to escape the market's 'law of one price', and to invite viewers to form their own estimation of 'use value', which individual retailers will attempt to match with a customized 'exchange value'. A slogan of this kind is 'Diamonds are forever', invented by Ayer for De Beers; it captures precisely the subjectivity and obligation implicit in the gift relation.[72] Thus, the advertising of the second half of the twentieth century is a form of mass production, exploiting economies of scale in media communications. As information becomes cheaper, marketers attempt to personalize their appeal, and to collect information about individual clients in so-called 'database marketing'. Procter & Gamble sends 'individualized' birthday cards for babies, and reminder letters to move up to the next size of disposable nappies.[73] The goal is to target promotions at the smallest possible market niche—the individual—in order to simulate a personal relationship between sellers and buyers. Customers are increasingly exposed to sales pitches disguised as personal communications.[74]

3

It is not only interpersonal relations that advertising attempts to appropriate. Art has a special credibility. It is assumed to be commercially disinterested, to possess integrity. Artists also practise deception, and invite us to suspend disbelief, to put ourselves, if only momentarily, in their hands. Hence their special attraction to advertising. Occasionally advertisers make use of well-known artists in their work. A Renault car is parked inside on the polished wooden floor of an art gallery, while a man (the owner?) contemplates Gainsborough's painting of Mr and Mrs Andrews, sitting under an oak tree framed by their broad acres. The copy

[72] 'Creating Intimacy with Customers', 'Ayer at 125' [advertising inset], *Advertising Age*, 4 Apr. 1994, A6.

[73] 'How to Turn Junk Mail into a Goldmine—or perhaps not', *The Economist*, 1 Apr. 1995, 81–2.

[74] 'Database marketing', *Business Week*, 5 Sept. 1994, p. 56; personal experience. Barclays Insurance Services Company to A. Ofer, Apr. 1993, author's collection.

says 'A PRIVATE VIEW, A STUDY IN REFINEMENT'.[75] Most commercial art is anonymous, however. It remains art nonetheless, and very distinct from photography (which in advertising has also striven increasingly for artistic effects). The illustrators of Ford car ads in the 1940s were paid upwards of 1,000 dollars for a colour illustration, at a time when a new car cost little more.[76] It is doubtful whether many 'pure' artists could command this kind of fee at the time.

In its quest for credibility, advertising has repeatedly sought to appropriate credible art. A prime example is Norman Rockwell. Between the 1920s and the 1960s, Rockwell presented a series of images of an idealized small-town America; almost invariably, his illustrations have a charming 'human touch', some kind of sympathetic human interaction or experience. On the covers of the *Saturday Evening Post* they gave Americans a picture of themselves as a community: they touched on childhood and its rites, young love, home and family, the past, Americans in uniform, at work, at play, American faces, and the ultimate gifting occasion, Christmas.[77] Rockwell provided his corny human interactions indiscriminately to editors and advertisers alike.[78] Indeed, he was not always clear in his mind about the distinction between the two. In 1946 and 1947 he engaged in a protracted correspondence with Ford's advertising agents, J. Walter Thompson, proposing to include a Ford car in a *Saturday Evening Post* cover, in return for a Ford station wagon. Cars were scarce at the time, and Ford had no trouble selling them. The offer was rejected.[79]

Advertising's search for credibility is highlighted by its relations with the media, and with the press in particular. The vast bulk of advertising expenditure (typically more than 90 per cent) is on space in editorial media.[80] On the other side, most editorial media (both broadcast and

[75] Renault, *Independent on Sunday*, 20 June 1993, 12–13.

[76] The artist Ronald Maclean charged $1,000 each for two advertising illustrations, but usually asked for and received considerably more. Walter Elton to George Strouse, 11 July 1946, Elton papers, JWT papers, Duke University. 'We usually figure that a drawing of a car in color will cost between $450 and $500', Elton to Strouse, 11 Oct. 1946, ibid.

[77] Based on the chapter headings in Finch (1975). [78] Stoltz (1986).

[79] Walter Elton to O'Neill Ryan, 21 Mar. 1946; George Strouse to Elton, 2 Apr. 1946; Walter Elton to Norman Rockwell, 5 Apr. 1946, Walter Elton papers box 5, JWT papers, Duke University.

[80] Excluding direct mail. In the UK between 1970 and 1992 it averaged 67 per cent on press advertising, and 27 per cent on TV: *Advertising Statistics Yearbook 1993*, table 4.1.2, 22. In 1982, direct advertising accounted for about 9 per cent of UK advertising (*World Advertising Expenditures, 1982*, table 8, 24–5). The American ratio of television to print was rather higher in 1982, standing at 0.6, compared with the British 0.41 (ibid.).

printed) depend on advertising for their survival. It is a firm convention that advertising is strictly demarcated from editorial. The reason is that advertising is not normally arresting in itself, except from people already contemplating the purchase of goods. For all their acquisitiveness, most people, most of the time, remain interested in personal interaction, culture, civic, social and political affairs, at least as much as they care for the price and quality of goods. In order to attract these readers or viewers, the good faith, or credibility of the editorial material is crucial. Editorial material provides the bread of credibility in the advertising sandwich.[81] On the whole, this boundary is respected by advertisers, because it is vital for the delivery of readers. But the more solid the boundary, the more credible the editorial, the greater the temptation for individual advertisers to free ride and to hijack editorial material for their own purposes.

In 1959 Ford launched the first of its compact cars, the Falcon. It was introduced in response to a buyer revolt against the Detroit 'dinosaurs', the staple cars which had reached a height of extravagance in the previous two years. To underpin the message of a return to basic values, and especially honesty, the JWT agency recruited Charles Schultz, creator of the 'Peanuts' cartoon series. Charlie Brown, Lucy, Snoopy, and their friends enlisted a wry homespun 'such is life' philosophy to sell Ford cars. As the account executive explained, 'the Peanuts strip has never been commercialized in an extensive or undesirable way . . . We have been careful to keep the Peanuts people in character so that references to Ford products will be made in terms of Schultz's philosophy.'[82]

This provoked a debate at the Newspaper Comics Council which provides a sense of some of the issues involved in the intermingling of culture and commerce. Phil Porter of the Cleveland *Plain Dealer*, gave the opening presentation, 'How Greedy Can You Get?' Most of those speaking shared his outrage, but they found it difficult to support with good reasoning. Two lines of argument emerged; both of them accused the commercialized cartoonist of free riding. One group of speakers (mostly on the editorial side of the press) simply objected to the blurring of the boundary between editorial and advertising. Editorial was impartial, and any sharing of contents across the boundary was bound to cast doubt on editorial integrity.

[81] See also Becker and Murphy (1993), 961.

[82] W. Elton to Philip Filhaber, 5 Apr. 1960, Wallace W. Elton Papers, JWT papers, Box 10, Duke University.

The advertisers are buying names, that's all. Just as they buy names of ball players—and faces too—for razor ads, or auto and cigarette ads. Let them buy these testimonials if they wish. We know that many of them are as phoney as a $3 bill, for some of the athletes don't smoke or are too young to shave. But let's not carry this thing into the holy of holies. Isn't there anything left for the reader these days, without a built-in commercial?[83]

Another editor chipped in, 'The battle to convince the public that news content is a pure and undefiled area has been made increasingly difficult by TV formats which allow the advertiser to control the content of the show.'[84]

For other speakers what was at stake was not only the public commons of the editorial side of the press, but also a much larger one, the commons of shared culture, in which these cartoon characters stood for emotional integrity.

Let them leave the characters we love alone. Our feelings about 'Peanuts', 'Blondie', 'Beetle Bailey' and 'Dick Tracy' are inextricably tied up with long standing mental associations deep inside each of us. Association with countless happy moments derived from reading our newspapers is what we want, not an association with motor cars, hair tonics, or underarm deodorants. 'Little Lulu' was once a character loveable for traits that certainly weren't related to Kleenex. I can't help but wonder just how much she was hurt by subconscious association with a runny nose.'[85]

Another editor said, 'those wonderful kids ought to stay out of the automobile selling racket.'[86] Several others spoke in the same vein. But Schultz was not without defenders. One of them pointed to the brutal reality, that editorial integrity was merely itself a marketing vehicle: 'Newspaper publishers are in business for just one reason—to deliver a big, responsive audience to advertisers. This determines whether you remain in business or close your doors.'[87]

Ford also made use of its own (rather effective) comic strips to convey little homely stories about the purchase decisions of its pick-up trucks. In its use of common culture, familiar cultural artifacts, and artistic expression, advertising will mobilize anything that has some emotive power (see Figure 10.3.)

In consequence, the boundary between art and commerce, especially in the United States, has been blurred; commercial products, cars, soft

[83] 'Open discussion of secondary rights to comics', Newspaper comics council meeting, 5 Feb. 1960, fo. 3. Wallace W. Elton Papers, JWT papers, Box 10.

[84] Ibid., Bill Steven, fo. 6.

[85] Ibid., William Hill, fo. 4.

[86] Ibid., Garry Byrnes, fo. 5.

[87] Ibid., Maurice T. Reilly, fo. 11.

FIGURE 10.3. *'Product placement has gotten so obtrusive'*
Source: *The Spectator* (30 Sept. 1995), 13. (artist: Nick Downes)

drinks, pervade the country's common culture. Coca-Cola is as much a national symbol as the Stars and Stripes.[88] Art also strives to mobilize the sources of emotive power, and it finds them in the immediate environment. It is a testimony to the success of advertising that by the 1960s artists were returning the compliment. Andy Warhol filled his canvasses with cans of Campbell's soup, bottles of Coca-Cola, boxes of Brillo; his banal images excited a surge of recognition, and made him into the best-known New York artist of the 1960s.[89]

Press and television editors, while no doubt guilty of other forms of

[88] Fox (1975: 78). [89] e.g. Honnef (1991).

excess, take pride in the credibility of their discourse, which is demarcated from advertising by well-kept fences. No wonder that advertisers yearn to let loose their cows on the lush pastures on the other side. Sometimes a cow will jump the fence on its own: occasionally advertisements appear that pretend to be editorial (or sometimes fiction). By convention, they carry a warning.[90] Occasionally advertisers attempt to influence editorial policy.[91] Much more important is the practice of *public relations*. Its purpose is to implant the marketing message in editorial media. This can be cheaper than buying space, but the greatest attraction is that viewer defences are down when taking in editorial materials. Public relations is a big enterprise. Unlike advertising, it extends well beyond the commercial world and a good deal of it is undertaken by in-house practitioners.[92]

4

If advertisers choose to be cavalier with the truth, the effect is primarily damaging to advertisers themselves. Advertising has low credibility. Many of its gambits are transparent. American respondents in the 1930s expressed a strong distrust of advertising messages, repeated in two surveys in 1969 and 1990.[93] In a European Commission survey (1975), 67 per cent of respondents agreed that much of advertising was misleading. In a French government survey in 1979, 66 per cent said that advertising tends to mislead.[94] Even children are aware that advertising deceives.[95] This is not inconsistent with the repertoire of persuasion and deception described before. At the level of reason, advertising is distrusted. Hence the importance, for advertisers, of *bypassing the filter of reason*. This accounts for our curious reaction to the medium: *we know that we are often misled, and yet we find it compelling.*

The longest-standing *economic* arguments both for and against advertising revolve around a single idea. On the one hand, it is said, advertising diffuses information about goods, which makes them attractive to

[90] But see 'Mountain Rescue—A True Short Story . . .' an ad masquerading as a short story with only a tiny small-print indication of provenance, reproduced in Schofield (1954: 131).

[91] 'Do Advertisers Often Try to Alter Editorial Policy?', *Campaign*, 17 Sept. 1993, 17.

[92] Ross (1959); Bentele (1992).

[93] Borden (1942: ch. 26); Reader's Digest Association (1970), Table 63, 186–7; Reader's Digest Association (1991), table 300, 466–9.

[94] Business International SA (1980), II-69.

[95] Schudson (1981: 110).

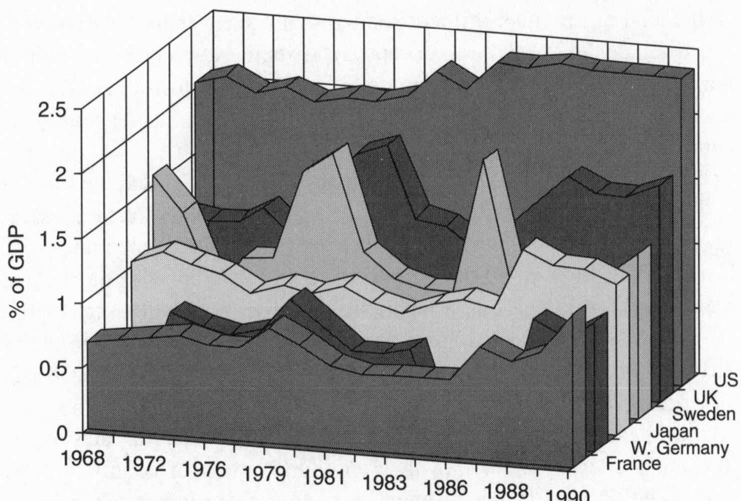

FIGURE 10.4. *Advertising as percentage of GDP in six affluent countries, 1968–1990*

Source: *Advertising Expenditures around the World* (1968–1990)

more people. With more people buying, it is possible to achieve economies of scale, and these economies of scale reduce the price of the good. On the other hand, there is no compulsion on successful advertisers to share their efficiency gains with the public; indeed, the more successful they are, the more of the market they capture, the higher the barriers to effective competition. There has been much research on the subject, and both the supporters and the critics have been vindicated empirically, but it is only natural to assume that advertising should cost less than its benefits at some times and places, and more at others.

Is advertising, however, a precondition of an affluent society? Is it vital in order to achieve modern levels of income and output? Some clues are provided by comparison of advertising outlays in different countries. The United States has spent more than 3 per cent of its GNP on advertising and promotion for most years from the 1900s to the 1930s, and more than 2 per cent since then.[96] Among the advanced industrial countries, the level of outlay on advertising has varied by a factor of three or more. Figure 10.4 compares advertising expenditure since the late 1960s in six industrial countries. The United States was

[96] Pease (1958: 13–14); *Advertising Expenditures around the World* (1960 ff.).

well ahead of the other affluent societies, and spent more than twice as much as any of the others, except for Britain. Nor are the quantities negligible. The percentage of national income spent just on advertising in the United States in 1971 was about one-quarter of the outlay on education at all levels.[97]

During this period several of the countries involved closed the income and productivity gap with the United States; at various times Sweden, Japan, and Germany matched or exceeded United States income levels. In other words, it was possible for them to catch up with the United States, without laying out comparable resources on advertising. Figure 10.5 extends the comparison (at one point in time) to a large sample of different countries. In terms of the relation between GNP per head and advertising outlays. Regression lines show three groups. In the poor countries, advertising outlays rise sharply with income, as they move into the market economy. In the 'middling' group of countries there is no relation, and in the 'affluent' countries there is a weak positive relation. The data suggest that outlays increase with economic *development*. As economic activity moves out of the household and into the market; as disposable income increases, and as the number of goods and volume of market transactions increase, as literacy and numeracy expand, more market information is required, and mass persuasion becomes more effective.

Economic performance in advanced economies does not depend on advertising. Countries at a comparable level of economic growth devote different shares of national income to advertising. The United States is an outlier, consistently devoting 2 per cent or more of national income. Other English-speaking countries, Australia, Canada, and the UK are in an intermediate position, with approximately 1 per cent. A number of strong European economies (France, Germany, Netherlands, Belgium) devote a much lower proportion of GNP to advertising; and the Japanese also restrict advertising to substantially less than 1 per cent of national income. Furthermore, the proportion of resources devoted to advertising has been relatively constant in the different countries during the post-war years, so that the absolute level of economic activity does not explain the share of advertising. In the 1960s, when the United States was as wealthy as Germany or the UK today, it still spent a higher proportion of its resources on advertising. Business culture and the general culture of different societies appear to determine different levels of

[97] United States Dept of Commerce (1980: table 6/6, 290).

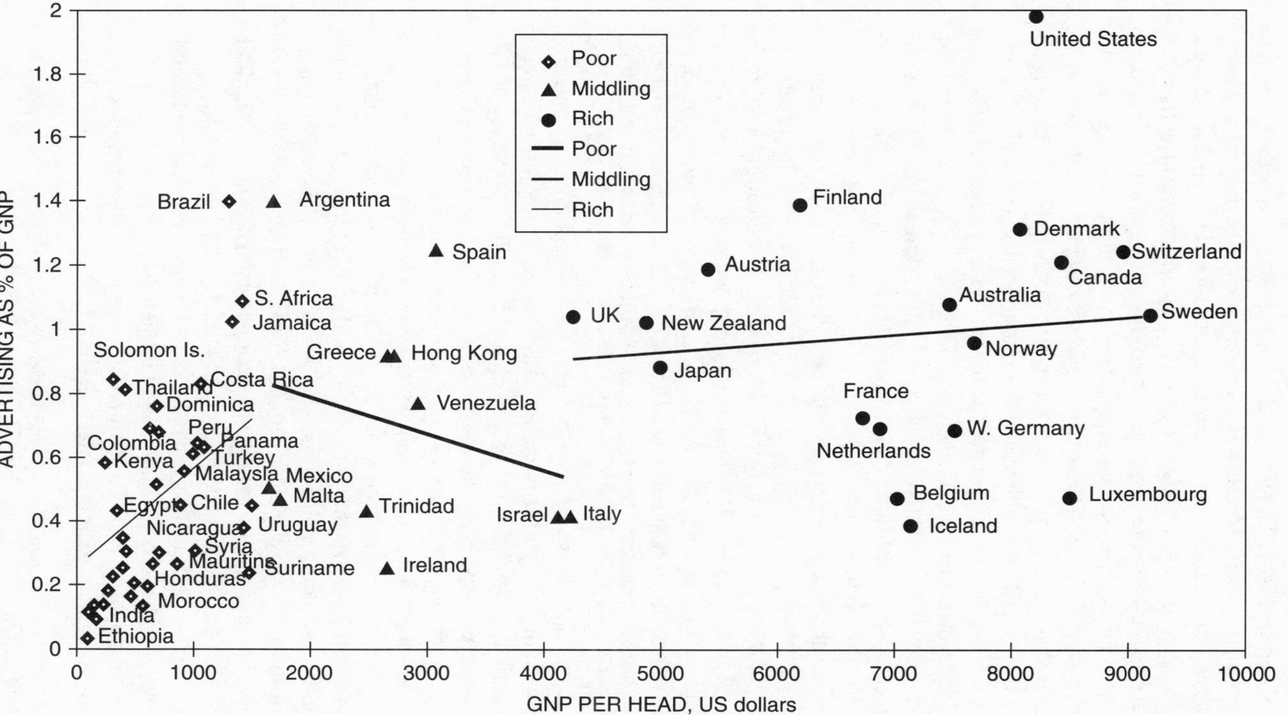

FIGURE 10.5. *Advertising as a percentage of national income and GNP per head, 1976*

Sources: *Advertising Expenditures around the World* (World Bank); International Bank for Reconstruction and Development

advertising intensity. Given that the United States is both the highest spender in terms of national income, and also the largest economy, advertising is dominantly an American institution. In 1980, for example, USA outlays on advertising formed 47 per cent of world outlays.[98]

Advertising uses the resources of credibility in order to transmit a message that is often deceptive. In using these resources, does advertising also *use them up?* Where does credibility come from? Robert Frank suggests that mankind is 'wired' for trust; that there is an innate capacity for trust which is facilitated by the emotions, just as linguists assume an innate capacity for language.[99] If that is the case, then advertising is *unlikely* to cause permanent damage, since the capacity to form trusting relations is a renewable resource. Another view is that the capacity for trust has to be nurtured and learned. There is some empirical evidence for this. An attitude survey in 1981–4 presented large samples of people in several countries with the following statement: 'speaking generally, other people can be trusted.' It then invited them to rate this statement as true or untrue. Replies aligned along a clear gradient, interpersonal trust rising with affluence. Three groups can be distinguished: Catholic countries, and poor as well as recently-poor countries rate low on interpersonal trust, regardless of income. English-speaking countries occupy an intermediate position. The Nordic countries, on the whole, show the highest levels of trust. The data are shown in Figure 10.6.

Is it possible, however, that by 'grazing' the commons of interpersonal trust and the common culture, advertising also actively degrades these resources, and diminishes the value of intangible but valuable *public* goods, and especially the resources of interpersonal trust? Could it be that by drawing on the resources of interpersonal trust for the purpose of commercial competition, advertising diminishes the capacity of society to engage in collective action, for both private and public ends?

Figure 10.7 shows that advertising outlay is correlated with interpersonal trust, controlled for income (which is not significant). On the face of it, this suggests that advertising is more attractive the higher the level of interpersonal trust; that advertising is using the general credibility of interpersonal discourse in order to interpolate its messages; that advertising is less attractive where mistrust is rife. The countries towards the bottom-right corner, which have high levels of trust and low levels of advertising, all operate fairly rigorous controls on advertising, seeking perhaps to protect their gullible citizens.

98 *Advertising Expenditures around the World*, 16th Survey (1981: table 1, 13–14).
99 Frank (1989).

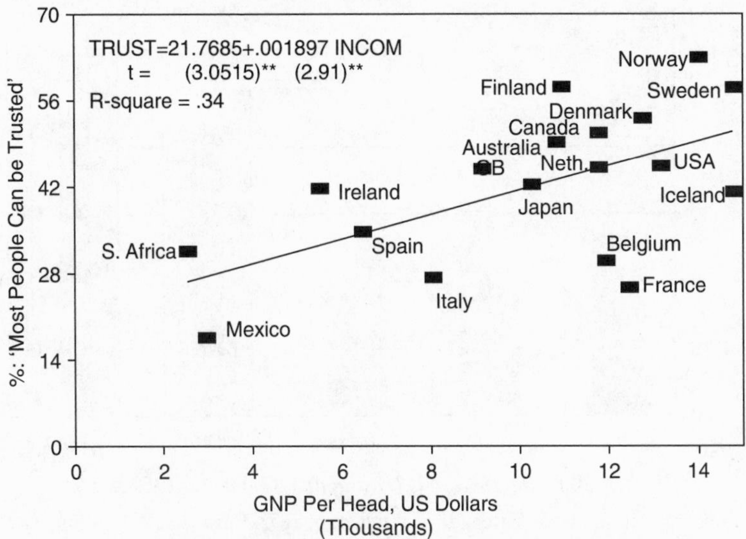

FIGURE 10.6. *Interpersonal Trust and GNP per head, 1981–1984*

Sources: European Values Survey data; *International Bank for Reconstruction and Development* (1990)

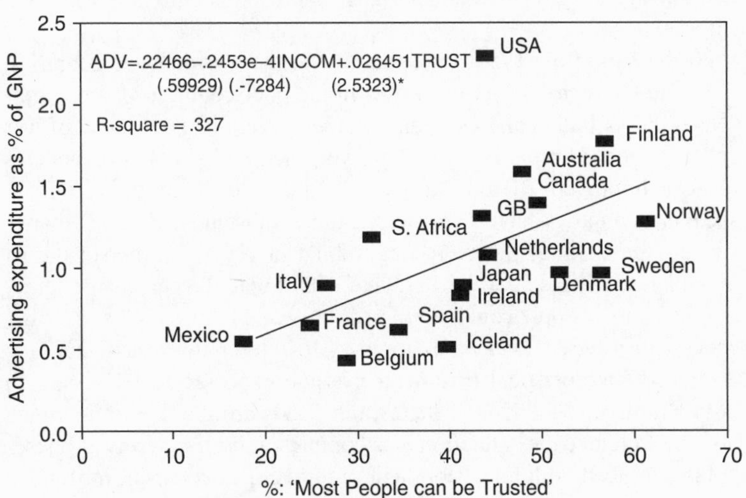

FIGURE 10.7. *Advertising Expenditure and Interpersonal Trust*

Source: European Values Survey data

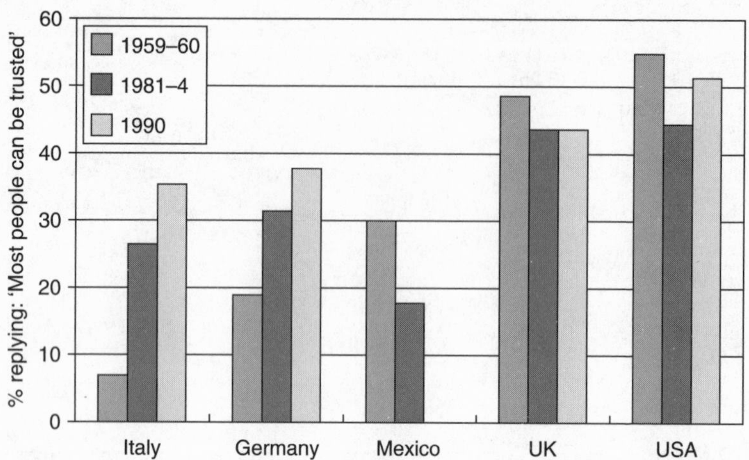

FIGURE 10.8. *Interpersonal Trust in Five Countries, 1959–1990*

Sources: Almond and Verba (1963: table 4, p. 267); European Values Survey, 1981–4 and 1990

There is some further evidence in the values survey, which provides three observations over thirty years for four countries. In addition to the two already mentioned, another values survey was carried out in 1990 (Figure 10.8).

At the end of the 1950s trust was low in the war-defeated countries, Italy and Germany, lower even than in the poor country, Mexico. Subsequently, as Italian and German societies overcame the trauma of war and experienced rapid economic growth, their social cohesion appears to have improved. Starting at a much higher level, the two English-speaking countries have experienced quite substantial declines, partly righted in the United States. A longitudinal survey of interpersonal trust in the United States between 1972 and 1989 found the percentage agreeing that 'most people could be trusted' hovering between 48 and 37 per cent, with a weak downwards trend.[100] It is tempting to associate the decline of interpersonal trust with massive exposure to television. In both Britain and the United States, the 1960s are the decade in which household television saturation was completed, both in terms of households equipped with television, and in terms of hours spent in front of the box. In terms of time use, television came to dominate leisure hours, with people spending an average of 20 to 35 hours a week in front of

[100] Wood (1990), 323 ff. I owe this reference to Robert Lane.

the box, depending on social class.[101] Television has a much larger transmission capacity ('bandwidth') than print, and achieved far greater viewer attention.

As this chapter was going to the press, important new evidence has emerged in support of this conjecture. Robert Putnam has measured the stock of 'social capital' in the United States, using a large longitudinal sample, the General Social Survey, for the years 1972–94. He has measured two variables in particular, membership of voluntary groups, and reponses to the statement 'most people can be trusted', which we have also used above. He has found a net decline since the early 1970s of voluntary group membership by about 15–20 per cent, and of trust by about 20–5 per cent.[102] The most powerful differentiator (apart from education), is *cohort*. The members of cohorts which turned 18 between the 1920s and the 1950s expressed positive trust at levels of between 50 and 60 per cent. Thereafter, there is a very sharp drop, with the latest cohort ('turned 18 in the 1970s') having a level of trust of between 20 and 30 per cent.[103] Similar patterns (at different levels) were found for voting turnout, newspaper readership, and group membership. The result was controlled for education and life-cycle effects, and is thus very robust. As Putnam points out, the downturn coincides with the first cohorts fully exposed to television. Furthermore, voluntary group membership is also found to vary inversely and strongly with hours of television viewing (and positively with education and newspaper readership). As television viewing increased, newspaper readership declined sharply, especially among the younger cohorts. Putnam notes substantial evidence that television viewing is associated with misanthropy, with a 'mean world view'. He has not considered the effect of advertising.[104]

Quite separately, there is also considerable evidence of the decline of trust in authority in the United States. Table 10.3 indicates the decline in the reputation of the main sources of social and political authority in American society since the 1960s.

Typically the percentage expressing a great deal of confidence in leadership declined by approximately one-half between the 1960s and the 1980s, and both government and politicians are rated low. Other sources have measured similar indicators of decline in authority, much of it taking place from the 1960s to the 1970s.[105] Similar expressions of distrust can be found in the United Kingdom.[106]

[101] Bowden and Offer (1994). [102] Putnam (1995: 668).
[103] Putnam (1995: 675). [104] Putnam (1995: 678–9).
[105] e.g. Yankelovich (1981: 184–6); Abramowitz (1980: 188–96).
[106] Kavanagh (1980: 145–7).

TABLE 10.3. *Confidence in leadership in the United States, 1966–1986: Percentage stating that they have a great deal of confidence*

Institution	1986	1973	1966
The military	36	40	61
Higher education	34	44	61
Medicine	33	57	73
Supreme Court	32	33	50
TV news	27	41	
Religion	22	36	41
Congress	21		42
Local govt.	21	28	
The press	19	30	29
White House	19	18	
State govt.	19	24	
Federal govt.	18	19	41
Major companies	16	29	55
Law firms	14	24	
Trade Unions	11	20	22

Source: Harris Polls, cited by Blumberg (1989: table 11.2, 204).

Now several things have made leadership a more intractable challenge in the post-1960s period. To mention some of them, the stagnation of real incomes, structural change in the economy, rising crime and social disintegration, and in the United States, the traumatic failure of Vietnam. But some of these failures might themselves be regarded as products of the failure of authority (and of social co-operation), rather than as independent variables. In all of this, the influence of advertising cannot be entirely ruled out.

Ever since Dwight Eisenhower's first Presidential campaign in 1952, marketing experts have increasingly controlled the format of American electoral campaigns. As David Ogilvy tells it, 'In 1952 my old friend Rosser Reeves advertised General Eisenhower as if he were a tube of toothpaste. He created fifty commercials in which the General was made to read out hand-lettered answers to a series of phony questions from imaginary citizens. Like this,

Citizen: 'Mr. Eisenhower, what about the high cost of living?'

General: 'My wife Mamie worries about the same thing. Tell her it's our job to change that on November 14th.'

Between takes the General was heard to say, 'To think that an old soldier should come to this.'[107]

The marketing of politics in the United States was stimulated enormously by the onset of television. Political campaigning has adapted to the television commercial format. The high cost of air time has inflated the price of political campaigning in the United States, and has raised the barriers to entry substantially.[108] The campaign itself is constrained by a format of thirty- or sixty-second 'spot' commercials. Political campaigning has thus adopted many of the attributes of commercial advertising: a slick, mass-appeal image, the use of jingles and puffs, and short, punchy 'soundbites'.[109]

The visuals of one thirty-second 1976 commercial show a horseman bursting out of the woods, and being joined by several cowboys, galloping across an open prairie. This was not a Marlboro commercial, but a political ad. The voice-over says,

> Come and join the Wallop Senate Drive.
> The Wallop Senate Drive!
> It's alert and its alive
> And it's Wyoming to the spurs.
> The Wallop Senate Drive![110]

Jimmy Carter's presidential campaign commercial of the same year is all faces and authenticity. 'My children will be the sixth generation on the same land'; 'We've always worked for a living. We know what it means to work'; 'I'll never tell a lie. I'll never make a misleading statement.' For all we know, unlike Eisenhower, Carter may have believed his lines, but they fall into a common advertising genre, 'the only straight player in the business'.[111] Carter's honesty was no match for the radiance of a real actor, Ronald Reagan, whose 'Morning in America' pitch evoked all the homely feel-good themes of margarine pretending to be butter. The Reagan presidency became a 'permanent campaign'.[112]

Political campaigning in America acquired both the benefits and the negative associations of marketing and advertising in general. The main benefit was in using a method of compelling attention, by means of a

[107] Ogilvy (1962: 156–7). [108] O'Shaughnessy (1990: 47).

[109] Kern (1989); Biocca (1992); Castleman and Podrazik (1982); O'Shaughnessy (1990); Diamond and Bates (1992).

[110] The Wallop Senate Drive, 1976, in Diamond and Bates (1992: 289–95).

[111] 1976: *Ford* vs. *Carter*, in Diamond and Bates (1992: 238–9); see above, p. 215.

[112] O'Shaughnessy (1990: ch. 9).

vast amplification of the cues of directness and intimacy. The drawback was that, on the face of it, the credibility of political leaders declined to the low level that is typical of business advertisers.

Even some of the greatest stalwarts of advertising have their doubts about its application in politics. John O'Toole, president of the International Association of Advertising, was on the campaign team for Nixon in 1972 and Reagan in 1980. He takes a strongly permissive view of advertising as a whole, but regards political advertising as a violation of the implicit contract with consumers. Towards the end of a campaign, he writes, the temptation to lie is overwhelming. He advocates limits on the candidates' television time.[113] Another advertising practitioner concluded a book entitled *The Duping of the American Voter* with the statement that political commercials of the 1960s and the 1970s were 'the most deceptive, misleading, unfair and untruthful of all advertising . . . the sky is the limit with regard to what can be said, what can be promised, what accusations can be made, what lies can be told.'[114] David Ogilvy, the best-known advertiser of the 1960s and 1970s, says that 'In a period when television commercials are often the decisive factor in deciding who shall be the next President of the United States, dishonest advertising is as evil as stuffing the ballot box.'[115] These honest advertisers have identified the social issue which arises from mass-media advertising. It is not so much the question of deception, which is widespread in human discourse.[116] Rather advertising in general, and political advertising in particular, by legitimizing deception by *social authority* undermines that very authority, and contaminates the trust that is necessary for compliance.

5

Mistrust of advertising is not restricted to its social critics, or to disgruntled marketing executives. All affluent societies have taken a variety of measures to protect themselves and their citizens. A survey of these protective measures also provides us with a sense of the guiding values of their different business, social, and political cultures.

Advertising is regulated at two different levels. Certain kinds of advertising are prohibited on normative grounds, because the *products*

[113] O'Toole (1981: 37–9).
[114] Spero (1980), cited by Ogilvy (1983: 211).
[115] Ogilvy (1983: 213).
[116] Nyberg (1993).

they promote are recognized as potentially harmful. Narcotics, alcohol, tobacco are all regulated in various ways. Certain kinds of *advertising* are also implicitly judged to be harmful or intrusive, and are regulated on these grounds. As we have noted, billboard [hoarding] advertising in the countryside was withdrawn by oil companies in response to public protest in the 1920s.[117] Cloudwriting was prohibited by law in Britain in the 1930s. But the central focus of advertising regulation in the West is on the same issue which is central to this essay, namely deception and truth.

Three dominant approaches to regulation may be characterized as the American, the British, and the Continental patterns. In the United States, advertising is assertive and aggressive. At the national level, it is regulated by a government agency, the Federal Trade Commission, by means of legal sanctions, which are vigorously contested by the industry. Britain has a large variety of legislation which restricts advertising, but active regulation is largely carried out by the advertising industry itself, by means of its own special agencies. Compliance with this regulation is much better. Advertisers on the Continent tend to be less assertive, and the state is more paternalistic. In the last three decades the European Commission (now the European Union) has embraced much of the critique of advertising, and has attempted to formulate a restrictive common policy, and to have it adopted by its members.

The conservative (and professional association) approach to advertising is a desire to trade with as little restriction as possible. Hence conservative parties in the English-speaking countries tend to see the advertisers' point of view, and to administer a lenient regulatory regime. This is generally supported by conservative economists on a variety of grounds.[118] In the United States and in Britain, the Democratic and Labour parties respectively have taken a more critical approach, and have been much more responsive to the social critique of advertising. The European approach reflects the more paternalist and prescriptive traditions of European politics, both on the social-democratic and communist left, and on the Christian-democratic right. Hence, European regulators have been much more forthcoming in their willingness to identify the disorders of advertising and to act against them. Finally, an important constraint on advertising is the enlightened self-interest of practitioners, of advertisers and their agents seeking to protect themselves against each other.

[117] Brown (1993). [118] e.g. Ekelund and Saurman (1988).

For many decades that was the motivation of advertising regulation in the United States. A practice code devised by *Printer's Ink*, the industry journal, went on the statute book in thirty-seven states even before the First World War. At the federal level, the Federal Trade Commission was created in 1914 by President Wilson, in the wake of the Progressive anti-trust movement of the turn of the century. Its remit was to monitor unfair competition, in other words, to protect not the consumer, but the market, from predatory actors. A parade of best-selling books during the 1920s and the 1930s exposed advertising as the exploiter of the consumer. The Consumer's Union was founded in 1936, and in 1938 the Federal Trade Commission was given jurisdiction to regulate advertising.[119]

During the 1950s the FTC continued to focus mainly on anti-competitive behaviour. Towards the end of the decade, in response to the rise of the consumer movement, the FTC shifted its attention to the consumer. In 1958 it began enforcing new guidelines against deceptive pricing. In the 1960s it attacked 'phony mock-ups', used in television commercials. In one case it challenged a television commercial which purported to show Colgate shaving cream being used to shave sandpaper clean. The demonstration actually used glass covered with wet sand. In another case the use of mashed potatoes to represent ice-cream was the subject of a 'cease and desist order'. In the early 1970s the agency began to focus on misleading claims: Listerine and Anacine, two reliefs for sore throats, were required to advertise extensively that they did not (as they had previously implied), cure colds. Other decisions were achieved against Wonder Bread and Geritol Iron Supplement for advertising which associated their products with health benefits. Much more radical restraints on advertising were enforced by state and federal law to curb not the medium, but the commodities it promoted. Cigarette packets were made to carry a health warning, and were banned from television. Automobile advertisements were made to carry certified performance figures, financial advertisements began to carry warnings and standardized interest rate figures (APRs).

The FTC relied on court orders to enforce its directives. This method had little effect. It was only on very rare occasions that companies were actually punished financially for disregarding directives; many of the directives were resisted, with cases taking several years to resolve, after proceeding all the way to the highest courts. By this time, the offending

[119] Pease (1958); Wagner (1971); Mulock (1979).

campaigns would have had time enough to run their course; and a loss in court rarely entailed a substantial financial penalty. The adversarial method of legal action encouraged defiance of the directives, and inhibited collective action. By the end of the 1970s the winds of the New Right were blowing strongly again, and the FTC retreated from activism. It lost funding and influence during the 1980s, and gave business a respite from regulation. In effect, it has succumbed to 'regulatory capture', in which the industry comes to control its regulators. Despite some pioneering legislative interventions, the United States gives advertisers more freedom than any other affluent country.

Things are radically different in Britain. Support for advertising is weaker than in the United States; in 1969, for example 59 per cent in an American Gallup survey supported the view that advertising was essential, but only 46 per cent thought so in Britain.[120] Large areas of the public domain are deliberately kept free of advertising. In the urban and rural environment, advertising is subject to strict planning regulation that, on the whole, has kept it from intruding in areas of substantial rural or urban beauty, though posters do add colour and vitality to the more nondescript urban landscapes, and have occasionally crept into the intermediate zones on the urban fringes. Likewise, much of the broadcasting spectrum has been kept free of advertising. Up to 1955 there was no commercial broadcasting except for foreign stations such as Radio Luxembourg. When commercial television was introduced in 1955, the duration and placing of advertising was constrained, with no more than six minutes per hour.[121] To this day, after sixteen years of Conservative rule, commercial-free television still controls two out of four available channels, and has a large slice of broadcast radio as well.

The contents of advertisements are regulated by a large body of statute law, some eighty-five statutes altogether, of which probably the most important recent pieces is the Trades Description Act of 1968. Some of this legislation corresponds to American law, as e.g. in controlling the advertising of tobacco and alcohol, claims for patent medicine, financial advertising, motor car performance, etc. Unlike the United States, there is no single agency charged with monitoring compliance. Instead, the advertising profession monitors itself, in accord with a British tradition of self-regulation, which also applies (with mixed results) in the commercial, financial and legal domains. The Advertising Association, which

[120] Reader's Digest Association (1970: table 63, 186–7).

[121] Great Britain, (1962*b*), 71, Pilkington Committee.

was founded in 1924, immediately set up a National Vigilance Committee, (subsequently the Advertising Investigating Department). In its first 17 months it dealt with more than 700 complaints, and continued to consider hundreds of complaints a year.[122]

American consumerism eventually reached out to Britain. The American Consumers' Union extended a loan to set up a British counterpart in 1956. Vance Packard's attack on advertising reverberated strongly across the Atlantic.[123] Several forms of public action followed: an official inquiry (the Molony Committee) reported in 1962, and recommended strong controls on advertising.[124] A Royal Commission on the Press examined the influence of advertisers.[125] Another government committee (the Pilkington Committee) looked again at commercial broadcasting, and decided to tighten the controls in 1962.[126] In the same year the Labour Party set up a committee of inquiry into advertising under the chairmanship of Lord Reith, legendary founder of the BBC, which took evidence for several years and finally reported in 1965.[127]

In response to this rising tide of criticism, the Advertising Association set up the Advertising Standards Authority in 1962.[128] This body is nominally independent, with representatives of consumers, labour and capital, though it is dominated by the advertising industry. This body attempts to strike a balance between the need to preserve the credibility of British advertising, and the creative and commercial freedom of its practitioners. Like the FTC, it accepts puffery, but polices the literal truth of factual claims. Complaints often fail when members of the public do not successfully make these distinctions. These constraints have not necessarily been bad for British advertising. Before the 1960s it was generally considered unadventurous and boring, an impression largely (if subjectively) confirmed by comparing e.g. American and British motor advertising. The emergence of a more constraining regulatory regime coincided with a 'creative revolution' in British advertising in the 1960s

[122] 'The Story of the Advertising Association' (typescript, 1949), fo. 6; Advertising Association Papers, 12/1–1, History of Advertising Trust.

[123] Box of papers on Motivation Research in the Mark Abrams papers, copy in possession of the author.

[124] Great Britain, (1962*a*), Molony Committee.

[125] Royal Commission on the Press; see Institute of Practitioners in Advertising, 'Replies to Questions posed by the Royal Commission on the Press', 4 Aug. 1961, AA 11/17/2, HAT.

[126] Great Britain, (1962*b*), Pilkington Committee.

[127] Labour Party (1966), minutes of evidence and submissions in Abrams Papers (in possession of the author).

[128] J. S. Williams, 'A Short History of the Advertising Association' (typescript, 16 Nov. 1973), fo. 3; Advertising Association papers, AA 12/3, History of Advertising Trust.

and 1970s, which has already been alluded to.[129] The more vulgar simulations of intimacy did not play a major role here; instead, the stress is on entertainment, humour, and surprise, though this may be another variant of the same: in the more reserved British society, humour is an accepted way of breaking the ice, and the first step for promoting trust.

In the 1970s and 1980s, as the audience became increasingly jaded and familiar with the standard advertising pitches, a more subtle form of advertising began to appropriate post-modernist approaches. Advertising will use anything that works, and imaginative agencies have captured the rising tide of disbelief in advertising, and incorporated it into their commercials.[130] On the whole, my subjective judgement is that the system of professional control and public constraint together have given Britain a system of advertising that has more of the positive aspects of advertising, and suffers less from its disorders, than the system of government regulation which is in force in the United States.[131]

In Britain, much of the 1970s and the 1980s were spent in fending off a much more earnest approach to regulation, emanating from the European Community. In 1968, the Community set up an international working party to ponder the problem of misleading advertising. After four years, the party made its first report:

> advertising, to be effective, must be striking and persuasive, qualities which can lead to aggression and exaggeration. Beyond certain limits aggression becomes unfairness and exaggeration becomes deception . . .[132]

After many iterations, this initiative eventually emerged in 1976 as a draft Community directive for harmonizing Community legislation on misleading advertising. The guiding principle was a strong one,

> Misleading advertising means any advertising which, having regard to the effect of the advertisement as a whole, either generally or in relation to any of its parts, misleads or is likely to mislead persons addressed or likely to be reached thereby.[133]

[129] For a sense of advertising development in Britain since the 1960s, see *Campaign 1968–1993*, 17 Sept. 1993.

[130] Myers (1986); Whitwell (1989); Goldman (1992).

[131] But this may be an expression of the general culture rather than the system of regulation; which may also be true of the system of regulation itself.

[132] Council of Europe, 'Consumer Protection: Report of the Working Party on Misleading Advertising', supplement to B (72) 21 (Strasbourg, Mar. 1972), 17.

[133] Commission of European Communities, 'Second Draft of the First Directive concerning the approximation of the Laws of Member States on Unfair Trading Practices', Misleading and unfair advertising. Working Document no. 6 (Brussels, Sept. 1976), article 3.

The way from a draft directive to the statute book of individual countries is long and tortuous, and the British advertising industry fought every foot of the way. Its objections were many and various, but they concentrated on two main points. The first was resistance to legislation.[134] The second issue was the right to puffery. The Community directive placed the locus of deception in the advertisement; the Advertising Association insisted that it was in the consumer's mind. People's preferences were opaque even to themselves,

> The thing they object to most in the memorandum, was [*sic*] the assumption that it is possible to define a wrong choice objectively.
>
> We do not believe it makes sense to describe a man as misled when he has got what he wanted. Choice is not a process which it is possible entirely to encompass in rational terms, and advertising which reflects the consumer's criteria by recognising that there are subjective satisfactions involved in any purchase (as well as objective ones) seems to us neither misleading nor unfair.[135]

In 1972 the Labour Party had made a commitment to control false or misleading advertising, and to promote the testing of advertisers' claims.[136] In 1978 the Labour minister for consumer affairs, Roy Hattersley, caused some alarm at the Advertising Association when he appeared to be preparing to endorse the Community's draft directive. The AA mobilized political and industrial lobbies, and hinted at more active forms of resistance. These fears were swept away when the Conservatives came into power in 1979. Hattersley's successor, Sally Oppenheimer, quelled these initiatives, and underlined the party's commitment to unfettered competition. Eventually the draft wended its way and became a binding directive in 1986. By that time, it had been toned down and interpreted so as to satisfy most of the objections of the advertisers, and to leave things, from a legal point of view, essentially unchanged.

Conclusion

Dissimulation is part of all discourse. But although few of us have not dissimulated at one time or another, we do not like to be deceived

[134] K. C. Hall, Dept. of Prices and Consumer Protection, to R. C. G. Hunt-Taylor, Secretary of the Advertising Association, June 1978, AA 17/12/1/1/ , HAT.

[135] AA, Revised comments on the EEC Memorandum . . . fo. 7. [Dec. 1976], AA 17/12/1/1, HAT.

[136] *Labour's Programme for Britain* (pamphlet, 1972?), 25; AA 11/9/1, HAT.

ourselves. Deception may sometimes be useful, or even necessary, but not as a *norm*. If truthfulness in discourse declines, it places an additional burden on society, yet another 'transaction cost'. In particular, it inhibits co-operation: interpersonal, social and political. It makes co-ordination and leadership more difficult. If some aspect of personal experience or of social performance is genuinely unsatisfactory, we can expect individuals to try to do something about it. At the start, they may be ridiculed and attacked, but eventually something gets done, often by the perpetrators themselves.

What should society do about misleading advertising? It already does a great deal, more in some countries than in others. An essay like this is part of the flow of comment that keeps society on its toes, that provides it with the evidence and the concepts to articulate responses to the torrent of marketing. For the historian and social scientist, this should be enough. But perhaps one ought to go a little further, to step into the fray, and to suggest what actions might be appropriate.

To understand the effects of advertising, it is also necessary to understand the psychic impact of goods and services. That is a larger project: much of our assessment of advertising and marketing depends on what we think of the goods it promotes. Should puffs be disallowed? I am in two minds about this. Perhaps they should come (like mortgages and motor cars) with a clear, footnoted health warning. One possibility is a voluntary warranty stamp on the part of advertisers ('Truth in Advertising'?), although that, like footnotes, is open to abuse. It is advertisers themselves who have a primary interest in credibility, as they have shown all along. They need help from the outside to govern their commons.

Apart from the question of *grazing* the common, there is also one of *litter*. Advertising unrestrained can be a form of pollution. It gives rise to congestion and clutter. Even David Ogilvy, the advertising guru, finds it all too much. He wrote that the average household in the United States watched 30,000 commercials a year, that on Sundays the *New York Times* carried up to 350 pages of advertising, and that some radio stations devoted 40 minutes in the hour to commercials. 'I don't know,' he writes, 'how all this clutter can ever be brought under control.'[137]

Freedom from advertising is a good, which people are willing to pay for. Unfortunately it is a public good, of which there is not always enough. After six decades of commercial broadcasting, the United States embarked in 1970 on an advertising-free Public Broadcasting system

[137] Ogilvy (1983: 208).

(though advertising has crept back in the form of 'sponsorship'). Boundaries are important: advertising is welcome to do its job, but should be clearly delimited. It should leave sufficient space which is free of advertising or 'sponsorship', in the environment, in the media, in the arts, sports, and public domains. How large this space should be is a matter for public negotiation and debate. Some people would have it larger, some might be content with less, yet others will be prepared to put up with no space at all. Finally, research must continue: it requires sustained attention to alert us to the seductions of intimacy, and to its continued costs.

REFERENCES

ABRAMOWITZ, A. I. (1980), 'United States: Political Culture Under Stress', in Almond and Verba (1980).

Advertising Association, *Advertising Statistics Yearbook* (annual, 1982 ff.). Henley-on-Thames: NTC Publications.

Advertising Expenditures Around the World (1960 ff.). Biannual survey, New York: International Research Associates; subseq. Starch Inra Hooper.

ALMOND, G., and VERBA, S. (1963), *The Civic Culture*. Princeton: Princeton University Press.

—— —— (eds.) (1980), *The Civic Culture Revisited*. Boston: Little, Brown Academic.

AXELROD, R. (1984), *The Evolution of Co-operation*. New York: Basic Books.

BAKER, S. S. (1968), *The Permissible Lie: The Inside Truth about Advertising*. London: Peter Owen.

BARTOS, R. (1989), *Marketing to Women around the World*. Boston: Harvard Business School Press.

BECKER, G. S., and MURPHY, K. M. (1993), 'A Simple Theory of Advertising as a Good or Bad', *Quarterly Journal of Economics*, 108/4 (Nov.), 941–64.

BELK, R. W., and POLLAY, R. W. (1985), 'Images of Ourselves: The Good Life in Twentieth Century Advertising', *Journal of Consumer Research*, 11 (Mar.), 887–97.

BENTELE, G. (1992), 'Ethik der Public Relations als wissenschaftliche Hersuforderung', in Avenarius and Armbrecht (1992), 151–70.

BIOCCA, F. (ed.) (1992), *Television and Political Advertising, 1. Psychological Processes. 2. Signs, Codes and Images*, Hillsdale, NJ: Lawrence Erlbaum Associates.

BLUMBERG, P. (1989), *The Predatory Society: Deception in the American Marketplace*. New York: Oxford University Press.

BODDEWYN, J. J. (1992), *Global Perspectives on Advertising Self-Regulation: Principles and Practices in Thirty-Eight Countries.* Westport, Conn.: Quorum Books.

BORDEN, N. H. (1942), *The Economic Effects of Advertising*. Chicago: Richard D. Irwin.

BORRIE, G. (1978), *Review of the UK Self-Regulatory System of Advertising Control*, A Report by the Director General of Fair Trading, London.

BOWDEN, S., and OFFER, A. (1994), 'Household Appliances and the Use of Time: The United States and Britain since the 1920s', *Economic History Review*, 47/4: 725–48.

BROMLEY, D. W. (1991), *Environment and Economy: Property Rights and Public Policy*. Oxford: Blackwell.

BROWN, D. E. (1991), *Human Universals*. Philadelphia: Temple University Press.

BROWN, R. (1993), 'Cultivating a "Green" Image: Oil Companies and Outdoor Publicity in Britain and Europe, 1920–1936', *Journal of European Economic History*, 22/5 (Fall), 347–65.

BULLMORE, J. (n.d. *c.*1993?), 'Advertising, What is it? What is it For?', in Advertising Association, *Advertising Matters*. London: Advertising Association.

——, and WATERSON, M. J. (1983), *The Advertising Association Handbook*, Eastbourne: Holt, Rinehard, and Winston.

Business International SA (1980), *Europe's Consumer Movement: Key Issues and Corporate Responses*, Geneva.

CASTLEMAN, H. and PODRAZIK, W. J. (1982), *Watching TV: Four Decades of American Television*. New York: McGraw-Hill.

CHASE, S., and SCHLINK, F. J. (1927), *Your Money's Worth*. New York: Macmillan.

DIAMOND, E., and BATES, S. (1992; 1st pub. 1984), *The Spot: The Rise of Political Advertising on Television*, 3rd edn. Cambridge, Mass.: MIT Press.

EKELUND, R., and SAURMAN, D. (1988), *Advertising and the Marketing Process: A Modern Economic View*, San Francisco: Pacific Research Institute for Public Policy.

EKMAN, P. (1985), *Telling Lies*. New York: W. W. Norton.

EWEN, S. (1976), *Captains of Consciousness*. New York: McGraw-Hill.

FINCH, C. (1975), *Norman Rockwell's America*. New York: Harry N. Abrams Inc.; Reader's Digest edn.

FOX, F. W. (1975), *Madison Avenue Goes to War: The Strange Military Career of American Advertising, 1941–45*. Charles E. Merrill Monograph Series, Provo, Utah: Brigham Young University Press.

FOX, S. (1990), *The Mirror Makers*, London: Heinemann.

FRANK, R. (1989), *Passions within Reason: The Strategic Role of the Emotions*. New York: Norton.

FREY, B. (1986), 'Economists Favour the Price System—Who Else Does?', *Kyklos*, 39/4: 537–63.

GALBRAITH, J. (1958), *The Affluent Society*, Harmondsworth: Penguin Books edn. 1962.

GILES, M. (1993), 'Indigestion: A Survey of the Food Industry', *The Economist*, 4 Dec., 1–18.

GOLDMAN, R. (1992), *Reading Ads Socially*. London: Routledge.

Great Britain (1962*a*), *Final Report of the Committee on Consumer Protection [Molony Committee]*, Cmnd. 1781, London.

—— (1962*b*), *Report of the Committee on Broadcasting, 1960 [Pilkington Committee]*, Cmnd. 1753, London.

HAUG, W. F. (1986), *Critique of Commodity Aesthetics: Appearance, Sexuality and Advertising*. Cambridge: Polity Press.

HECKER, S., and STEWART, D. W. (eds.) (1988), *Nonverbal Communication in Advertising*. Lexington, Mass.: Lexington Books.

HONNEF, K. (1991), *Andy Warhol 1928–1987: Commerce into Art*. Cologne: Benedikt Taschen.

International Bank for Reconstruction and Development (1990), *World Tables 1989–90: Socio-economic Time-Series Access and Retrieval System [STARS]*. [Software].

JACOBY, J., and HOYER, W. D. (1982), 'Viewer Miscomprehension of Televised Communication: Selected Findings', *Journal of Marketing*, 46/4 (Fall), 12–26.

—— —— (1987), *The Comprehension and Miscomprehension of Print Communications: An Investigation of Mass Media Magazines*. New York: Advertising Educational Foundation.

—— —— (1989), 'The Comprehension/Miscomprehension of Print Communication: Selected Findings', *Journal of Consumer Research*, 15 (Mar.), 434–43.

—— —— 'The Miscomprehension of Mass-Media Advertising Claims: A Re-Analysis of Benchmark Data', *Journal of Advertising Research* (June/July), 9–15.

—— ——, and SHELUGA, D. A. (1980), *Miscomprehension of Televised Communications*. New York: American Association of Advertising Agencies.

KALDOR, N. (1950–1), 'The Economic Aspects of Advertising', *Review of Economic Studies*, 18.

KAVANAGH, D. (1980), 'Political Culture in Great Britain: The Decline of the Civic Culture', in Almond and Verba (1980).

KERN, M. (1989), *30-Second Politics: Political Advertising in the Eighties*. New York: Praeger.

Labour Party (n.d., 1966), *Report of a Commission of Enquiry into Advertising* (mimeo), London: Labour Party.

LEARS, J. (1995), *Fables of Abundance: A Cultural History of Advertising in America*. New York: Basic Books.

LEISS, W., KLINE, S., and JHALLY, S. (1990), *Social Communication in*

Advertising: Persons, Products and Images of Well-Being, 2nd edn. London: Routledge.

MARCHAND, R. (1986), *Advertising the American Dream: Making Way for Modernity, 1920–1940*. Berkeley and Los Angeles: University of California Press.

MAUSS, M. (1954), *The Gift: Forms and Functions of Exchange in Archaic Societies*. London: Cohen & West.

MILGRAM, S. (1974), *Obedience to Authority: An Experimental View*. London: Tavistock.

MULOCK, B. (1979 (9 July)), 'Advertising Regulation by the Federal Trade Commission', Congressional Research Service Report No. 79–145-E, Washington, DC.

MYERS, K. (1986), *Understains: The Sense and Seduction of Advertising*. London: Comedia.

NYBERG, D. (1993), *The Varnished Truth: Truth Telling and Deceiving in Ordinary Life*. Chicago: University of Chicago Press.

OFFER, A. (1996), 'Between the Gift and the Market: The Economy of Regard', Oxford University Discussion Papers in Economic and Social History, 3 (Jan.).

OGILVY, D. (1962), *Confessions of an Advertising Man*. New York: Atheneum.

—— (1983), *Ogilvy on Advertising*. New York: Crown Publishers.

O'SHAUGHNESSY, N. J. (1990), *The Phenomenon of Political Marketing*. London: Macmillan.

OSTROM, E. (1990), *Governing the Commons: The Evolution of Institutions for Collective Action*. Cambridge: Cambridge University Press.

O'TOOLE, J. (1981), *The Trouble with Advertising*. New York: Chelsea House.

PACKARD, V. (1960), *The Hidden Persuaders*. Harmondsworth: Penguin Books.

PEASE, O. (1958), *The Responsibilities of American Advertising: Private Control and Public Influence, 1920–1940*. New Haven: Yale University Press.

POLLAY, R. W. (ed.) (1979), *Information Sources in Advertising History*. Westport, Conn.: Greenwood Press.

—— (1986), 'The Distorted Mirror: Reflections on the Unintended Consequences of Advertising', *Journal of Marketing*, 50 (Apr.), 18–36.

—— (1988), 'Promotion and Policy for a Pandemic Product: Notes on the History of Cigarette Advertising', Vancouver: University of British Columbia, History of Advertising Archives, *Working Papers and Research Reprints* (Jan.).

—— (1990), 'More Chronological Notes on the Promotion of Cigarettes', Vancouver: University of British Columbia, History of Advertising Archives, *Working Papers and Research Reprints* (Aug.).

PRESTON, I. L. (1975), *The Great American Blow-up: Puffery in Advertising and Selling*. Madison: University of Wisconsin Press.

—— (1994), *The Tangled Web They Weave: Truth, Falsity and Advertisers*. Madison: University of Wisconsin Press.

PUTNAM, R. D. (1995), 'Tuning In, Tuning Out: The Strange Disappearance of Social Capital in America', *PS: Political Science & Politics*, 28/4 (Dec.), 664–83.

Reader's Digest Association (1970), *A Survey of Europe Today*. London: Reader's Digest Assocation.

—— (1991), *Reader's Digest Eurodata: A Consumer Survey of 17 European Countries Sponsored by The Reader's Digest Association Inc*. London: Reader's Digest Assocation.

ROSS, I. (1959), *The Image Merchants: The Fabulous World of American Public Relations*. London: Weidenfeld & Nicolson.

SCHLINK, F. J., and KALLET, A. (1933), *100,000,000 Guinea Pigs*. New York: Vanguard Press.

SCHOFIELD, P. (1954), *100 Top Copy Writers and their Favorite Ads*. New York: Printer's Ink Publishing Co., Inc..

SCHUDSON, M. (1986), *Advertising: The Uneasy Persuasion. Its Dubious Impact on American Society*, Pbk edn. New York: Basic Books.

SELDIN, J. J. (1963), *The Golden Fleece: Selling the Good Life to Americans*. New York: Macmillan.

SHORRIS, E. (1994), *A Nation of Salesmen: The Tyranny of the Market and the Subversion of Culture*. New York: Norton.

SPERO, R. (1980), *The Duping of the American Voter: Dishonesty and Deception in Presidential Television Advertising*. New York: Lippincott & Crowell.

STOLTZ, D. (1986), *The Advertising World of Norman Rockwell*. New York: Harrison House; distributed by Crown Publishers.

TAYLOR, M. (1987), *The Possibility of Cooperation*. Cambridge: Cambridge University Press.

TEDLOW, R. S. (1990), *New and Improved: The Story of Mass Marketing in America*. New York: Basic Books.

THOMPSON, D. (1943), *Voice of Civilization*. London: Muller.

TUFTE, E. R. (1983), *The Visual Display of Quantitative Information*. Cheshire, Conn.: Graphics Press.

TUNNARD, C., and PUSHKAREV, B. (1963), *Man-Made America: Chaos or Control? An Inquiry into Selected Problems of Design in the Urbanized Landscape*. New Haven: Yale University Press.

TVERSKY, A., and KAHNEMAN (1974), 'Judgment under Uncertainty: Heuristics and Biases', *Science*, 185: 1124–31.

United States Department of Commerce, Bureau of the Census (1980), *Social Indicators III: Selected Data on Social Conditions and Trends in the United States*, Washington, DC.

WAGNER, S. (1971), *The Federal Trade Commission*. New York: Praeger.

WHITEHEAD, F. (1973), 'Advertising', in Denys Thompson (ed.), *Discrimination and Popular Culture*, 2nd edn. Harmondsworth: Penguin, 51–77.

WHITWELL, G. (1989), *Making the market: The Rise of Consumer Society*. Melbourne: McPhee Gribble.

WIGHT, R. (1972), *The Day the Pigs Refused to be Driven to Market: Advertising and the Consumer Revolution*. London: Hart-Davis, MacGibbon.

WOOD, F. (ed.) (1990), *An American Profile: Opinions and Behaviour, 1972–1989*. Detroit: Gale Research.

YANG, C., and STERN, W. (1995), 'Maybe They Should Call Them "Scammers"', *Business Week* (16 Jan.), 30–1.

YANKELOVICH, D. (1981), *New Rules: Search for Self-Fulfilment in a World Turned Upside Down*. New York: Random House.

11

Quality of Life and Quality of Persons: A New Role for Government?[1]

ROBERT E. LANE

> If the obstacles to human development lie in the paucity of resources, in insuperable technical barriers, the task would be hopeless. We know instead that it is too often a lack of political commitment, not of resources, that is the ultimate cause of human neglect.
>
> United Nations, *Human Development Report 1991*

In order to improve the quality of life of the poor the government builds (or used to build) public housing but that housing has often deteriorated into slums. Between 1970 and 1985 the United States doubled its real expenditures on education without measurable improvement in learning. We enlarge our police forces and expand our prisons and yet crime increases and the urban quality of life on the streets diminishes. Even when there is a political will, government efforts to improve the external features of quality of life often fail because quality of life, as I shall argue, is dependent on a companion quality that is often unacknowledged, the quality of persons (to be defined below).[2]

[1] I herewith express my thanks for useful comments from panel participants at the Annual Meeting of the International Society of Political Psychology (Helsinki, July 1991), the Yale Faculty Political Theory Seminar (Feb. 1992), and the members of the Nuffield Seminar on Quality of Life (15 June 1993). David Miller has kindly cautioned me (in vain) against confidence that governments can reform character. I am also grateful to the editor of *Political Theory* for permission to reprint this article from volume 22, no. 2, May 1994.

[2] Although the social indicator movement was interested in the qualities of persons only in so far as these qualities influenced subjective well-being, and economists were interested primarily as human capital and consumers, philosophers have recently enriched the discussion of the way qualities of persons influence quality of life. See, for example, Nussbaum and Sen (1993), Nussbaum (1992), and Griffin (1986).

CONCEPTS OF QUALITY OF LIFE AND OUTLINE OF AN ARGUMENT

Quality of life is not a condition, such as relative prosperity, nor a state of mind or of being, like happiness, nor yet a quality of person, such as wisdom or virtue. Rather, 'quality of life' is the name we give, or should give, to the *relation* between quality of conditions and quality of persons. A high quality of life has intrinsic value and may be considered an ultimate good largely (but not wholly) because it reflects and influences the qualities of persons which themselves have intrinsic value. In contrast, a high quality of conditions, the circumstances of one's life, do not have intrinsic value.

The many disciplines relevant to quality of life live well together: philosophy as a source of concepts of the good and of their defence, psychology as the source of most of what we know about the causes of subjective well-being, of human development, and of concepts of mental health, and the other social sciences for their insights into how such institutions as government and markets might contribute to better qualities of life and of persons. Like Sen, I will employ an 'engineering approach',[3] as much concerned with policy as with conceptual clarification.

After a brief discussion of the background of treatments of quality of life, I will explicate the relational theory of quality of life, define the quality of persons and quality of conditions that comprise the two basic elements of this relational theory, and discuss the nature of this relationship in the context of theories proposed by Sen, Nussbaum, and Griffin. There follows a brief discussion of the failures of utilitarian theory and the limitations of empirical studies of 'subjective well-being'. I will then analyse several reasons for thinking that quality of life *necessarily* implies qualities of persons. If government is to have a role in promoting higher quality of persons, we must also understand how outsiders can have an appropriate jurisdiction over the qualities of their citizens; I turn to that next. Finally, I deal with the government's competence and responsibilities in these matters: what technology is available to governments and what are the main resistances to their acceptance of these responsibilities.

[3] Sen (1987: 4).

Background

Concern for something called 'the quality of life' (temporarily defined as subjective well-being and personal growth in a healthy and prosperous environment) is a relatively recent phenomenon. Prior to World War II (in the West), *democratic politicism* (the idea that if we could perfect democratic government the quality of life would take care of itself), *economism* (the utilitarian assumptions that economic prosperity would produce a sense of well-being—the utilitarian's supreme good), and *ethicism* (the assumption that improvement of individual and social morals would produce both better social institutions and better quality of life) dominated the scene. Political scientists, economists, and philosophers all worked within this framework. Although the relation between government and markets was intensely debated, the links between good government and prosperity, on the one hand, and the quality of life, on the other, were not explored. And, because ethics and justice were goods in themselves, the links between these goods and other aspects of quality of life were generally ignored.

The post-war history of empirical research on what was often called 'the quality of life' shows a steady accumulation of measures, each reflecting a change of concept or emphasis and none substituting for previous measures. The first measures tended to be wholly economic and objective. These measures of per capita income and wealth are still useful especially as supplemented by measures of other objective aspects of life, such as rates of pollution, life expectancy, drug abuse, and crime—external to the individual (and considered externalities in standard market theory, as well). In the 1960s and 1970s new concepts of *subjective well-being* ('happiness', 'satisfaction with life-as-a-whole') added an internal dimension to the measured concept of quality of life, a dimension thought by its advocates to capture the most important meaning of this term.[4] The movement was world-wide.[5] Under criticism from

[4] Bradburn and Caplotvitz (1965), Andrews and Withey (1976), Campbell *et al.* (1976), Freedman (1980), Andrews (1986). In 1986 Alex Michalos reported a review of 2,545 articles and books on various aspects of subjective well-being. See also Isen (1987) and Diener (1984).

[5] See, for example, Allardt (1975), Argyle (1987), Veenhoven (1989), Strack *et al.* (1991), Hankiss (1980), and Mukherjee (1989). It may be noted that some scholars, e.g. Bestuzhev-Lada *et al.* (1987: 139), in command economics saw the emphasis on quality of life as a way of reducing material welfare, 'The real purpose of talk about "the qualitative side of life" is to counteract the struggle of the working class for higher living standards. The German communists call on workers to resolutely oppose attempts to make "the quality of life" an alternative to living standards'.

ethicists and others, a further dimension of human development became salient and, chiefly prompted by the philosophically minded economist, Amartya Sen. In the 1990s the United Nations Development Programme issued a series of cross-national reports on 'human development'. Thus, economic standard of living, social, ecological, and physological circumstances, utilitarian happiness, and humanistic standards of human development all claim to represent quality of life. Part of the purpose of this chapter is to offer a way of thinking about these various claims.

THE QUALITY OF LIFE

Quality of life (QL) is properly defined by the relation between two subjective or person-based elements and a set of objective circumstances. The subjective elements of a high quality of life comprise: (1) a sense of subjective well-being and (2) personal development, learning, growth (QP). (The relation between these two subjective elements will be treated below.) The objective element is conceived as quality of conditions (QC) representing opportunities for exploitation by the person living a life. The basic concept can be expressed in a simple formula: $QL = f(QC, QP)$. This relational definition is supported by both evaluative and explanatory analysis.

Evaluation

Whether one focuses on the circumstantial features of the quality of condition or on the dispositional features of the person living a certain life is a question dealing with the location of value. Does value inhere in the object valued or in the valuing person? The problem has other venues: is beauty in the eye of the beholder or in the 'beautiful' object? The matter is complex because persons have intrinsic value, but within the framework of a process of evaluation where objects are also said to have value, the value of persons does not absorb all concepts of value. Some theorists (e.g. deontologists) may disagree but I concur with Rescher and Perry: it is the *relation* between objects and persons that makes an object valuable.[6] This proposition offers a framework within which to understand how there can be no quality to life except as that quality is perceived and appraised by living persons, though not necessarily by the person living that life. Note, again, that while quality

[6] Rescher (1969: 52); Perry (1954: 12).

of persons is intrinsically valuable, the environmental aspects of life included in quality of condition have (with the exception of justice and life itself) no such intrinsic value.

The source of value in persons has many aspects beyond Kantian dignity. As both Bay and Sen point out,[7] freedom is worthless without capacities and willingness to choose. High culture is but a set of artefacts without persons who can appreciate and interpret it. Without piety, religion is merely dogma and ritual. We cannot even think of virtue without the idea of virtuous persons. As the Austrian school pointed out long ago, even commodities are valueless without valuing persons.

Explanation

If a person likes a movie, is it because of the taste or mood of the person or because of the excellence of the movie? To cognitive psychologists, the references to joint control of quality of life by an environmental quality of condition and by personological qualities of persons will suggest the familiar twofold aspects of causal attribution: attribution to circumstances (QC) and attribution to dispositions (QP). Following a tendency to assign causal force to individual traits (QP), there was a shift in the early 1970s to 'situational psychology' when, like economists with their emphasis on price (QC), some cognitive psychologists held that emphasis on dispositions was the 'fundamental attribution error'.[8] But later research agrees that it is at the intersection of circumstances and traits that the most interesting phenomena take place.[9] Inevitably, the relationship between circumstance (QC) and disposition (QP) must be assessed; neither is sufficient alone.

If it is true that it is the value of persons that carries the principal weight of value, does quality of life become merely a means to enhance the value of persons? I am sympathetic to this idea, but it does not relieve us of concern for the quality of life, for three reasons: (1) in an age when questions of foetal personhood and miserable incapacity for the elderly seeking release from life are issues, it is commonly (though not universally) agreed that compared to life itself or the qualities of the persons (or 'persons' if we refer to foetuses) involved, the *quality* of a life is often a superordinate value; (2) persons possessed of all the high qualities that we might care to assign them do themselves care about the kinds of lives they lead, *being* and *doing* are inseparably interlocked;

[7] Bay (1965), Sen, (1985*a*: 169); (1993: 32–3).
[8] Ross (1977).
[9] Bem and Fundor (1978).

and (3) even as means, that portion of quality of life composed of those qualities of conditions facilitating or inhibiting human development are a natural concern for those who believe that only persons have value. Here we echo W. D. Ross, who invites us to imagine a world without mind and holds that 'you will fail to find anything in it that you can call good in itself'. But that empire of the mind is not empty of objects for 'the existence of a material universe may . . . be a necessary condition for the existence of many things that are good in themselves'.[10] Whether or not a high quality of life is good in itself, the relational concept of QL would necessarily lead us to search for the circumstances (QC) necessary to maximize the intrinsic good of persons.

Specification of and relations among the qualities of persons

Postponing for the moment a discussion of the utilitarian value of subjective well-being, I turn to the second of the two person-based elements of quality of life, the development of the individual. Few values have been so widely endorsed: human development is a dominant theme from Aristotle through the Enlightenment to such modern philosophers as Frankena, Frankfurt, Galston, Hardin, Macpherson, Nussbaum, Sen, and Held. Quality of persons is more important than well-being, because it is at the same time an element of the quality of life, a cause of a high quality of life, and a consequence of it, as we shall see in analysing the causal relations among these components. To return to an example from aesthetics, I find this tripartite analysis no more circular than to say that the beholder's appreciation of beauty in a painting is at the same time *a part* of the experience, a disposition that contributes to or causes the experience, and one that is further enriched by the experience.

Analysis of the qualities of persons contributing to or inhibiting a high quality of life requires three things: specification of the *elements* themselves, consideration of the *relations of the elements* to each other, and *justification* or derivation of the qualities included. Each of these, of course, is dependent on the purposes to be served by the analysis.

The elements

Prepared to accept all reasonable substitutes and emendations (for my purposes the details are not important), I will employ the concept of a better *quality of person* to mean development of nine qualities derived from studies of mental health: capacity for enjoying life, cognitive

[10] Ross (1930: 140).

complexity, a sense of autonomy and effectiveness, self-knowledge, self-esteem, ease of interpersonal relations, an ethical orientation, personality integration, and, to take advantage of opportunities for work and income, a productivity orientation.[11] This list of qualities of persons includes skills or *capacities* (cognitive complexity, ease of interpersonal relations), *beliefs* and *knowledge* (belief in one's own effectiveness, self-knowledge), *emotions* and *evaluations* (self-esteem, ethical orientation), and *states of being* (personality integration). Should we not also include subjective well-being or happiness as a quality of person reflected in the phrase, a 'sunny disposition', thus collapsing the two parts of the internal, person-based term, QP, into one? We defer an answer to the later discussion of the relation of quality of persons to subjective well-being.

My conception of quality of persons is to be distinguished from three other approaches, Sen's capability approach, Nussbaum's essentialist functionings, and various characterizations of basic needs. Each approach, of course, is dominated by the purposes it is designed to serve.[12]

Over the past twenty years, Sen has created and argued for an approach to national and international development based on people's capabilities.[13] In a statement with Drèze, Sen claims 'the object of public action can be seen to be the enhancement of the capability of people to undertake valuable and valued "doings and beings"'.[14] And coming very close to a major theme of this essay, Sen says: 'A person's well-being is not really a matter of how *rich* he or she is . . . [for] commodity command is a *means* to the end of well-being, but can scarcely be called the end in itself'.[15] Although the capabilities approach has the advantage of stressing the active, agency aspect of personality, it does not serve as an adequate statement of the attitudinal, emotional, and integrative aspects of the whole person whose development is the central theme of

[11] In general, efficiency values are omitted from this list, but the 'quality of industriousness' has been found to be central to occupational success. See Jencks *et al.* (1979). I have employed a broader term, taken from Fromm (1947). I may also be remiss in not including love or a loving disposition, valued in romantic and Christian thought alike. For my purposes, the nine qualities mentioned have the additional advantage of having been the subject of much recent research.

[12] Crocker (1992) compares Rawls' concept of primary goods to Sen's capabilities approach and Nussbaum's essentialist functioning approach, but because Rawls (1971) is more concerned with justice than with quality of life, I shall not do so, except to object to Rawls' characterization of material resources as the grounds for defining the better-off and the least advantaged. Although Rawls (1988) later expands his list of primary goods, this expansion does not change the materialist criteria employed for the difference principle. Among his other criticisms of Rawls, Sen (1984) makes a similar point.

[13] Sen (1993). [14] Sen and Drèze (1989: 12), quoted in Crocker (1992: 287).

[15] Sen (1985*b*: 28).

my understanding of what is necessary for a high quality of life. People are much more than their abilities or capabilities.

In response to 'an evaluative inquiry into what is deepest and most indispensable in our lives',[16] Martha Nussbaum has developed a concept of 'essentialist functioning' for evaluating well-being. To some degree, the point of essentialism is to surmount the difficulties imposed by relativistic arguments that make every local norm sovereign[17] and by subjectivistic arguments that impose the criteria of methodological individualism on what is to be considered good, criteria which state that in order to be considered good something must be chosen by the persons involved. The point of an emphasis on functioning is to make the relevant qualities of persons active, agency-oriented qualities implying autonomous choices. Nussbaum derives her list of the qualities of persons necessary, first, for a life to be considered fully human and, second, for a *high* quality of life from the human condition, that is, from an interpretative evaluation of life itself.[18] Although there is a heartening correspondence between Nussbaum's list and my own ('being able to imagine, think, and to reason', 'being able to laugh, to play, to enjoy recreational activities'), without such basic qualities as self-esteem and personality integration, I believe the list is inadequate for the purpose of designing a plan of human development. The emphasis on capabilities serves the useful purpose of emphasizing potential, but fails to define a desired outcome for human development. Both Sen's and Nussbaum's concepts of human beings fail to correspond to concepts of personality development to be discussed later.

Among others,[19] James Griffin has developed an approach to well-being through a set of proposals designed to meet moral criteria.[20] The version of well-being to be used for moral judgement, he says, is defined by 'the measure to which basic needs are met so long as they retain their importance'[21] where 'importance' refers to the quality of the life a person leads. In Griffin's treatment, 'basic needs' are those that are common to all people and not particular to any one person, although some flexibility must be allowed. Like Nussbaum, Griffin defines his list

[16] Nussbaum (1992: 208).

[17] Evidence accumulates that many things we think of as essentially Western are, in fact, shared with countries whose histories are very different from our own. See, for example, Schwartz and Bilsky (1990), Heath (1977). On the other hand, it seems that French culture (France and Quebec) evaluates money more highly than American and Anglo-Canadian culture. See Lane (1991: 542).

[18] Nussbaum (1992: 222–3).

[19] Braybrooke (1987), Streeton *et al.* (1981).

[20] Griffin (1986).

[21] Ibid. 52.

of basic needs as those meeting the problems of human existence.[22] In the end, the list is a fairly conventional statement of 'prudential values' cognate to Nussbaum's 'practical reason': accomplishment in public or private life; autonomy, including 'having basic capabilities'; understanding, including 'self-knowledge'; enjoyment, including 'enjoyment of the day-to-day textures of life'; 'deep personal relations'; 'freedom from the inexorable working of appetite', and morality interpreted as a conception of the good and the right (which Griffin finds absorbed by the good).[23] Griffin's list is specifically designed to fit into a framework of well-being, does deal with the problem of 'minimalism' (the risk that given the general achievement of a particular standard the 'haves' will think their job is done), and is well grounded in the problems of existence. Nevertheless, for our purposes, Griffin's list does not embrace the central problems of human development (such as personality integration), his idea of 'understanding' is not specifically addressed to cognitive functioning in, say, problem solving, and the elements in this list are insufficiently related to the circumstances of life. As Sen suggests, the basic needs concept, which was, indeed, Sen's starting-point, 'is a more passive concept than "capability," and it is arguable that the perspective of positive freedom links naturally with capabilities (what can the person *do*?) rather than with the fulfilment of their needs (what can be *done for* the person?)'.[24]

Relations among the elements

With multiple ingredients in the quality of life, can more of one compensate for less of another? Such questions involve matters of commensurability, ordering, weighting, compatibility, and so forth, reaching beyond the scope of my treatment. On the narrower question of trade-offs, opinions differ: Griffin says trade-offs are possible if we know 'how central [an element] is to our living a human existence, and just how greatly we value our humanity, even at the cost of our happiness'[25] but in her account of quality of life as a product of human functioning, Martha Nussbaum says: 'You cannot pay for the absence of one function by using the coin of another'.[26] I would agree that in dealing with

[22] Ibid. 67. [23] Ibid. 67–8. [24] Sen (1984: 514).

[25] Griffin (1986: 91).

[26] Nussbaum (1992: 231). The point is that each person should be helped to develop minimal capabilities in each of the ten areas of functioning specified. But I suspect that the alleged Aristotelian proscription of trade-offs might weaken if, for example, a person were to fall short of the minimal standard in the use of one or more of the five senses

subjective well-being and the qualities of persons, a greater sense of well-being does not, for example, compensate for a weak ethical orientation.[27] But among the nine qualities of persons, the diversity of humankind requires us to acknowledge that people may develop their potentials by developing one element, say, greater cognitive complexity, while sacrificing another, say, ease of interpersonal relations. Although they should be limited, trade-offs are needed. (Two tentative principles emerge: ethical goods cannot be exchanged for prudential goods; and one cannot exchange the welfare of others for the welfare of the self, but one can exchange the welfare of the self for the welfare of others.)

The limits will involve priorities. Ethicists would give an ethical orientation (including a sense of injustice and benevolence) priority on the grounds that among these elements only the ethical component is an intrinsic good. Utilitarians would give priority to a capacity to enjoy life, since pleasure and the avoidance of pain are sovereign. Specialists in human development would make personality integration the chief element on the grounds that the other elements all depend on the functioning of the whole person and on having 'conflict-free energy'. We must leave such ordering unsettled and permit each analyst and culture to assign weights, providing that they do not assume, without investigation, compatibility, or even identity among the elements. For example, it is important to divorce sense of well-being from an ethical orientation or moral virtue (Aristotle—allowing for the different meanings of 'virtue'—and Spinoza to the contrary notwithstanding), for virtue interpreted as a strong 'sense of duty' has been found to be *negatively* related to subjective well-being[28] (as Freud also claimed). On the other hand, prosocial behaviour has been found to be more likely to occur when a person is happy (as Kant predicted)[29] and, in turn, that prosocial behaviour creates a better mood in the prosocial actor.[30]

in order to develop further capabilities 'to form a conception of the good. . . .' In their 'Introduction' to their edited volume (1993: 3), Nussbaum and Sen say, 'The capability of a person refers to the various alternative combinations of functionings, any one of which (any combination, that is) the person can choose to have. In this sense, the capability of a person corresponds to the freedom that a person has to lead one kind of life or another.'

[27] See, for example, Sen (1979).

[28] Kugler and Jones (1992), Tangney *et al.* (1992).

[29] Kant (1920), 277, says, 'To secure one's happiness is a duty, at least indirectly; for discontent with one's conditions, under a pressure of many anxieties and amidst unsatisfied wants, might easily become a great temptation to transgression of duty.'

[30] Isen (1987). Of course, there will be exceptions familiar to readers; these reports are of statistical regularities in samples of the American public.

Justifying the elements

One way to justify the selection of elements is to seek consensus among those who have thought about the problem of human development. With some free translation whereby cognitive complexity may be identified with 'reason', ease of interpersonal relations is implied by 'friendship', self-esteem is partially cognate to 'dignity', and, of course, self-knowledge follows from 'an examined life', many of these qualities find support in philosophical definitions of the good. (I stress this point because I am seeking to build a bridge across the chasm that separates behavioural research and philosophy.) There are better ways. Although in general, the basic needs approach tends to be intuitive and *ad hoc*, Griffin, like Nussbaum, derives his list of elements from conceptions of what is necessary to live a full life. Sen agrees, but his 'engineering approach' leads him to focus more particularly on what governments and international agencies can and should do for the people of developing countries. All would agree with Nussbaum that there is no metaphysical grounding for concepts of essential functions or of basic needs and that the foundations of these things must be based on 'the exchange of reasons and arguments by human beings within history, in which, for reasons that are historical and human but not the worse for that, we hold some things to be good and others bad, some arguments to be sound and others not sound'.[31]

In contrast, my specification of the qualities of persons derives from empirical studies of mental health[32] and human development.[33] Few of the psychologists who analyse mental health have any illusions that their conceptions of mental health are purely scientific. Marie Jahoda, for example, says: 'By this label [mental health], one asserts that these psychological attributes are "good". And, inevitably, the question is raised: Good for what? Good in terms of middle class ethics? Good for democracy? For the social *status quo*? For the individual's happiness? For mankind? For survival? or mediocrity and conformity? The list could be continued.'[34] Nevertheless, there is a *functional* basis for concepts of mental health, for the test is whether the individual can hold a job, marry and sustain a family, avoid clinical depression, in short to function well in modern society. Rooted in observation by trained, if fallible, analysts of the qualities required for (admittedly evaluative)

[31] Nussbaum (1992: 213). [32] Srole *et al.* (1962: 62), Scott (1968).

[33] See, for example, Bronfenbrenner (1979), Hurrelmann (1988), Bolger *et al.* (1988).

[34] Jahoda (1958: 77).

concepts of healthy and fruitful living, this kind of justification or foundation seems to me to be preferable for an engineering approach such as this one.

Subjective well-being and the quality of persons

One reason why subjective well-being (SWB) is confounded with quality of life (QL) is that its basic formula is identical with that of quality of life mentioned above: SWB = *f* (QC, QP). That is, peoples' basic moods depend upon the relation between their circumstances and their dispositions, as we shall see in more detail later. But QP must be defined as something much larger than capacity for enjoying life which leads directly to the utilitarian solution. What, then, is the relation between the two *subjective* components of quality of life, subjective well-being and human development? Most significantly, a pure subjective well-being standard is inadequate because it does not include development of the qualities of persons that give to the quality of life much of its value. If we follow the traditional utilitarians, we find so flat or even empty a concept of the human personality that, even with due care for the pleasures of others, the life to be lived promises to be monothematic, following the pleasure principle or what Martha Wolfenstein once called 'the fun morality'.[35] Sen and Williams say that the utilitarian version of humanity is limited to 'the sites at which such activities as desiring and having pleasure and pain take place'.[36]

There are, therefore, good reasons for maintaining the separation of subjective well-being and the related concept of capacity to enjoy life: (1) were we to unite the two in the same class of things, we would also collapse the main utilitarian good with the concepts of the good of such non-utilitarian philosophers as Frankena, Sen, and Nussbaum; (2) the empirical studies focusing on human development seek emphatically to distinguish their explicandum and chief value from those of studies making subjective well-being the explicandum;[37] (3) there is a clear difference in a capacity to enjoy life and the fulfilment of that capacity; we should not confound a skill with the products of that skill; and (4) in fact, the two variables, subjective well-being and personality development, are empirically somewhat dissociated.

Although a sense of well-being generally contributes to human development, there are many situations where this is not the case, as,

[35] Wolfenstein (1968). [36] Sen and Williams (1982: 4).
[37] See, for example, Bronfenbrenner (1988).

for example, in the early stages of study when studying is perceived as unpleasant. Subjective well-being may hinder as well as help human development, for hedonic factors may lead to poor learning or to learning the wrong things. For example, the benefits of security derived from a guaranteed income certainly promise hedonic gains but, as research shows, a guaranteed income has a tendency to encourage dependency and, if suddenly introduced, to disrupt beneficial social practices, such as stable marriages.[38] Thus, some sources of well-being injure the capacity to develop in ways of which the beneficiaries, in their 'pursuit of happiness', are unaware.

The third element of the definition of quality of life is a set of *qualities of conditions* that represent the external means to the superordinate values of the subjective elements.

QUALITY OF CONDITION

From the mercantilists' reserves of gold, to the current emphasis on Gross National Product and per capita GNP, economic indicators have, until recently, dominated most discussion of quality of life. But the familiar irony still prevails: in the short run the greater the expenditure on armaments the higher will be a nation's GNP—but presumably not the higher the quality of life of its citizens.[39] As Edward Land has pointed out, such objective measures as GNP per capita have 'failed to reflect the quality of life, the dimension of equity, or such side-effects of economic prosperity as environmental pollution [and failed to capture] psychological satisfaction, happiness, or life fulfilment'.[40] And per capita GNP also suffers from what I have called the *economistic fallacy*, the belief that a sense of well-being is measured by income. Evidence set forth at length elsewhere shows that beyond a decent minimum there is almost no relation in Western societies between higher income and higher subjective well-being.[41]

As reflected in the epigraph to this chapter, the relation between

[38] See Robins *et al.* (1980).

[39] In the early 1970s two economists, Nordhaus and Tobin (1973), devised a measure of Net Economic Welfare which attempted to address this problem by subtracting expenditures on such disamenities as urban stress, crowding, and long hours commuting and such 'regrettable necessities' as defence to give a purer measure of the useful national product.

[40] Land (1983: 3).

[41] Lane (1991: 524–7).

objective indicators themselves also shows the perils of an exclusive attention to income and wealth: in 1977, for example, the people of Sri Lanka, one of the 'poorest' countries in the world in terms of per capita output, actually lived longer and had a higher literacy rate than the citizens of most other developing countries, including some oil-rich countries with much higher per capita incomes.[42]

The limits of objective indicators were recognized early. In framing their research project, the Manpower and Social Affairs Committee of the OECD stated (1973) their purpose as identifying matters that were of 'fundamental and direct importance to human well-being as opposed to a matter of instrumental or indirect importance'. They noted their omission of important matters that they could not quantify, such as 'aesthetic values, love and comradeship', matters on which they could not agree (such as family life), and, at that early stage of research, 'the perception which individuals and groups have of fundamental aspects of their well-being', which they regarded as 'a necessary and important component of the social indicator program' but did not have the means to ascertain.[43] In summary form, their list included: health, education ('Individual development through learning', including adult learning), favourable employment and quality of working life, time and leisure, command over goods and services, a good physical environment, personal safety, the fair administration of justice, and social opportunity and participation (including degree of social equality). Other lists have included the absence of the use of drugs and alcohol, of suicides by teenagers, of pollution of air and water, and much else.

Remaining quite agreeable to substitutes and corrections, but in the interest of specificity and without further defence, I will outline the kinds of environmental features that seem to me to foster both a sense of well-being and better qualities of persons. In harmony with the empirical literature cited in footnotes 4 and 5 and with the OECD 1973 report (and keeping in mind Maslow's somewhat inadequate concept of a hierarchy of needs),[44] the following nine opportunities and assets may be said to comprise a high quality of condition: adequate material support, physical safety and security, available friends and social support (including secure and accepted membership in society or at least in some niche in that society), opportunities for the expression and receipt

[42] *New York Times* (1977). [43] OECD (1973: 9).

[44] Maslow (1968). This concept of a hierarchy of needs has stimulated much comment, but further research has failed to validate the hierarchical relations of the elements. See Wahba and Bridwell (1976).

of love (because satisfaction with family life makes a large contribution to subjective well-being), opportunities for intrinsically challenging work marked by discretion and self-direction, the kinds and amounts of leisure that give scope to skills, creativity—and relaxation, available set of values (especially moral values) that can give meaning to life, opportunities for self-development with the assistance of such help as may be needed, and objective justice, that is, justice assessed by a disinterested, competent judge or other assessor.[45] But these favourable qualities of condition can only be exploited by persons with the appropriate personal qualities.

We may test the role of subjective well-being and reveal the dominance of quality of persons over quality of conditions by two contrasting cases. No matter how creditably people may develop their potentials, or how propitious their circumstances and opportunities, if they are miserable we would not say they have a high quality of life. Even if their misery is a personal construction on a set of circumstances that would make most other people happy, their quality of life would not be highly rated.[46] This is because the internal resources they bring to their situations are inadequate, for they do not permit them to enjoy a life of high quality. The opposite case, where a person achieves subjective well-being and a moderate degree of personal development in the face of unfavourable circumstances, is more difficult to interpret. On the one hand, one might say (as did one helpful referee) that the quality of their lives was poor because they did not have the external advantages necessary to develop their potentials to the full. On the other hand, if people living in squalor with every material disadvantage can yet maintain an authentic cheerful disposition and improve their capabilities beyond those that characterized their origins, I would rate the qualities of their lives favourably because they *overcame* their material disadvantages. It is not what is given ('resourcism') but what people *do* with what is given that is essential to my conception of a high quality of life. And incidentally we see how quality of persons trumps quality of conditions in evaluating quality of life. Bear this in mind when we turn to governmental policy.

[45] For a similar definition of the circumstances that favour mental health, see Leighton *et al.* (1963). In my opinion, this remains one of the best studies of how quality of conditions influences quality of persons (mental health) and therefore of life itself.

[46] In a personal communication, David Miller takes exception to this interpretation, 'Such a person does have a high quality of life, on the view I am defending, just because their misery is a personal construction which we as policy-makers cannot take into account.'

HOW CONCEPTS OF THE QUALITY OF LIFE IMPLY CONCEPTS OF THE QUALITY OF PERSONS

We may examine further the influence of environmental opportunities on behaviour, mood, and thought by a brief reference to a literature on the psychology of situations. Occasional research findings that situations account for more of the variation in behaviour and thought than do personality traits[47] create special problems for the argument that quality of persons is an essential ingredient in promoting a better quality of life. If situations, more than dispositions, can account for more of the variance in sense of well-being and learning, we do not need to bother with the causal influence of qualities of persons. Much of my agenda is made otiose. In fact, the effort to create a 'psychology of situations'[48] (such as is implicit in economic reasoning about the effects of price) has been found to be inadequate. Because situational effects do vary with personal dispositions, the common-sense view has come to prevail: 'it is interaction between the person and the situation that supplies the . . . interesting variance in behaviour'.[49]

Ways in which the quality of life implies the quality of persons

In this section I aim to show that one cannot even conceive of a quality of life without considering the qualities of a person living that life. By this route I hope further to show that the emphasis on life quality will fail of its purpose without an equivalent emphasis on human development.[50] We turn first to the complex relation between quality of life (QL) and the two independent variables: environmental quality of conditions (QC) and quality of persons (QP).

QL as the history of interaction between QC and QP

Recall the formula summarizing the basic definition of quality of life as a relation between quality of condition and quality of person: QL = f (QC, QP). To convert this static definition to a more plausible historical or dynamic definition we may think of QL as a product of past experiences with their combined changes in circumstances and dispositions.

[47] Mischel (1973). [48] See Magnusson (1981), Bem and Fundor (1978).

[49] Bem and Fundor (1978: 485).

[50] The relations between institutions and cultures, on the one hand, and personality, on the other, have been well explored in an extensive if somewhat dated literature. See, for example Kardiner and associates (1945), Whiting and Child (1953), Hsu (1961), LeVine (1973), Smelser and Smelser (1963).

A person's personal history of favourable and unfavourable environments, of initial and learned capabilities and beliefs, and of positive or negative attitudes toward life make quality of life at stage two dependent on these qualities at stage one:

$$QL_2 = f\ (QL_1) = f\ (QC_1,\ QP_1).$$

Quality of person is also a historical function of both quality of conditions and, reflexively, the capacity of a person to learn and develop. Both socialization and maturation are essential ingredients of this process. A person's qualities at stage one influence his or her qualities at stage two, as may be illustrated by the consequences of adolescent incompetence in choosing and preparing for a career and marriage.[51] If there is, indeed, personal development, this change would take place even if QC were to remain constant:

$$QP_2 = f\ (QC_{1=2},\ QP_1).$$

Quality of conditions also change with recurring economic recessions and inevitably with changes in the life-cycle: marriage and divorce, the presence and departure of children, illness, and old age. These changes are partially independent of dispositions, although their interpretation is dispositional. If we italicize the most important variable, we get: $QC_2 = f\ (\mathit{QC_1},\ QP_1)$. But in some ways an explanation of conditions without at least partial reliance on qualities of persons would assume the lack of human development, for human development implies that personality, endowed by this development with greater capacity to process information and cope with adversity, plays an increasingly greater explanatory role. One common element of personality development is the strengthening of internal attribution, the belief that one is the cause of events impinging on the person. Thus: $QC_2 = f\ (QC_1,\ \mathit{QP_1})$.

The problem, and also one of the main points of this discussion, is, as mentioned, that quality of persons (QP) is an element, a cause, and a consequence of a high quality of life.

Subjective well-being as a historical product

In our model subjective well-being (SWB) is a separable part of the quality of persons and not confined to the capacity to enjoy life. Although subjective well-being is a relatively stable quality, it may change over time, especially over the life-cycle. We must, therefore, conceive

[51] See Clausen (1991).

of this relationship historically, where not only do the QC and QP at stage one produce a change in subjective well-being (SWB) at stage two, but also where SWB at stage one also influences SWB at stage two. To some extent one learns moods and they become habitual: $SWB_2 = f(QC_1, QP_1) + SWB_1$.

Assets and income in the quality of life

The relational character of the value of a quality of life may be illustrated by an economic metaphor. One might think of the list of opportunities and available resources available in the quality of conditions as representing no more than a set of assets that may be used by those living in situations with those opportunities. It is not the assets but the psychic income, whether in the form of well-being or of learning extracted from those assets, that is the proper source of value of any given quality of life. It is conventional to value assets according to the income they yield to either their actual or potential owners and it is the availability of skills (QP) that determines the value of assets, in this case the quality of conditions. We are all entrepreneurs in the economy of life, extracting from our opportunities and endowments whatever hedonic and developmental yields we can.

Put differently, the *objectivist* claim mentioned earlier is fallacious because it mistakes assets for income or mixes the two in a sum that has no clear meaning. Thus, the objectivist fallacy is a mistake in accounting.

For every external feature of life there must be an internal receptor. Even a primitive knowledge of biology recognizes the jigsaw puzzle pattern of cells such that to be effective a cell of a certain kind must find its matching receptor cell. Analogously, 'opportunities' in the environment contribute to quality of life only if there are matching receptive properties in the persons involved. Although the elements of quality of conditions and quality of persons were each designed for independent theoretical reasons, to be successful in their joint operations to promote a high quality of life they must have this effector-receptor matching character:

Opportunities (Quality of Conditions)	***Qualities of Persons to Exploit Opportunities***
Adequate material support	Cognitive complexity, sense of effectiveness, productivity orientation

Opportunities (Quality of Conditions)	***Qualities of Persons to Exploit Opportunities***
Physical safety & security	
Available friends & social support	Ease of interpersonal relations, self-esteem
Opportunities for expressing love	Ease of interpersonal relations, personality integration, self-esteem
Opportunities for intrinsically challenging work	Cognitive complexity, sense of autonomy and effectiveness
Leisure for creativity & relaxation	Self-knowledge (knowledge of own values)
An available set of values in the community	An ethical orientation, personality integration, self-esteem
Opportunities for self-development	Personality integration, self-knowledge, self-esteem
Justice (objective)	An ethical orientation

At the most general level, these opportunities imply choices, but choices are worthless without that cognitive complexity that permits both rational and imaginative (counterfactual) reasoning, on the one hand, and 'informed desire', on the other—although the benefits of cognitive complexity apply only to human development and, as we shall see, not to subjective well-being. Self-knowledge and self-esteem, personality integration, and autonomy and sense of one's own effectiveness generally inform the performance of effective, happy persons. Those who believe that the quality of conditions implied by 'adequate material support' will always find a 'materialist' receptor will be disappointed in a post-materialist society.[52] For receptors change with changing conditions. It is likely that people with a productivity orientation will find their happiness in their work to a degree far greater than what they find in their incomes.[53] The self-direction at work that gives joy and increases cognitive flexibility and even empathy can be exploited only by those with a sense of personal control and self-attribution. The availability of candidates for friendship is valueless without some 'ease of interpersonal relations'. Finally, objective justice is unrecognizable without an ethical orientation. Each feature of the quality of conditions calls for some general or specific matching feature of the quality of persons.

[52] Inglehart (1990).

[53] Lane (1991: 524–47). I have been asked why a 'maintenance orientation' does not qualify as a criterion of high personal quality. The answer is that a maintenance orientation rarely leads to further learning; work is or can be a source of increasing skills in self-direction and autonomy. See Kohn and Schooler (1983).

As we shall see in a later discussion of developmental technology, there are two kinds of personal qualities called for: those that have general application to several opportunities and those specific qualities that are useful in exploiting only one or two opportunities.

Receptors for Positive Moods or Subjective well-being

Recall that the subjective well-being (SWB) is a quality of person unlike other such qualities in that it represents an intrinsically desirable product of interaction of QC with the other aspects of QP. But the 'capacity for enjoying life' is, as the literature on mental health makes clear, an essential quality for a person to enjoy subjective well-being. It is not the only one, however: choices will yield subjective well-being only with that kind of self-knowledge that knows the real, authentic values of the self. Modern utilitarians recognize that in order to convert the proffered 'welfare' into well-being, the persons to whom the welfare goods are available must have these and other matching receptor qualities. But the utilitarian theory of welfare is underdeveloped, partly because of unresolved philosophical questions.[54] But even more because the acknowledged subjectivity of welfare implies that 'the substantive content of a theory of human welfare must depend on the nature of the human person'.[55] A deficient theory of personality is a fundamental impediment to a proper utilitarian assessment of the quality of life.[56]

The contribution of cognitive complexity to a person's capacity to find happiness among the qualities of conditions is not impressive. As we have seen in the references to cognitive complexity, capacities for reason are relevant as tools for assessing life quality, but not, as Sidgwick[57] and others have thought, for increasing a sense of well-being. As measured—inadequately—by education and IQ, capacities for reasoning are, at most, only weakly associated with well-being.[58]

I have called the sense of well-being a stable and enduring disposition, but, in fact, positive and negative moods have more ephemeral, situationally specific elements, as well as enduring, trait-like elements. The sense of well-being embraced in the concept of a high quality of life refers to both but, because it is a life and not just an experience that is at stake, my concept of well-being refers more aptly to the more

[54] These questions include the following: How should a person's welfare be assessed when the person's own assessment is based on social comparisons? How should we treat failed continuity of identity? And, What weight should attach to a person's welfare if a person's own assessment is heteronymous? Hardin (1988: 157–207).

[55] Ibid. 191. [56] Ibid. 191–2. [57] Sidgwick (1907).

[58] Michalos (1986: 62). Michalos is reporting work in Sigelman's 1981 study and Kamman's 1978 studies.

enduring, trait-like elements than to transient moods. In one study this enduring disposition was called a 'talent for happiness' whose presence explained much of the variance in the measures of happiness employed.[59] Its opposite is a chronic 'negative effectivity' which also may be an enduring personality trait.[60] In fact, these enduring, trait-like qualities conditioning responsiveness to quality of conditions may be a physiologically based disposition.[61] 'It is clear', says Diener in a review article on subjective well-being, 'that at some level hormonal and biological events must mediate mood and Subjective Well-Being'.[62] Without entering this complex literature,[63] I will simply note that an authority on the physiology of moods, Jan Fawcett, says of joylessness: 'We seem to be measuring a biological characteristic, like blue eyes, that doesn't change'.[64] For the joyless, no quality of conditions can produce happiness, that is, convert even the most favourable circumstances into a perceived high life quality. The lesson could not be more patent: the hedonic features of quality of life depend on established features of the personalities living those lives.

THE ROLE OF OUTSIDERS IN INTERPRETING QUALITY OF LIFE AND QUALITY OF PERSONS

Who decides whether a life is of a high quality? The issue is important in meeting the charge of paternalism against the argument on behalf of a governmental responsibility for fostering higher quality persons as well as higher qualities of conditions and of life itself.

The question of who is to decide whether or not a life is of a high quality is a modern, not a classical issue. Utilitarians assume that a person is the best judge of the quality of his or her own life and Rawls also makes the decision of a life plan an individual matter.[65] More generally, the idea of a social contract was devised to legitimize governmental decisions by referring them back to hypothesized individual decisions. Classical philosophers, on the other hand, faced no such problem of legitimizing a judgement or its application by reference to individual or

[59] Freedman (1980).

[60] 'NA [negative affectivity] is a stable and pervasive personality dimension—high NA individuals report more stress, distress, and physical complaints, even in the absence of any objective stressor or health problems.' Watson *et al.* (1986), 141.

[61] Fawcett (1975), Ruse (1980).

[62] Diener (1984), 561.

[63] For a more extended treatment, see Lane (1991), 548–72.

[64] Klein and others (1983).

[65] Rawls (1971).

popular choice. For this reason, among others, classical philosophers are more prepared than modern philosophers to see governments assume responsibility for human development. For example, in claiming that 'virtue must be the serious concern of a state which truly deserves the name',[66] Aristotle was prepared to have the state educate its citizens in the qualities that comprise civic virtue.

The question of self-assessment versus external assessment has answers differing according to what is to be assessed.[67] Among the elements of quality of life, moods such as *happiness* might be thought to be assessable only by the owner of the mood. For this purpose, self-definition is certainly necessary. But it is not sufficient. We know from empirical studies that people sometimes eulogize their victimized statuses and sometimes have trouble labelling their own feelings.[68] When they attempt to assess the *causes* of their own moods, their self-assessments are particularly vulnerable. For example, people tend to believe that it is their own religious faith or their sense that they are well governed that makes them satisfied with their lives whereas the quality of life studies show that for most people neither piety nor civic satisfactions are related to overall feelings of well-being.[69]

The second subjective element of quality of life refers to personal development and learning. Although much learning is not like school learning, some of the same *caveats* apply. For the same reason that we do not let students grade their own performances on examinations we would not let people be the sole assessors of their learning in other life situations. Not only are they likely to have self-serving biases, they are also likely to have poor knowledge of relative standards and to misunderstand their own potentials. This is particularly the case in the matter of learning skills that have rising marginal utilities and, therefore, need external persuasion to overcome the initial pains of learning. The presentation of a quality of life alternative to the one that now satisfies a person represents just such external persuasion. Still, we all have had the experiences of private knowledge of personal growth of which others are unaware. Assessing qualities of persons and explaining moods must be a collaborative engagement between the persons themselves and outside assessors.

Assessing quality of conditions is more obviously a public matter,

[66] Aristotle (1908), 1280b.

[67] Filipp and Klauer (1991), 217 adopt 'the value position that the perceiving self ought to be the litmus test for the quality of life.'

[68] Lane (1991), 548–72.

[69] Campbell *et al.* (1976), 83.

although, for the reasons given above, judging the effects of these conditions on mood and personality is again a joint enterprise. One element in our roster of conditions stands out as different: *justice*. It is well understood why a person should not be the final judge of the justice of his or her own case. Similarly, because distributive justice is necessarily comparative but individuals are insufficiently familiar with the circumstances of others to assess whether or not they themselves have been fairly treated, outsiders' judgements must be enlisted. Nevertheless, there is also a purely internal feature to justice: the sense of having been fairly treated, although again self-serving biases intrude. Another common bias, the belief in a just world,[70] disqualifies assessment of self and others, for it invites complacency.

As for the standards to be applied in judging a life, the question of whether a given quality of life is 'adequate' (or less or more than adequate) enlists the combined judgements of outsiders and of the person living that life, for although individuals may be thought to have privileged (though corrigible) information on what, given their potentials, might be the appropriate standards in their own cases, outsiders have information on alternative lives, information that may derive from a wider set of ideals, from knowledge of other societies or, to borrow a term from the economists, from some notional 'possibility frontier'. Rescher makes a similar point on the objective standing of values: 'In our view', he says, 'values are founded upon a vision of how life ought to be lived. The quality of the sorts of lives that they facilitate thus becomes the arbiter of values. Perfectly objective standards are operative here, revolving around the concepts of human welfare: health, well-being, comfort, security, freedom of action, etc.'[71] Objective standards, of course, are as visible to outsiders as they are to the persons living those lives. Whereas I located *justice* among the conditions of life and *an ethical orientation* among the qualities of persons living a life, *standards* are features of the assessor, whether that be the person involved or some outsider.

Liberal humanists, who place high on their order of values a person's autonomy, that is, reliance on the individual's own self-assessment of his or her quality of life, fear that admitting outsiders as judges will jeopardize this value. The grounds for this legitimate fear are undermined in two ways: first, the qualities of persons to be developed include 'a sense of autonomy and effectiveness' designed to heighten a person's

[70] Lerner (1980). [71] Rescher (1969), 10.

power to resist the manipulation of his or her life qualities. Second, reliance on an individual's unaided judgement implies judgmental qualities that are, in fact, rare, a circumstance that affects the degree to which we can count on cognitive complexity in exploiting the opportunities presented in the above parallel lists of qualities of persons to be used in exploiting qualities of conditions. Self-knowledge is even more important and equally rare, for we know from the empirical studies of 'quality of life' (see footnote 69) that people often disguise from themselves their authentic moods and exaggerate their growth and ethical contributions. The studies' exposition of these illusions is helpful in giving perspective to the value of self-assessment of the quality of life and in making room for what otherwise seems to be intrusive or paternalistic assessments by outsiders, even by governments. If governments can help to develop the human personality, including the skills necessary for autonomous judgements and action, obstructing that help by invoking the values of autonomy is to mistake a symbol for its reality; it is self-defeating. It is a commonplace to ask that each person live a life calling forth his or her own potentials—a commonplace often ridiculed as an application of economistic, resource-exploiting policies. I am seeking to replace that commonplace with analysis.

LEARNING THE PRODUCTION FUNCTIONS OF QUALITY OF PERSONS

I will limit discussion here to three matters: the generalization of capacities and moods, the relative importance of skills (as in the capabilities approach) and motives, and a sampling of the kinds of knowledge or technology that governments may use in helping to develop desirable qualities of persons.

Qualities of persons: specific or general

For policy as well as for conceptual purposes it is important to know whether a programme of human development would have to improve human capacities in each area of behaviour and mood and thought separately or whether some overwhelming features of the human personality serve to guide people in multiple situations. Do cognitive capacities generalize from one situation to another? Are there general personality constellations that help a person to achieve a better quality of life?

We know that 'massive general transfer can be achieved by appropriate learning'[72] and that what is learned in school is applied in situations that are even subjectively very unlike schools. Level of education and related cognitive complexities are, therefore, a good predictor of performance in many tasks including those involving the level of moral reasoning.[73] Objective measures of levels of education such as those included in the United Nations Development Program's *Human Development Reports* do serve as rough indicators of a very broad range of capabilities. But, of course, some well-educated persons are immature and make a mess of their lives.

The most valuable quality of person is the broad personality constellation summarized by the concept of *ego-development*, a form of development that improves many kinds of performance, thought, and mood in a variety of situations. Something of the flavour of conceptions of ego-development is seen in an account of Jane Loevinger's idea of the higher stages of development. At these higher stages people begin to perceive and to develop for themselves long-term goals and accept responsibility for their own acts; they become achievement oriented and think in terms of more complex configurations. With the relaxation of guilt (characterizing an earlier 'conscientious stage') and the development of a greater understanding of and tolerance towards the self, they may develop to the highest stages, 'autonomous' and 'Integrated' (stages 6 and 7), whose chief characteristics are complex thought processes, awareness and acceptance of internal conflicts, a combination of independence and interdependence, and consciously seeking self-development and the fulfilment of one's potentials.[74] Thus, the better qualities of persons I have in mind do have some general properties.

Skills and motives

In defining situations people tend to see situations as similar (thereby enhancing the transfer of teamed skills) when they require similar behaviour. People choose to enter and apply their knowledge in situations

[72] Bruner (1963), 6.

[73] See Hyman and Wright (1975), Kohlberg (1981). Inferences from the correlations between level of education and stages of moral reasoning must be qualified by the fact that there is often a difference in attitudes and cognitions among those still in high school between those who plan to go to college and those who do not, that is, a recruitment effect, as well as a treatment effect, is here at work.

[74] Loevinger (1976). For critical but generally supportive reviews of Loevinger's work and its associated measures, see Hauser (1976) and Holt (1980). For an alternative, cross-culturally tested, conception of human development, see Heath (1977).

where they believe they have some expertise.[75] In these circumstances, improving quality of life rests in substantial part on improving skills. For example, if work is to be made more enjoyable and more conducive to human development, workers need certain skills to experience their work as enjoyable and to learn something of value from it. As mentioned, this emphasis on skill also applies to the ethical sensitivities and capacities of the persons involved. While one must not underrate the motivational components, it is a relief to find that changing skills is sometimes sufficient, for we are better at changing skills than in changing motivation.

Human development: a segmented, partial technology

Brief consideration of the means employed by governments to rectify their current 'mindlessness' is important to relieve anxieties about possible invasions of privacy and excessive paternalism.[76] The many means available to governments should be employed first in infusing our growing knowledge of, for example, socialization for cognitive complexity, pro-social behaviour, and capacities for self-direction, into governmentally supported institutions such as the military, courts, penal institutions, bureaucracies—and schools. Of course, governments do shape the qualities of persons through their educational programmes but we have only to look around us to see how inadequate are these programmes. While it is true that most measures of ethical as well as cognitive development show strong positive relations with years of schooling, emotional maturity and ease of social interaction are less clearly helped by education. Still, in and out of schools, there is a record to build on. The army has had some success in teaching racial tolerance;[77] pupils in certain experimental Head Start programs were, ten years later, materially less likely to become delinquent (boys) or pregnant (girls); high school students taught systematically to observe the consequences of their own acts were much more likely than matched others to continue their studies during the temporary absence of their teachers;[78] bullies have been led to change their behaviour by self-observation following correction of their perceptions of others;[79] the development of capacities for self-direction at work has been well studied.[80] We know something about how these

[75] Cantor and Kihlstrom (1987), Bem and Funder (1978).
[76] Griffin (1986), 10, 71, Nussbaum and Sen (1993), 4.
[77] See Lovell and Stiehm (1989), 188. [78] DeCharms (1976).
[79] Bower (1991). [80] Kohn and Schooler (1983).

things are taught and learned and, because science is self-correcting, we are improving our knowledge all the time.

We do not need a 'nanny government' or administration by behavioural scientists; what is missing is the sense that governmental agencies are responsible for trying to improve the qualities of persons, infusion of the relevant knowledge from the appropriate sciences into normal procedures—and the will to do in an informed way what is being done haphazardly anyway.

If a high quality of life, intensely desired by all, is thus dependent upon the qualities of persons leading those lives, we should expect the public to demand governmental programmes devised to promote cognitive complexity, a sense of autonomy and effectiveness, self-knowledge, self-esteem, and so forth. Why is this not the case?

FAILURE OF SUPPORT AND OF POLITICAL WILL

The failure of will: historical causes

There are some general historical causes for a lack of interest in human development. Poverty is the principal cause, for poverty makes the quality of condition dominant over quality of person. Religion is another. For a long time the salvation of the soul rather than the development of the person was exigent, but piety does not value several of the traits we have assigned to the concept of a developed personality, especially cognitive complexity, autonomy, and self-direction. Nor has *Gemeinschaft*, the circumstance of most people for most of our post-hunting and gathering history, ever been congenial to human development, for the aim of solidarity with a group and of winning the approval of others specifically outlaws autonomy and greatly inhibits self-knowledge and cognitive development.[81] Authoritarian regimes also tend to inhibit human development, both by their discouragement of a sense of effectiveness, and, it seems, cognitive development, as well.[82]

Modernity, including democracy, has undermined most of these large-scale societal deterrents, but the demand for human development still languishes. The idea that government should accept responsibility for

[81] For example, people with strong solidary relations in small communities in the American South have IQs about two points lower than do people with matched backgrounds in more cosmopolitan areas. Nunn *et al.* (1978).

[82] Witkin *et al.* (1962), 145–6.

improving the qualities of persons is frightening to many. Let me summarize some causes of this reluctance.

Features intrinsic to human development

The goal of general human development is a very old one but it has never gone much beyond the philosophers' library;[83] with a few exceptions such as recent California state efforts to promote self-esteem, it has not been institutionalized. Although Aristotle, Durkheim, and Mill all thought that the test of government was the quality of its people,[84] governments have been reluctant to accept this criterion for evaluating their performances. One reason is that people so cherish their identities that the idea of changing their features is threatening. However they may welcome the idea of general development, any particular change invites what the psychoanalysts call *resistance*. Thus, the idea of *self*-development, where the individual's self is in control of particular changes, dominates the field.

There is only limited immediate satisfaction to be derived from many personality changes which, nevertheless, have long-term value. Although the empirical quality of life studies shows that the degree of people's satisfaction with their own general development does contribute to their sense of well-being,[85] the specific features of development included in my definition usually make smaller contributions to feelings of well-being. For example, people's satisfaction with their 'contributions to the lives of others' (a surrogate measure for 'identification with moral values') made little difference in their sense of well-being, and their satisfaction with their own 'sincerity' and 'honesty' made almost no difference at all.[86] In contrast, there is a close relation between self-esteem and sense of effectiveness on the one hand, to well-being on the other, but this relationship will be experienced as simply the rewards of

[83] 'The philosophical debates [on a 'thriving human life'] have not had much impact on the making of public policy in much of the world . . .' Nussbaum and Sen (1993: 2).

[84] Mill (1944*a*: 127), says, 'The most important point of excellence which any form of government can possess is to promote the virtue and intelligence of the people themselves.' Durkheim's views may be found in his *Formes et essence du socialisme* quoted in Lukes (1973: 324).

[85] Andrews and Withey (1976: 135–6), Freedman (1980: 41 ff.). One suspects, however, that as the *Zeitgeist* of the 1960s waned the priority for self-development declined; at least this was true in colleges where the service ideals of 1970 gradually gave way to self-avowed ambition to make money. See Yankelovich (1974: 61).

[86] Andrews and Withey (1976: 135). On the other hand, as mentioned above, once we depart from perceptions we find that there is a reciprocal relationship between positive affect and prosocial behaviour. See Isen (1987).

being oneself by most persons; the sources of their well-being are usually obscure. For two of the elements of human development, cognitive development and self-knowledge, there is no relationship; as mentioned, these two qualities do not yield immediate hedonic rewards. The tragedy and irony of dysfunctional patterns of mental performance are that these patterns are themselves the causes of failed self-help. This is true for capabilities or capacities (as distinct from opportunities) for enjoyment as well as for a sense of effectiveness, self-esteem, better human relations, and greater personality integration.

At least three other factors inhibit any great effort by people to improve themselves as a means to greater well-being. People subjectively upgrade the circumstances of their lives as a protection against self-criticism and criticism by others—they inflate their quality of condition.[87] People do not know what makes them happy, greatly reducing their demands for even those things that do make people happy. And even if people knew the sources of their own happiness, they would not know how to achieve them. Nisbett and Ross point out that it is not experience but *theories* of the sources of well-being that control hedonic behaviour,[88] and most people, partly because of the misleading character of market doctrine, have inferior theories.

There are institutional causes, as well. Because of the generality and dispersion of the benefits of human development, no single agency or firm finds it 'profitable' to undertake the effort to help people to develop themselves. If firms invest in developing the general skills of their employees, other firms, at no expense to themselves, will poach these developed persons. Finally, the sheer difficulty of the task imposes obstacles. It is much harder to change persons and their behaviour than it is to change the circumstances of life.

Doctrinal resistances to institutional programmes for human development

While personal and institutional resistances to human development retard its progress, doctrinal resistances or deficiencies in our psychological, economic, philosophical, and political theories also play a part. In this partly psychological domain, *psychology* presents a case of mixed support and incapacity. Although, as illustrated above, the discipline is increasingly providing a segmental set of 'production functions' of

[87] Campbell *et al.* (1976: ch. 6). [88] Nisbett and Ross (1980: 197).

selected qualities of persons (such as prosocial behaviour and cognitive development) and more general models of personalities with superior capacities for development, illustrated by work on 'ego development' mentioned above, it still lacks a theory of 'societal psychology' linking psychology with institutional functions.[89]

Nor have the applied fields of psychology undertaken the task. For example, political psychologists study the effects of psychological processes on political processes; they rarely consider how society influences qualities of persons and even more rarely allow themselves to define better and worse models of human personality. The field of economic psychology explains economic behaviour, not the effects of economic institutions on individuals.

Like all our theories, *economic theory* has multiple branches: while business schools are concerned with the effects of institutions on those qualities of persons directly influencing demand and production (e.g. human capital), the central body of micro-economics retains the universalistic assumptions of rationality and greed.[90] The economistic fallacy, or more generally, the objectivist fallacy, concentrates attention on the quality of conditions and inhibits concentration on human development. A little like their utilitarian companions, both economists and political scientists focus on *interests* [91] rather than on persons, on stakes rather than on realized satisfactions and possibilities for growth. Dominant economic theory would, if it were applied to the problem, suggest that human development is a do-it-yourself or *laissez-faire* process.

Philosophers are concerned largely with the ethical qualities of persons and with human dignity or personhood, not with the whole person. For example, although there is reason to believe that the value of human development is inherent in the concept of personhood, which is the intrinsic value of most deontologists and the defenders of rights,[92] much ethical theory is inhibited from analyzing human development both by its fear of consequentialism and by its belief that analysis of qualities of persons requiring the comparison of one person with another will violate the intrinsic value of human dignity.

Political philosophy, to which we must appeal, stresses the value of

[89] Himmelweit and Gaskell (1980).

[90] Recently Robert Frank (1988) joined the hardy band of distinguished contemporary dissidents (Boulding, Hirschman, Myrdal, Simon, Tversky, etc.).

[91] Hardin (1988: 201).

[92] I believe that within Kant's (1920: 38) own doctrine of moral imperatives there is implied a set of human qualities that open the door to concepts of human development.

autonomy mentioned above and therefore emphasizes a (reasonable) fear of governmental intrusion into our private lives. Since human development is as 'self-regarding' as any of Mill's illustrations, there is philosophical support for *laissez-faire* in this apparently intimate process. Isaiah Berlin puts the matter in a perspective particularly appropriate to the questions posed here. In an ironic voice, he says: 'The sage knows you better than you know yourself, for you are the victim of your passions . . . You wish to be a human being. It is the aim of the state to satisfy your wish.' This, says Berlin, is the argument of every dictator who seeks to rationalize his power.[93]

Berlin's concern is appropriate: communist regimes sought to impose on their subjects the personality features of 'the new socialist man' and fascist regimes sought to stamp out all human individuality.[94] But application of Berlin's fears of totalism to democratic governments concerned with improving their citizens' quality of life by improving the qualities of their persons is a category error. Concern for individuals is not totalism but an application of democratic values. I know of no immanent forces that make political concern for developed individuals endowed with greater cognitive skills, sensitive moral characters, and the capacities for self-direction a condition favouring decline into totalitarianism. Quite the opposite.

Utilitarianism is a special case. Because utilitarians define a high quality of life in terms of happiness (if others share it) and because they have not, until recently, enquired into other qualities of persons, their focus tends to be on the objective features of a life, that is, on the quality of conditions that contribute to happiness. This focus on externals is congenial to a concern for governmental facilitation of quality of condition for two reasons: in their pursuit of happiness, people may be expected to *demand* from government the things that they believe will make them happy, and governments understand how to improve external qualities of life far better than they understand how to improve qualities of persons.

The recent development within the camp of the utilitarians, whose philosophy often presides over concepts of quality of life, of a self-

[93] Berlin (1969: 149–50).

[94] 'The man of Fascism is an individual who is nation and fatherland, which is a moral law, . . . [leading] a life in which the individual, through the denial of himself, through the sacrifice of his own private interests, through death itself, realizes that completely spiritual existence in which his value as a man lies.' Mussolini (1947: 164).

conscious recognition of their need for a personality theory, offers some hope.[95] But utilitarians, fearing paternalism, seem to be committed to the idea that the quality of life can only be interpreted by the individual living that life[96]—even though we have shown that individuals are often not good interpreters of their own welfare or of the quality of the lives they lead. If the goal is maximum welfare for all, it may be that philosophical fear of paternalism stands in the way of the overarching good of a better quality of life for all.

Democratic theory is only partially receptive to the idea of state responsibility for human development. The various branches of theories of democracy offer conflicting concepts of the proper scope of governmental activities, some holding that the concept of the sovereign public binds government to perform only those functions demanded by the public. They would share the embarrassment of the economists over the evidence that people do not know the sources of their own well-being. Others, more respectful of the idea of governmental trusteeship, might find people's confusion on the sources of their own welfare less disturbing and accept that the government is independently responsible for the welfare of the public. For example, Mill's idea that those who have superior knowledge of the 'lower' and 'higher' forms of pleasure should help those who don't have such knowledge to choose the 'higher' forms[97] opens the way to non-coercive government encouragement and even facilitation. Note, too, that Edmund Burke's concept of representation as a kind of trusteeship for the well-being of the representative's constituency is a tenable theory of the way democracies (or republics) may deal with the welfare of their publics. Recently, others, arguing that democracy never did rely on the dictates of a sovereign public in policy matters, have found a limited paternalism congenial to democratic theory.[98] And, quite apart from policy, democracy itself is said to have some of the 'self-transformative' qualities we have been discussing[99] —a belief that in my opinion is ill founded and certainly minimalist. Finally, many social philosophers have extended the concept of rights

[95] Held (1989: 15); Hardin (1988).

[96] For example, only where it can be supposed that 'paternalistic' laws might 'be enacted at the behest of those who wish to control themselves by imposing external discipline on their actions by having the state do for them what they know they would not do well for themselves' would state intervention be admissible. Hardin (1988: 199).

[97] Mill (1944*b*: 8, 10).

[98] See, for example, Sunstein (1991), Hardin (1988: 199).

[99] See Warren (1992).

to include the right of 'self-development' and 'human development'[100] which democratic governments are bound to protect and, by extension, to favour.

Acknowledging the risks, I believe there are reasons, in addition to the intrinsic value of human development, for assigning to governments a responsibility for seeking to develop the qualities of the people in their jurisdictions: a high quality of life cannot be achieved without human development, government policies fail when they ignore the capabilities of the people involved, and *laissez-faire* policies of self-development are inadequate to the task. All this makes it necessary to add to the public concern for quality of life an equal concern for the qualities of those who will inevitably live those lives.

REFERENCES

ALLARDT, E. (1975), *Dimensions of Welfare in a Comparative Scandinavian Study.* University of Helsinki: Research Group for Comparative Sociology, Report No. 9.

ANDREWS, F. M. (ed.) (1986), *Research on the Quality of Life.* Ann Arbor: Institute for Social Research of the University of Michigan.

——, and WITHEY, S. B. (1976), *Social Indicators of Well-Being: Americans' Perceptions of Life Quality.* New York: Plenum.

ARGYLE, M. (1987), *The Psychology of Happiness.* London: Methuen.

ARISTOTLE (1908), *Politics,* Jowett translation. Oxford: Clarendon Press.

BAY, C. (1965 [1958]), *The Structure of Freedom.* New York: Atheneum.

BEM, D. J., and FUNDOR, D. C. (1978), 'Predicting More of the People More of the Time: Assessing the Personality of Situations', *Psychological Review,* 86: 485–501.

BERLIN, I. (1969), 'Two Concepts of Liberty', in his *Four Essays on Liberty.* London: Oxford University Press, 149–50.

BESTUZHEV-LADA, I. V., BATYGIN, G. S., and GRISHAYEVA, N. P. (1978), 'The Category of "Quality of Life" in Present-Day Western Sociology', in Bestuzhev-Lada and N. M. Binov (eds.), *The Modern Conception of Level*

[100] Thus, Held (1989: 184), emphasis added, proposes that the concept of rights extends beyond 'economic and social rights [to] . . . a decent life, [and] *adequate self-development*'. Earlier, Macpherson (1973: 42, 138), argued that the power to develop one's own capacities was the crucial political power and claimed that people have the 'right to a set of power relations that permits a full life of enjoyment and development of one's human capacities'.

of Life. Moscow: Academy of Sciences of the USSR, Institute for Social Research: Soviet Sociological Association.

BOLGER, N., CASPI, A., DOWNEY, G., and MOOREHOUSE, M. (eds.) (1988), *Persons in Context: Developmental Processes*. Cambridge: Cambridge University Press.

BOWER, G. (1991), Research reported in Kathleen McCarthy, 'Moods—Good and Bad—Color all Aspects of Life', *APA Monitor,* 22: 13.

BRADBURN, N. M., and CAPLOVITZ, D. (1965), *Reports on Happiness: A Pilot Study of Behavior Related to Mental Health*. Chicago: Aldine.

BRAYBROOKE, D. (1987), *Meeting Needs*. Princeton, NJ: Princeton University Press.

BRONFENBRENNER, U. (1979), *The Ecology of Human Development: Experiments by Nature and Design*. Cambridge; Mass.: Harvard University Press.

—— (1988), 'Interacting Systems in Human Development. Research Paradigms: Present and Future', in Bolger *et al*. (1988), 25–49.

BRUNER, J. S. (1963), *The Process of Education*. New York: Knopf/Vintage.

CAMPBELL, A., CONVERSE, P. E., and RODGERS, W. L. (1976), *The Quality of American Life*. New York: Russell Sage.

CANTOR, N., and KIHLSTROM, J. F. (1987), *Personality and Social lntelligence*. Englewood Cliffs, NJ: Prentice-Hall.

CLAUSEN, J. S. (1991), 'Adolescent Competence and the Shaping of the Life Course', *American Journal of Sociology,* 94: 805–42.

CROCKER, D. A. (1992), 'Functioning and Capability: The Foundations of Sen's and Nussbaum's Development Ethic', *Political Theory,* 20: 584–612.

DECHARMS, R. (1976), *Change in the Classroom*. New York: Irvington.

DIENER, E. (1984), 'Subjective Well-Being', *Psychological Bulletin,* 95: 542–75.

FAWCETT, J. (1975), 'Biochemical and Neuropharmacological Research in the Affective Disorders', in E. James Anthony and Therese Benedek (eds.), *Depression and Human Existence*. Boston: Little Brown, 21–52.

FILIPP, S-H., and KLAUER, T. (1991), 'Subjective Well-Being in the Face of Critical Life Events: The Case of Successful Copers', in Strack *et al*. (1991).

FRANK, R. (1988), *Passions within Reason: The Strategic Role of the Emotions*. New York: Norton.

FREEDMAN, J. (1980), *Happy People*. New York: Harcourt, Brace.

FROMM, E. (1947), *Man for Himself*. New York: Rinehart.

GRIFFIN, J. (1986), *Well-Being: Its Meaning, Measurement, and Moral Importance*. Oxford: Clarendon Press.

HANKISS, E. (1980), 'Structural Variables in Cross-Cultural Research on the Quality of Life', in Alexander Szalai and Frank M. Andrews (eds.), *The Quality of Life: Comparative Studies*. Beverly Hills, Calif.: Sage, 41–56.

HARDIN, R. (1988), *Morality within Limits of Reason*. Chicago: University of Chicago Press.

HAUSER, S. (1976), 'Loevinger's Model and Measure of Ego Development: A Critical Review', *Psychological Bulletin,* 83: 928–55.

HEATH, D. (1977), *Maturity and Competence: A Transcultural View.* New York: Wiley.

HELD, V. (1989 [1984]), *Rights and Goods: Justifying Social Action.* Chicago: University of Chicago Press.

HIMMELWEIT, H. T., and GASKELL, G. (eds.) (1980), *Societal Psychology.* Newbury Park, Calif.: Sage.

HOLT, R. R. (1980), 'Loevinger's Measure of Ego Development: Reliability and National Norms for Male and Female Short Forms', *Journal of Personality and Social Psychology,* 39: 909–20.

HSU, F. L. K. (ed.) (1961), *Psychological Anthropology* (Homewood, Ill.: Dorsey Press.

HURRELMANN, K. (1988), *Social Structure and Personality Development: The Individual as a Productive Processor of Reality.* Cambridge: Cambridge University Press.

HYMAN, H. H., and WRIGHT, C. (1975), *The Enduring Effects of Education.* Chicago: University of Chicago Press.

INGLEHART, R. (1990), *Culture Shift in Advanced Industrial Society.* Princeton, NJ: Princeton University Press.

ISEN, A. M. (1987), 'Positive Affect, Cognitive Processes, and Social Behavior', in L. Berkowitz (ed.), *Advances in Experimental Social Psychology,* 20, San Diego, Calif.: Academic.

JAHODA, M. (1958), *Current Concepts of Positive Mental Health.* New York: Basic Books.

JENCKS, C., BARTLETT, S., and associates (1979), *Who Gets Ahead? The Determinants of Economic Success in America.* New York: Basic Books.

KANT, I. (1920), *Preface to the Fundamental Principles of the Metaphysic of Morals*, ed. and trans. T. K. Abbott. Published as *Kant's Theory of Ethics.* London: Longmans, Green, 6th edn. Reprinted in T. M. Greene (ed.), *Kant: Selections.* New York: Scribner's Sons.

KARDINER, A., with the collaboration of LINTON, R., DUBOIS, C., and WEST, J. (1945), *The Psychological Frontiers of Society.* New York: Columbia University Press.

KLEIN, D., FAWCETT, J., *et al.* (1983), reported by Abby Avin Belson, 'Studying the Chemistry of Joylessness', *International Herald Tribune*, 17 Mar. 1983.

KOHLBERG, L. (1981), *The Philosophy of Moral Development: Moral Stages and the Idea of Justice.* New York: Harper & Row.

KOHN, M., and SCHOOLER, C. (1983), *Work and Personality: An Inquiry into the Impact of Social Stratification.* Norwood, NJ: Ablex.

KUGLER, K., and JONES, W. H. (1992), 'On Conceptualizing and Assessing Guilt', *Journal of Personality and Social Psychology,* 62: 318–27.

LAND, K. C. (1983), 'Social Indicators', *Annual Review of Sociology,* vol. 9. Palo Alto, Calif.: Annual Reviews.

LANE, R. E. (1991), *The Market Experience.* NewYork: Cambridge University Press.

LEIGHTON, D. C., HARDING, J. S., MOCKLIN, D. B., MACMILLAN, A. M., and LEIGHTON, A. H. (1963), *The Character of Danger. The Stirling County Study of Psychiatric Disorder and Sociocultural Environment,* vol. iii. New York: Basic Books.

LERNER, M. J. (1980), *The Belief in a Just World: A Fundamental Delusion* New York: Plenum.

LEVINE, R. A. (1973), *Culture, Behavior, and Personality: An Introduction to the Comparative Study of Psychosocial Adaptation.* Chicago: Aldine.

LOEVINGER, J. (1976), *Ego Development.* San Francisco: Jossey-Bass.

LOVELL, J. P., and STIEHM, J. H. (1989), 'Military Service and Political Socialization', in Sigel (1989), 172–202.

LUKES, S. (1973), *Emile Durkheim: His Life and Work.* London: Allen Lane/ Penguin.

MACPHERSON, C. B. (1973), *Democratic Theory: Essays in Retrieval.* Oxford: Clarendon Press.

MAGNUSSON, D. (ed.) (1981), *Toward a Psychology of Situations: An Interactional Perspective.* Hillsdale, NJ: Erlbaum.

MASLOW, A. H. (1968), *Toward a Psychology of Being.* Rev. edn. Princeton, NJ: Van Nostrand.

MICHALOS, A. C. (1986), 'Job Satisfaction, Marital Satisfaction, and the Quality of Life: A Review and a Preview', in Frank M. Andrews (ed.), *Research on the Quality of Life.* Ann Arbor: Institute for Social Research.

MILL, J. S. (1944*a* [1910]) *Representative Government,* in *Utilitarianism, Liberty, and Representative Government.* London: Dent.

—— (1944*b* [1910]), *Utilitarianism [1861*], in *Utilitarianism, Liberty, and Representative Government.* London: Dent.

MISCHEL, W. (1973), 'Toward a Cognitive Social Learning Reconceptualization of Personality', *Psychological Bulletin,* 80: 252–83.

MISCHEL, W. (1976), *Introduction to Personality.* New York: Holt, Rinehart, & Winston.

MUKHERJEE, R. (1989), *The Quality of Life: Valuation in Social Research.* New Delhi: Sage.

MUSSOLINI, B. (1947), *The Doctrine of Fascism.* Repr. in Michael Oakeshott, *The Social and Political Doctrines of Contemporary Europe.* New York: Macmillan.

New York Times (1977), 'A New Index of the Quality of Life', 13 Mar.

NISBETT, R., and ROSS, L. (1980), *Human Inference: Strategies and Shortcomings of Social Judgment.* Englewood Cliffs, NJ: Prentice-Hall.

NORDHAUS, W. D., and TOBIN, J. (1973), 'Is Growth Obsolete?', in Milton

Moss (ed.), *The Measurement of Economic and Social Performance,* Studies in Income and Wealth, 38. New York: National Bureau of Economic Research.

NUNN, C. Z., CROCKETT, H. J., Jr., and WILLIAMS, J. A., Jr. (1978), *Tolerance for Nonconformity.* San Francisco: Jossey-Bass.

NUSSBAUM, M. C. (1992), 'Human Functioning and Social Justice', *Political Theory*, 20: 202–46.

——, and SEN, A. (eds.) (1993), *The Quality of Life.* Oxford: Clarendon Press.

OECD (Organization for Economic Co-operation and Development) (1973) *List of Social Concerns Common to Most OECD Countries.* Paris: OECD.

PERRY, R. B. (1954), *Realms of Value: A Critique of Human Civilization.* Cambridge, Mass.: Harvard University Press.

RAWLS, J. (1971), *A Theory of Justice.* Cambridge, Mass.: Harvard University Press.

—— (1988), 'The Priority of Right and Ideas of the Good', *Philosophy and Public Affairs*, 17: 251–76.

RESCHER, N. (1969), *Introduction to Value Theory.* Englewood Cliffs, NJ: Prentice Hall.

ROBINS, P. K., SPIEGELMAN, R. G., WIENER, S., and BELL, J. G., (eds.) (1980), *A Guaranteed Annual Income: Evidence from a Social Experiment.* New York: Academic.

ROSS, L. (1977), 'The Intuitive Psychologist and his Shortcomings', in L. Berkowitz (ed.), *Advances in Experimental Psychology,* vol. x. New York: Academic.

ROSS, W. D. (1930), *The Right and the Good.* Oxford: Clarendon Press.

RUSE, M. (1980), 'Genetics and the Quality of Life', *Social Indicators Research,* 7, 419–42

SCHWARTZ, S. H., and BILSKY, W. (1990), 'Toward a Theory of the Universal Content and Structure of Values: Extensions and Cross-Cultural Replications', *Journal of Personality and Social Psychology*, 58: 878–91.

SCOTT, W. A. (1968), 'Conceptions of Normality', in Edgar Borgatta and William W. Lambert (eds.), *Handbook of Personality Theory and Research.* Chicago: Rand McNally.

SEN, A. (1979), 'Utilitarianism and Welfarism', *Journal of Philosophy*, 76: 463–88.

—— (1984), *Resources, Values and Development.* Cambridge, Mass.: Harvard University Press.

—— (1985*a*), 'Well-Being, Agency, and Freedom: The Dewey Lectures, 1984', *Journal of Philosophy*, 82: 169–221.

—— (1985*b*), *Commodities and Capabilities.* Amsterdam: North Holland.

—— (1987), *On Ethics and Economics.* Oxford: Blackwell.

—— (1993), 'Capability and Well-Being', in Nussbaum and Sen (1993), 30.

——, and DRÈZE, J. (1989), *Hunger and Public Action.* Oxford: Clarendon.

——, and WILLIAMS, B. (1982), 'Introduction' to Sen and Williams (eds.), *Utilitarianism and Beyond.* Cambridge: Cambridge University Press.

SIDGWICK, H. (1907), *The Methods of Ethics,* 7th edn. London: Macmillan.

SIGEL, R. S. (ed.) (1989), *Political Learning in Adulthood: A Sourcebook of Theory and Research.* Chicago: University of Chicago Press.

SMELSER, N. J., and SMELSER, W. T. (eds.) (1963), *Personality and Social Systems.* New York: Wiley.

SROLE, L., LANGNER, T. S., MICHAEL, S. T., OPLER, M. K., and RENNIE, T. A. C. (1962), *Mental Health in the Metropolis: The Midtown Manhattan Study,* vol. i. New York: McGraw-Hill.

STRACK, F., ARGYLE, M., and SCHWARZ, N. (eds.) (1991), *Subjective Well-Being: An Interdisciplinary Perspective.* Oxford: Pergamon.

STREETON, P., with BURKI, S. J., UL HAQ, M., HICKS, N., and STEWART, F. (1981), *First Things First: Meeting Basic Needs in Developing Countries.* New York: Oxford University Press.

SUNSTEIN, C. R. (1991), 'Preferences and Politics', *Philosophy and Public Affairs,* 20: 3–34.

TANGNEY, J. P., WAGNER, P., FLETCHER, C., and GRAMZOW, R. (1992), 'Shamed into Anger? The Relation of Shame and Guilt to Anger and Self-Reported Aggression', *Journal of Personality and Social Psychology*, 62: 659–75.

VEENHOVEN, R. (ed.) (1989), *How Harmful is Happiness?* Rotterdam: University Press of Rotterdam.

WAHBA, M. A., and BRIDWELL, L. G. (1976), 'Maslow Reconsidered: A Review of Research on the Need Hierarchy Theory', *Organizational Behavior and Human Performance*, 15: 210–40.

WARREN, M. (1992), 'Democratic Theory and Self-Transformation', *American Political Science Review,* 86: 8–23.

WATSON, D., PENNEBAKER, J. W., and FOLGER, R. (1986), 'Beyond Negative Affectivity: Measuring Stress and Satisfaction in the Workplace', *Journal of Organizational Behavior Management*, 8: 141–57.

WHITING, J. W. M., and CHILD, I. (1953), *Child Training and Personality: A Cross Cultural Study.* New Haven: Yale University Press.

WITKIN, H. A., DYK, R. B., FATERSON, H. F., GOODENOUGH, D. R., and KARP, S. A. (1962), *Psychological Differentiation.* New York: Wiley & Sons.

WOLFENSTEIN, M. (1968), 'The Emergence of Fun Morality'. Repr. in E. Larrabee and R. Meyersohn (eds.), *Mass Leisure.* Glencoe, Ill.: Free Press.

YANKELOVICH, D. K. (1974), *Changing Values in the 1970s: A Study of American Youth.* New York: John D. Rockefeller 3rd Fund.

INDEX